Managing Diversity in Education

NEW PERSPECTIVES ON LANGUAGE AND EDUCATION

Series Editor: Professor Viv Edwards, *University of Reading, Reading, Great Britain*
Series Advisor: Professor Allan Luke, *Queensland University of Technology, Brisbane, Australia*

Two decades of research and development in language and literacy education have yielded a broad, multidisciplinary focus. Yet education systems face constant economic and technological change, with attendant issues of identity and power, community and culture. This series will feature critical and interpretive, disciplinary and multidisciplinary perspectives on teaching and learning, language and literacy in new times.

Full details of all the books in this series and of all our other publications can be found on http://www.multilingual-matters.com, or by writing to Multilingual Matters, St Nicholas House, 31–34 High Street, Bristol BS1 2AW, UK.

Managing Diversity in Education

Languages, Policies, Pedagogies

Edited by
David Little, Constant Leung and Piet Van Avermaet

MULTILINGUAL MATTERS
Bristol • Buffalo • Toronto

Library of Congress Cataloging in Publication Data
Managing Diversity in Education: Languages, Policies, Pedagogies/Edited by David Little, Constant Leung and Piet Van Avermaet.
New Perspectives on Language and Education: 33.
Includes bibliographical references and index.
1. Multilingualism. 2. Multiculturalism. 3. Language policy. 4. Linguistic minorities. 5. Language and education. 6. Mainstreaming in education. I. Little, D. G., editor of compilation.
P115.M36 2013
306.44'6071–dc23 2013025854

British Library Cataloguing in Publication Data
A catalogue entry for this book is available from the British Library.

ISBN-13: 978-1-78309-080-8 (hbk)
ISBN-13: 978-1-78309-079-2 (pbk)

Multilingual Matters
UK: St Nicholas House, 31–34 High Street, Bristol BS1 2AW, UK.
USA: UTP, 2250 Military Road, Tonawanda, NY 14150, USA.
Canada: UTP, 5201 Dufferin Street, North York, Ontario M3H 5T8, Canada.

The policy of Multilingual Matters/Channel View Publications is to use papers that are natural, renewable and recyclable products, made from wood grown in sustainable forests. In the manufacturing process of our books, and to further support our policy, preference is given to printers that have FSC and PEFC Chain of Custody certification. The FSC and/or PEFC logos will appear on those books where full certification has been granted to the printer concerned.

Typeset by Techset Composition India (P) Ltd., Bangalore and Chennai, India.
Printed and bound in Great Britain by the Lavenham Press Ltd.

Contents

Part 2

Contributors

Nathalie Auger is a full professor of language sciences at the University of Montpellier, France. Her research focuses on second and foreign language acquisition in France and Canada, and she leads a team working on this topic at Praxiling, a National Centre for Scientific Research (CNRS). She is a strong advocate of the use of immigrant pupils' home languages at school, a subject on which she has published a number of books and articles; she is also responsible for a prize-winning film, *Comparons nos langues*. She works closely with the French Ministry of Education to implement plurilingual and intercultural approaches as part of general language education, and she has contributed to Council of Europe projects in this area.

Jan Blommaert is Professor of Language, Culture and Globalization and Director of the Babylon Center at Tilburg University, The Netherlands. He also holds appointments at the University of Ghent (Belgium), the University of the Western Cape (South Africa), Beijing Language and Culture University (China), and is coordinator of the Max Planck Sociolinguistic Diversity Working Group. Major publications include *Language Ideological Debates* (Mouton de Gruyter, 1999), *Discourse: A Critical Introduction* (Cambridge University Press 2005), *Grassroots Literacy* (Routledge, 2008), *The Sociolinguistics of Globalization* (Cambridge University Press 2010), and *Ethnography, Superdiversity and Linguistic Landscapes: Chronicles of Complexity* (Multilingual Matters, 2013).

Bronagh Ćatibušić was awarded a PhD in Applied Linguistics by Trinity College Dublin in 2011. A book based on her PhD research, *Immigrant Pupils Learn English: A CEFR-related Empirical Study of L2 Development*, co-authored with David Little, is published by Cambridge University Press. She lectures on teaching English as a second language at St. Patrick's College of Education, Dublin, and is involved in work on language test development. She has previously worked on the production of assessment resources for children from immigrant backgrounds as part of the English Language Support programme provided by the Irish Department of Education and Skills. She has also taught English in Bosnia and Herzegovina, Japan and Ireland.

Tracey Costley is currently a visiting assistant professor in the Department of English at City University of Hong Kong. Her PhD research was concerned with the social construction of policy and practice and adopted an ethnographic perspective in order to understand the ways in which learners of English as an Additional Language are conceptualised within mainstream educational settings in London. Her current research interests include exploring the interface between education policy and curriculum practices. She is also interested in academic literacies, processes of academic socialisation, academic genres, and student identity in writing at university.

Jim Cummins is a professor at Ontario Institute for Studies in Education at the University of Toronto. His research focuses on literacy development in educational contexts characterized by linguistic diversity. He is the author (with Margaret Early) of *Identity Texts: The Collaborative Creation of Power in Multilingual Schools* (Trentham Books, 2011).

Daniel Faas is head of the Department of Sociology and a member of the University Council at Trinity College Dublin. His research and teaching interests are in the sociology of migration with particular emphasis on the intersection of migration and education. His work focuses on youth identities in relation to immigrant integration, national identity, multiculturalism and social cohesion in Europe, diversity management in educational sites and work places, curriculum design and development, and comparative case study methodologies. He was awarded the 2012 Provost's Teaching Award at Trinity College and the 2009 European Sociological Association award for best journal article. He is the author of *Negotiating Political Identities: Multiethnic Schools and Youth in Europe* (Ashgate, 2010).

Rachael Fionda is academic director at a large Dublin language school. She was awarded her PhD by Trinity College Dublin in 2010 for a thesis entitled *English Language Support for Migrant Students in Irish Post-Primary Schools*. She worked as a part-time English language support teacher in a disadvantaged post-primary school in Dublin for three years. Before coming to Dublin she was a full-time lecturer in English Language and Linguistics at the University of Innsbruck, Austria. She completed her MPhil in Applied Linguistics at the same institution, and her BA in Linguistics and Italian at the University of Leeds, UK.

Nelson Flores is assistant professor in Educational Linguistics at the University of Pennsylvania Graduate School of Education. His research seeks to problematize oppressive language ideologies that inform current approaches to the education of language-minoritised students, develop new research methodologies for analysing language practices of language-minoritised populations outside these oppressive frameworks, and re-imagine language education pedagogy in ways that resist these ideologies. He has collaborated on several studies related to the education of emergent bilingual students at public schools in New York City and Philadelphia.

Ofelia García is professor in the PhD programs of Urban Education and Hispanic and Luso-Brazilian Literatures and Languages at The Graduate Center, City University of New York. She has been professor at Columbia University's Teachers College and Dean of the School of Education at Long Island University. Among her recent books are: *Bilingual Education in the 21st Century; Bilingual Community Education and Multilingualism* (with Zeena Zakharia and Bahar Otcu); *Handbook of Language and Ethnic Identity, I and II* (with Joshua A. Fishman); *Educating Emergent Bilinguals* (with Joanne Kleifgen); and *Additive Schooling in Subtractive Times* (with Lesley Bartlett). She is the Associate General Editor of the *International Journal of the Sociology of Language*.

Patrick Grommes is a post-doctoral researcher in the Department of Language, Literature and Media at the University of Hamburg in the area of German as a Second/Foreign Language. From 2009 to 2011 he participated in the project 'Multilingual Language Development in Educational Institutions', which was part of the university's 'Linguistic Diversity Management in Urban Areas (LiMA)' research cluster. He studied German linguistics at Humboldt University Berlin and completed his PhD on the topic of coherence in spoken dialogue in 2005. His research interests include multilingualism, second language acquisition and teaching, and aspects of speech and text production.

Fiona Kearney is an Inspector of Special Education (Primary/Post-primary) with the Department of Education and Skills, Ireland. Previously she was seconded from Castleknock Community College to the position of National Coordinator with the Special Education and Support Service. Prior to her secondment she was a mainstream teacher of English, English Language Support coordinator, and Learning Support and Special Educational Needs teacher and coordinator. She helped the Special Educational Needs Dublin 15 and Dublin 7 Cluster Group to design and deliver seminars relating to special educational needs, Child Protection Guidelines, and the induction of new-comer students. She was also a lecturer and teacher in early childhood education for 16 years. She has conducted research on the issue of inclusion.

Déirdre Kirwan is principal of Scoil Bhríde Cailíní, Blanchardstown, Dublin. 70% of the school's enrolment consists of pupils from more than 40 cultural and linguistic backgrounds. In 2008 she received the *European Ambassador for Languages* award for her promotion of cultural and linguistic diversity in the school. In 2009 she received a PhD from Trinity College Dublin for her research in the area of language education. She has presented papers on the topic of multilingual education at national and international conferences, and has delivered courses to teachers at undergraduate and post-graduate levels. She is strongly committed to promoting plurilingualism at primary level and is currently exploring, with teachers, parents and pupils, the benefits of an integrated approach to language teaching and learning in Scoil Bhríde Cailíní.

Stergiani Kostopoulou specializes in Applied Corpus Linguistics, English for Specific/Academic purposes, and Second Language Pedagogy. She has published a number of articles and given numerous presentations in these areas. She taught modules on Applied Linguistics, English Language Teaching and English for Academic Purposes at Trinity College Dublin from 2007 to 2011. She was also a member of the English Language Support Programme of the Trinity Immigration Initiative (2007–2010). She is currently a research associate at the Centre for Intercultural and Migration Studies, University of Crete, and a teacher of English for Academic Purposes at MBS College in Greece.

Constant Leung is Professor of Educational Linguistics at King's College London. He also serves as deputy head of the Department of Education and Professional Studies. Before taking up teaching positions in higher education he taught in schools and worked as an advisory teacher and manager in local government. His research interests include education in ethnically and lin-guistically diverse societies, second/additional language curriculum develop-ment, language assessment, language policy, and teacher professional development. He has written and published widely on issues related to ethnic minority education, additional/second language curriculum, and language assessment nationally and internationally.

David Little retired in 2008 as Associate Professor of Applied Linguistics and head of the School of Linguistic, Speech and Communication Sciences at

Trinity College Dublin. His principal research interests are the theory and practice of learner autonomy in second language education, the exploitation of linguistic diversity in schools and classrooms, and the use of the *Common European Framework of Reference for Languages* to support the design of second language curricula, teaching and assessment. From 2001 to 2008 he was director of Integrate Ireland Language and Training, which was funded by the Irish government to provide intensive English language programmes for adult immigrants with refugee status and to support the teaching of English as an Additional Language in primary and post-primary schools. From 2007 to 2010 he led the Trinity Immigration Initiative's English Language Support Programme, which created the post-primary EAL learning materials available at http://www.elsp.ie.

Zachary Lyons is a lecturer in Language Learning, French and Maths, a post-primary teacher of Maths, French and ICT, and a former research fellow with the Trinity Immigration Initiative's English Language Support Programme for Post-Primary Schools, Trinity College Dublin. He has been involved in language, literacy and numeracy teaching for over 24 years and currently works in Lausanne for an international organisation as a language consultant developing multilingual learning materials and programmes.

Bríd Ní Chonaill is a lecturer at the Institute of Technology Blanchardstown, Dublin. She has delivered courses and carried out research on French culture and society with a particular focus on linguistic diversity in France, language policy, and issues concerning immigration. Having broadened her research interests to immigration in the Irish context she currently lectures and researches in this area. She completed an IRCHSS project entitled 'Perceptions of Migrants in the Blanchardstown Area: Local Views' in 2007 and a two-year funded project on migrant parents and the transition to third level education in Ireland in 2011.

Sven Sierens has a Master's degree in Communication Science from the Free University of Brussels and a special degree in Social and Cultural Anthropology from the University of Leuven. He started working as a researcher at the University of Leuven and is currently attached to the Centre for Diversity and Learning at the University of Ghent. He has carried out a number of studies on intercultural education and immigrant minorities and diversity in education. He is presently involved as researcher and coordinator in research projects that focus on linguistic diversity and multilingualism in elementary education in Flanders, Belgium.

Shelley K. Taylor is associate professor at Western University (Ontario) where she teaches courses on Minority Languages, Issues in Language and Literacy, and Teaching English and French as Second Languages. Her research interests include longitudinal studies of the development, maintenance and evolution of plurilingual students' linguistic repertoires in various contexts internationally, and classroom-based explorations of how plurilingual learners fare in educational language programs that are out of step with superdiversity in Canada and Denmark. She has published in the *Canadian Journal of Applied Linguistics, TESOL Quarterly, Race, Ethnicity and Education* and *Writing and Pedagogy*, and she is Associate Convention Program Chair of TESOL 2015 in Toronto.

Piet Van Avermaet has a PhD in Applied Linguistics and teaches Multicultural Studies at the University of Ghent, Belgium, where he also directs the Centre for Diversity and Learning. His expertise and research interests are: diversity and social inequality in education, educational linguistics, multilingual and multicultural education, language and the integration of immigrants, sociolinguistics, and language testing. He worked for many years at the Centre for Language and Education at the University of Leuven, where he was coordinator of the Certificate in Dutch as a Foreign Language (CNaVT).

Fie Velghe is currently a PhD student at Tilburg University and a member of the Transformations in the Public Sphere (TRAPS) research group in the Tilburg School of Humanities, Department of Culture Studies. Her research focuses on mobile phone use and mobile phone literacies amongst middle-aged women in impoverished communities in Cape Town, South Africa. She has Master's degrees in African Languages and Cultures and Conflict and Development, both from the University of Ghent.

Introduction

David Little, Constant Leung and Piet Van Avermaet

Diversity comes in many forms – cultural, social, ethnic and linguistic – and poses a challenge to all educational systems. Some authorities, schools and teachers look upon it as a problem, an obstacle to the achievement of national educational goals, whereas for others it offers new opportunities. The primary objective of educational systems is to help children and adolescents to develop the competences – knowledge, skills and attitudes – that they need if they are to function successfully in society. Competences are also acquired outside school, of course, at home, from friends, on the street, by belonging to youth clubs and so on; but out-of-school environments vary enormously, and one of the emancipatory functions of educational systems is to compensate for this variation. Yet the results of several consecutive PISA studies (Programme for International Student Assessment) carried out by the OECD (Organisation for Economic Cooperation and Development) lay bare the relative lack of success in responding to the diversity of school-going populations.

This book originated in the language strand of *New Migrations, New Challenges*, an international conference held at Trinity College Dublin in the summer of 2010. The conference was organised by the Trinity Immigration Initiative, a network of five loosely linked research projects: National Policy Impacts; Migrant Careers and Aspirations; Migrant Networks; Children, Youth and Community Relations; and the English Language Support Programme. Most contributions to the language strand of the conference reflected on aspects of the educational response to the unprecedented levels of immigration Ireland had experienced since the mid-1990s: policy and practice at primary, post-primary and tertiary levels. Historically, Ireland has been a country of emigration rather than immigration; and although significant numbers of migrants came from new EU member states, especially Poland, Latvia and Lithuania, overall the migrant population was extremely diverse. As the international contributions to the conference showed, however, Ireland's emerging educational experience was strikingly similar to that of other countries. This is further confirmed by the additional international contributions to the book, from Canada, France, The Netherlands, Germany and the United States.

The book is divided into three parts that deal in turn with policy and its implications, pedagogical practice, and responses to the challenge of diversity that go beyond – in some cases a long way beyond – the language of schooling.

Part 1

The relationship between education and national development in a knowledge-based economy motivated the OECD to initiate PISA. This has highlighted the extent of immigrant students' underachievement in many affluent countries and also the considerable variability across countries in the extent to which these students succeed academically. The first chapter, by Jim Cummins, analyses the ways in which Canada and the United States have incorporated the PISA data and other research findings into their educational policy. In both countries little consideration has been given to the role of societal power relations and their manifestation in patterns of teacher–student identity negotiation. Policy-makers have also largely ignored research related to the role of immigrant students' first language as both a cognitive tool and a reflection of their identity, and the importance of reading engagement as a major factor determining reading achievement. The chapter outlines an empirically based theoretical framework that explicitly addresses the roles of literacy engagement and identity negotiation as determinants of student achievement.

Chapter 2, by Tracey Costley and Constant Leung, considers how policy is used to manage diversity in state-funded education in England, and how it shapes and informs local schooling practices. The authors are particularly concerned with English as Additional Language (EAL) students, and the professional and institutional processes through which policy is rendered 'on site' by teachers in local schools. The chapter traces policy dispositions and social values regarding the teaching of EAL, and draws on ethnographic data to provide an account of the ways in which a London primary school conceptualised and organised EAL provision. Costley and Leung explore the ways in which the learners' needs were construed by the school and how the views of the staff were translated into curriculum arrangements and classroom pedagogy. In the final part of the chapter they suggest that a pedagogic and curricular vacuum has been engendered by a 'symbolic policy' on EAL, and argue that the symbolic nature of policy allows a school community to engage in curriculum and teaching practices that are commensurate with educational segregation on the basis of students' language and cultural backgrounds.

Since the 'PISA shock' in 2001, Germany has embarked on a contentious debate that has led, among other things, to the evaluation of student competences and educational progress. In Chapter 3 Daniel Faas draws on interviews with seven educational policy-makers to discuss the challenges and transformations that followed the 'PISA shock' and presents their views on how to balance cultural diversity and social cohesion in 'post-PISA' Germany. The interview material is triangulated with curriculum documents for History, Geography and Citizenship. Faas's study found that importance is attached to national, European and multicultural values and to making interculturalism a 'lived reality' in the classroom. But as regards cultural autonomy, there was disagreement between ministry officials on the one hand and curriculum planners and educational evaluators on the other. The chapter reveals that despite the efforts at educational reform that followed PISA, Germany still has some way to go if it is to close the gap between ethnic majority and migrant minority students, especially those from Turkish communities. Many of the questions raised in this chapter are also raised in debates elsewhere in Europe.

Chapter 4, by Rachael Fionda, presents findings from a small-scale empirical exploration of the English language support provided for EAL students in Irish post-primary schools. Working within the framework of the Trinity Immigration Initiative's English Language Support Programme, Fionda began by analysing the provision of funding for English language support. A preliminary survey of ten schools then revealed that many of them struggled to devise programmes apt to develop students' English language proficiency and give them access to curriculum content. Finally, the provision of English language support in three of the ten schools was studied longitudinally through the school year 2008–2009. Informed by a broadly Gramscian perspective, Fionda's research supports the view that education systems reproduce dominant cultural ideology and in doing so maintain the disadvantage of minority cultural groups. A key argument concerns the 'gap' between the knowledge presented by the school system and the knowledge and experience that marginalised students bring to school.

The scale and speed of inward migration to Ireland have had a major impact on the working lives of teachers. In Chapter 5, Fiona Kearney presents the findings of a study that used a questionnaire survey and semi-structured follow-up interviews to investigate the attitudes of Irish post-primary teachers to the presence of migrant students in their classrooms. Kearney found that teacher attitudes are mediated by ideological and structural factors such as personal experience and school context, and she argues for the importance of training and support in moderating teacher resistance to inclusion. Her chapter reminds us that teachers play a critically important role in any attempt to address issues of diversity in education.

Like other English-speaking countries, Ireland has a long tradition of recruiting higher education students from beyond its national borders. On the whole, international students have been expected to arrive in Ireland with a level of proficiency in English appropriate to their chosen programme of study. High levels of immigration over the past decade and a half mean, however, that there is now a population of EAL students who still need English language support when they enter third-level education. Chapter 6, by Bríd Ní Chonaill, offers an overview of the English language support provided to third-level students from migrant backgrounds in the academic year 2009–2010. Of the 27 designated institutions of Ireland's Higher Education Authority (HEA), only 10 offered English language classes or other forms of language support to students for whom English was an additional language. Ní Chonaill's study raised questions about the need to provide English language support for students who are not native speakers of English, whether they are recruited internationally, are participating in an exchange programme, or come from immigrant families resident in Ireland; the deficit in terms of academic English that can contribute to underachievement; and the question of who is responsible for bringing such students' English language proficiency to the necessary level – the student, the institution or the state? The study concluded that given the HEA's aim to promote equality of opportunity in higher education, the question of language support for migrants, and indeed all non-native speakers of English, needs to be addressed.

Part 2

Although some chapters in Part 1 address matters of classroom practice, their primary orientation is to policy. The four chapters in Part 2, on the other hand, are concerned with pedagogy, though in some cases policy provides an essential framework. Chapter 7, by Bronagh Ćatibušić, reports on research into English L2 acquisition among immigrant pupils in three Irish primary schools. Focusing on the development of oral skills, it compares empirical evidence of L2 development with the L2 learning outcomes specified in the *English Language Proficiency Benchmarks for non-English-speaking pupils at primary level.* These are officially sanctioned guidelines for the provision of English language support that are based on the first three proficiency levels of the *Common European Framework of Reference for Languages* (CEFR). The research took the form of a longitudinal study of 18 EAL pupils' acquisition of English L2 over a 10-month period and involved a mixed-methods form-function analysis of about 80 hours of recorded classroom talk. The results show that a clear relation exists between the learning outcomes defined by the *Benchmarks* and actual patterns of L2 acquisition evident among the participating pupils. Bearing in mind the diversity of the participants and the range of possible internal and external influences on the acquisition of English L2 oral skills, the *Benchmarks* may thus be said to offer a flexible 'map' of L2 proficiency development appropriate to the individual language learning needs of EAL pupils. This chapter points to the need for empirical validation of transnational language proficiency scales.

In Chapter 8 Patrick Grommes outlines the German vocational training system and its accessibility to students from migrant backgrounds, then discusses the aims and objectives of one particular sector as regards migrant students' language development. The concept of *Bildungssprache* (academic language) informs the analysis of written texts by two students, one Polish and the other Turkish. Although both students show sufficient general language competence, they lack appropriate skills in *Bildungssprache*. Comparing these skills, the aims and objectives of the training programme and its implementation, Grommes concludes that conflicting goals may be built into the system.

The next two chapters originated in the work of the Trinity Immigration Initiative's English Language Support Programme, which was concerned with the development of migrant students' proficiency in English as language of schooling at post-primary level. In Chapter 9 Stergiani Kostopoulou reports on a corpus linguistic analysis of textbooks in six curriculum subjects: English, Geography, History, CSPE (Civic, Social and Political Education), Mathematics and Science. The chapter begins by outlining the rationale for the research and summarising the aims of corpus analysis. It then describes the six textbooks-derived corpora and the methodological procedures employed to analyse them, and presents the principal empirical findings. These include the most frequent content words together with their significant collocates and the most frequent 4-word clusters in each corpus. Lexical features are discussed in relation to their semantic value and functional utility in individual corpora. Overall, the empirical analysis reveals the lexical variation that exists across subjects and provides pedagogically useful information on curriculum language as a whole.

Post-primary subject teachers often report that their students are not maximising their learning potential and are unable to engage with subject-specific content at a level that ensures comprehension. In Chapter 10 Zachary Lyons describes the development of a website that delivers a large array of learning materials based on the findings of the corpus analysis presented in Chapter 9. The website offers a new approach to the teaching and learning of subject-specific language across the first four proficiency levels of CEFR. The second part of the article reports on an empirical study that sought to measure the impact of these materials on teachers' daily practice.

Part 3

A large proportion of the policy and practice that seeks to address the challenge of linguistic, cultural and ethnic diversity focuses on the need to ensure that children and adolescents from migrant backgrounds develop adequate proficiency in the language of schooling. This is no doubt understandable as a first response to the challenge, but effective diversity management must address a number of issues in addition to the language of schooling. The chapters in Part 3 focus on three such issues: making use of migrants' languages to enhance their cognitive growth but also to enhance the language awareness of all pupils; responding to a legal requirement simultaneously to teach through several different languages; and developing awareness of the potential of mobile phone technology to create new opportunities for informal learning, with clear implications for formal education.

In Chapter 11 Déirdre Kirwan describes the evolution of policy and practice in the primary school in Blanchardstown, Dublin, of which she is principal. The school has always given priority to ensuring that EAL pupils have access to their peers and to the curriculum as quickly and efficiently as possible. As a result of their experience of multilingual classrooms, some teachers have begun to develop plurilingual awareness among both newcomer and indigenous pupils. Using the diverse languages present in the classroom, they cultivate an environment where children learn to communicate while increasing their awareness of the analytical elements involved in language learning in an informal way. This has aroused pupils' interest in the exploration of language and seems to aid their understanding at more complex levels of thinking and learning. Such an approach can flourish, however, only when teachers are committed to valuing all languages equally.

Specialists emphasise the importance of multilingualism as an added value for those aiming for an international career in Europe. Children are encouraged to learn French, English, German, Spanish and Italian and, if possible, to use these new languages at home, with friends and on holiday. On the other hand, the multilingualism of immigrant minority children, adolescents and their parents is often considered to be an obstacle to success at school. In Flanders parents are sometimes encouraged to abandon their own language and talk Dutch to their children; in some schools children are forbidden to speak any language other than Dutch. Chapter 12, by Sven Sierens and Piet Van Avermaet, responds to this situation by arguing that three strategies are necessary in order to manage linguistic diversity at school: a constructive language policy, linguistic sensitisation, and functional multilingual learning. This last is conceptualised as an alternative to the binary opposition between monolingual and multilingual education: a new pedagogical approach that exploits children's plurilingual repertoires as didactic capital for learning.

A similar argument is developed by Nathalie Auger in Chapter 13. Despite interesting experiments in the promotion of language awareness ('éveil aux langues') and research findings on both sides of the Atlantic that support the view that learners' L1 is always a good foundation for the learning of second/additional languages, the use of learners' L1 proficiency in multilingual classrooms has still to find a secure place on the educational agenda in France. Indeed, until 2002 the French educational system treated mother tongues other than French as a handicap. Auger reports on a study that set out to discover whether immigrant pupils' mother tongues were used in classrooms; classroom observation was complemented by interviews with pupils, teachers and parents. Her analysis confirms that the use of migrant languages is rare, and leads into a discussion of how such languages can be used in schools and what benefits such an approach can bring.

In the United States as in Europe language may be one of the few areas where overt discrimination is still permissible: it is common for people to insist that only Standard American English should be used in public life, and equally common for bilingual American students to be given to understand that their language practices are inappropriate in US society. Aware of the difficulties experienced especially by emergent bilingual students – that is, students who are still developing English – well-meaning educators insist on teaching Standard American English, often with the unintended consequence of delegitimizing the students' home language practices (similar practices are reported in France and Flanders by Auger and Sierens and Van Avermaet respectively). In Chapter 14, Nelson Flores and Ofelia García propose an alternative pedagogical approach that embraces the fluid language practices of bilingual and multilingual students. Focusing on the alternative language practices of two English teachers at a school for Spanish-speaking immigrants in New York City, they argue that the linguistic 'third spaces' constructed by these teachers transcend the hegemonic language ideologies that emerged within the nation state paradigm.

Complex multilingual societies are the norm in many parts of the world. Accordingly, UNESCO (2003) describes societal multilingualism as a way of life, not a problem to be solved; and it argues that any 'problems' posed by multilingualism should not be attributed to culturally or linguistically diverse children, but to educational systems that have not adapted to complex realities and do not provide quality education that takes learners' needs into consideration. Countries that may at first seem worlds apart, such as Canada, Ireland and Nepal, face similar challenges in the management of diversity in education. In Chapter 15 Shelley Taylor introduces a model of multilingual language education designed to manage linguistic diversity in Nepal and summarises the reactions of minority and dominant group members to the model. A unique aspect of the Nepali initiative is that there are some 140 reported languages in the country, which makes L1-based instruction for all a major undertaking and many-layered process. The chapter considers whose interests the initiative serves, how it has been implemented, and what other countries that are grappling with diversity management can learn from the Nepali response.

Education is intuitively understood as being located in the institutional realm of schools and adjacent formal learning environments. It is thus good to remind ourselves that formal learning environments are always surrounded by complex informal learning environments, and that learning and teaching are features of an enormous range of everyday social practices performed individually as well as in small peer groups and (increasingly) in large virtual networks. The boundaries between formal and informal learning environments are porous, and skills and knowledge acquired in one seep through into the other. New technologies – the internet and mobile communication devices – have complicated and intensified the development of informal learning environments, shaping a space for new literacy and numeracy practices. Where access to formal learning environments is or has been constrained, such new technologies often promote the acquisition of skills and forms of knowledge not otherwise available. The last chapter in the book, by Fie Velghe and Jan Blommaert, engages with these issues. It explores the ways in which mobile phones have acquired communicational prominence in a township near Cape Town, South Africa, becoming a resource that has acquired specific functions by virtue of its 'ecological' insertion into broader local economies of knowledge and resources. The chapter is thus an attempt to situate the use of mobile phones as learning devices in the broader local communicative, social and cultural framework.

Reference

UNESCO (2003) *Education in a Multilingual World.* http://unesdoc.unesco.org/images/0012/001297/129728e.pdf (accessed 9 August 2013).

Part 1

1 Language and Identity in Multilingual Schools: Constructing Evidence-based Instructional Policies

Jim Cummins

Since the mid-1990s, educational underachievement among immigrant and other marginalized social groups has increased in significance for policy-makers in many countries because of the demonstrated relationship between education and national development in a knowledge-based economy. This relationship motivated the Organisation for Economic Cooperation and Development (OECD) to initiate the Programme for International Student Achievement (PISA) which provides member countries with a 'report card' on the effectiveness of their educational systems, including the relative success of students from immigrant backgrounds. PISA has highlighted the extent of immigrant students' underachievement in many affluent countries and also the considerable variability across countries in the extent to which these students succeed academically. This chapter analyses the ways in which the PISA data and other research findings have been incorporated into educational policy in the Canadian and United States contexts. In both contexts, there exists a considerable gap between policies and research evidence. Specifically, there has been little consideration given to the role of societal power relations and their manifestation in patterns of teacher–student identity negotiation. Policy-makers have also largely ignored research related to the role of immigrant students' first language as both a cognitive tool and a reflection of student identity. Finally, little attention has been paid to the importance of reading engagement which has consistently emerged in the PISA research as a major determinant of

reading achievement. The chapter outlines an empirically-based theoretical framework that explicitly addresses the roles of literacy engagement and identity negotiation as determinants of student achievement.

Introduction

Underachievement among immigrant and other minority group students
is by no means a recent phenomenon. Students from groups that have experienced persistent discrimination in the wider society over several generations
are particularly vulnerable to educational failure (Ogbu, 1992). In the United
States context these groups include African American, Native American and
Latino students. In Europe, Roma and Traveller communities as well as more
recent immigrant communities have experienced widespread discrimination,
which is reflected in students' educational performance. Schools tend to
reflect the values of the societies that fund them and thus it is not surprising
that societal discrimination is frequently also reflected within the educational system. This discrimination expresses itself both in the structures of
schooling (e.g. curriculum and assessment practices) and in patterns of
teacher–student interaction. The subtle ways in which societal biases express
themselves in patterns of teacher–student interaction are illustrated in a
large-scale study conducted by the US Commission on Civil Rights (1973)
in the American southwest. Classroom observations revealed that Euro-
American students were praised or encouraged 36% more often than
Mexican-American students and their classroom contributions were used or
built upon 40% more frequently than those of Mexican-American students.

The link between societal discrimination and school performance was
clearly expressed in the judgment of the federal court in the United States
versus the State of Texas (1981) case which documented the 'pervasive, intentional discrimination throughout most of this century' against Mexican-
American students (a charge that was not contested by the State of Texas in
the trial). The judge noted that:

> the long history of prejudice and deprivation remains a significant obsta-
> cle to equal educational opportunity for these children. The deep sense
> of inferiority, cultural isolation, and acceptance of failure, instilled in a
> people by generations of subjugation, cannot be eradicated merely by
> integrating the schools and repealing the 'no Spanish' statutes. (1981: 14)

Indigenous communities throughout the world have similarly experienced
'generations of subjugation', which is also manifested in poor school

performance. In the Canadian context, for example, First Nations and Inuit students were taken from their communities, often against their parents' will, and placed in residential schools operated by religious orders. The physical, sexual and psychological abuse that occurred in these schools has been well-documented. Eradication of Native identity was seen as a prerequisite to making students into low-level productive Christian citizens.

This brief historical sketch of the educational experiences of minority group students illustrates one of the main themes of this chapter, which can be stated as follows:

> The academic achievement of minority group students is directly influenced both by the structures of schooling, which tend to reflect the values and priorities of the dominant group, and by the patterns of identity negotiation students experience in their interactions with educators within the school. Teacher–student interactions are never neutral – in contexts of social inequality these interactions either reinforce the devaluation of minority group culture, language and identity in the broader society or they challenge this devaluation. This implies that in order to reverse underachievement among minority group students, classroom instruction must affirm students' identities and challenge patterns of power relations in the broader society.

Efforts to reverse underachievement among low-income and minority group students were initiated in several countries during the 1960s, motivated primarily by renewed commitment to equity and social justice. These efforts have met with limited success. For example, data from the United States show that the achievement gap between low-income and more affluent students and between Euro-American and most groups of minority students remains large (Darling-Hammond, 2010).

However, during the past 15 years, educational underachievement has assumed greater significance for policy-makers in many countries because of the demonstrated relationship between education and economic development in a knowledge-based economy. The economic implications of increasing diversity derive from the fact that immigrants represent human capital, and school failure among any segment of the population entails significant economic costs. The relationship between education and the economy motivated the Organisation for Economic Cooperation and Development (OECD) to initiate the Programme for International Student Achievement (PISA), which provides member countries with a 'report card' on the effectiveness of their educational systems, including the relative success of first- and second-generation immigrant students. The PISA research has highlighted the extent of immigrant students' underachievement in many affluent countries (e.g. Germany, the United States) and also the considerable variability across countries in the extent to which these students succeed academically (Christensen & Segeritz, 2008; Stanat & Christensen, 2006).

An economic growth projection published by the OECD (2010a) estimated that even minimal improvements in the educational performance of socio-economically disadvantaged students would result in very significant long-term savings for member countries. OECD projections suggest that a 1% increase in adult literacy levels would translate into a 1.5% increase in a country's gross domestic product, which, in Canada's case, would amount to $18 billion per year (Coulombe et al., 2004). Thus, it is not surprising that the relatively poor literacy performance on the PISA tests by 15-year old first- and second-generation immigrant students in many of the more affluent European countries has given rise to intense debate about how to improve students' literacy skills.

Efforts to improve school achievement in general and among any segment of the school population are always premised on hypotheses regarding the causes of underachievement. Unfortunately, in many cases, these hypotheses derive more from ideological convictions than from rigorous analysis of the empirical data. This reality is not altogether surprising; there are obvious ideological complexities associated with social policies generally, and particularly with respect to issues of equality, income distribution, immigration and priorities within public education systems. Consequently, ideological presuppositions frequently influence what research is considered relevant and how that research is interpreted.

In this chapter, I attempt to critically assess the extent to which educational policies in relation to immigrant students (and minority group students more generally) are based on empirical evidence. In the first section, I review the outcomes for immigrant students in the 2003 and 2006 PISA studies and the recommendations for educational reform that have been made on the basis of these data. I then present an alternative analysis of the causal factors underlying the underachievement of certain groups of immigrant and minority students that draws on a wider range of research data than has typically been considered in relation to the PISA data. Finally, I examine the extent to which relevant research findings have been incorporated into educational policy in two national contexts: Canada and the United States. In each context, there exists a considerable gap between policies and research evidence. In no case have considerations related to teacher–student identity negotiation or patterns of societal power relations been explicitly integrated into causal or intervention frameworks despite the extensive research evidence attesting to the significance of these factors. By the same token, policy-makers have largely ignored research related to the role of migrant students' first language (L1) as both a cognitive tool and a reflection of student identity. The absence of identity negotiation and power relations from policy consideration is particularly notable given the prominence of these constructs in recent applied linguistics research and theory focused on second language learning and literacy development (see, for example, the review by Norton & Toohey, 2011).

Patterns of Immigrant Student Achievement

The 2003 and 2006 PISA reading achievement of 15-year-old first- and second-generation immigrant students in 15 countries is presented in Figure 1.1. Christensen and Segeritz (2008: 15) summarize the overall pattern of results as follows:

> With regard to reading, first- and second-generation students lag significantly behind their native peers in all of the assessed countries, except Australia and Israel, and second-generation students in Canada, New Zealand, and the United Kingdom.

The PISA data reveal major differences between countries in how well first- and second-generation immigrant students are doing in school. Students' performance tends to be better in countries such as Canada and Australia that have encouraged immigration over the past 40 years and that have a coherent infrastructure designed to integrate immigrants into the society (e.g. free adult language classes, language support services for students in schools, rapid qualification for full citizenship, etc.). In Canada (2003 assessment) and Australia (2006 assessment), second-generation students performed slightly *better* academically than native speakers of the school language. Some of these positive results in both countries can be attributed to selective immigration that favours immigrants with strong educational qualifications. First-generation immigrant students in Ireland exhibit relatively strong performance parallel to the patterns in Canada and Australia, which is likely related to the minimal differences in socioeconomic status between immigrant and native-born students (OECD, 2010b).

Christensen and Segeritz (2008: 18) point out that the poor performance of second-generation students in many countries should be a cause of concern to policy-makers: 'Of particular concern, especially for policy-makers, should be the fact that second-generation immigrant students in many countries continue to lag significantly behind their native peers despite spending all of their schooling in the receiving country.'

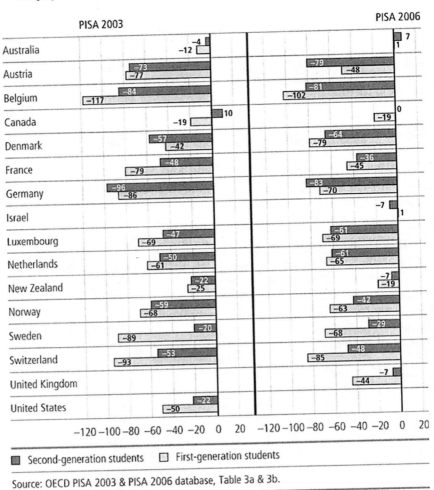

Figure 1.1 PISA Reading scores 2003 and 2006 (from Christensen & Segeritz, 2008: 16)

Barth and colleagues (2008), in commenting on the PISA data, identify some of the dimensions along which both policy-makers and educators can implement effective instruction for a diverse student body. Obviously, providing language support and an inclusive curriculum that integrates language and content are core elements. However, they also emphasize the necessity for schools to view diversity as a resource and to establish respectful collaborative partnerships with parents and the community. The OECD (2010b) also highlights the importance of capitalizing on the resources of immigrant communities and valuing and validating students' proficiency in their mother tongues. Little (2010) has expressed a similar perspective which is reflected in Council of Europe initiatives in this area: 'The language, ethnicity and culture that children and adolescents from migrant backgrounds bring to school are assets that must be exploited first for their own benefit as individuals and then for the benefit of the larger school community' (2010: 31).

However, this emphasis also highlights a major challenge for implementing educational change. As noted earlier, schools reflect the values and priorities of the societies that fund them. Thus, if the prevalent sentiment in a society is one of hostility to immigrants and diversity, then it is likely that a significant number of educators, who belong to that wider society, will also reflect the dominant discourse in their attitudes and practice. It is probably no coincidence that second-generation students tend to perform very poorly in countries that have been characterized by highly negative attitudes towards immigrants (e.g. Belgium, Denmark, Germany) and relatively well in countries such as Australia and Canada that have explicitly endorsed multicultural philosophies at the national level and which expedite integration into the society (e.g. in Canada immigrants become eligible for citizenship after three years residence).

Thus, a deeper analysis of the causes of immigrant and minority group underachievement is necessary if we are to understand the kinds of school-based changes and reforms that are required to promote equity of educational provision and outcomes. In the next section I document intersections among socioeconomic status (SES), societal power relations and teacher–student identity negotiation and argue that schools *do* have the power to push back at least some of the negative impact of out-of-school variables associated with SES.

Intersections Among Socioeconomic Status, Societal Power Relations and Identity Negotiation

Socioeconomic status

SES has emerged in virtually every study of school achievement as one of the strongest and most consistent predictors of student outcomes. In a large-scale longitudinal study, Kieffer (2011) has reported that the effect of SES on reading achievement appears to vary according to the grade level of the student:

> Findings from this study suggest that children's socioeconomic backgrounds and those of their classmates do not exert uniform effects on reading across development. Rather, students from lower SES backgrounds start lower in reading achievement, but then make more rapid growth in the primary grades, and go on to demonstrate slower growth in the upper-elementary and middle school grades, compared to their peers with higher SES. Students in schools with high concentrations of poverty can be expected to make even slower growth in later grades.

This pattern of findings may be related to the fact that early reading instruction and assessment tend to focus on decoding skills which are largely rule-governed and sensitive to instruction whereas at later grades the focus of instruction and assessment is on reading comprehension, which is strongly related to vocabulary knowledge and less capable of being developed through direct instruction. Vocabulary knowledge also varies extensively across social class groups (Hart & Risley, 1995).

However, SES does not fully explain differences in students' reading performance. This is illustrated by the pattern of PISA performance observed in many countries.

> Socio-economic background is strongly associated with student performance; performance differences are substantially reduced after accounting for socio-economic factors such as the occupation and education level of students' parents. However, it does not fully explain the observed performance disadvantage for immigrant students, and in most countries, substantial performance gaps for immigrant students remain even after accounting for socio-economic backgrounds. (OECD, 2010b: 37)

As an explanatory factor SES is complex. It tends to be viewed as a static inherent characteristic of students and their families but, in reality, reflects a dynamic confluence of in-school and out-of-school variables intimately linked to current and historical patterns of societal power relations. The link between SES and patterns of social exclusion experienced by many immigrant communities is acknowledged by the OECD (2006: 7–8) as follows:

> Moreover, disadvantaged background characteristics of immigrant students may, at least in part, themselves be outcomes of past public policies, such as when a low usage of the language of assessment at home is

due to insufficient language support of immigrant families or when difficulties in the access to labour-markets lower the occupational status of the parents of immigrant students.

Among the SES-related factors that have been highlighted in the United States context as directly affecting students' educational prospects are less access to maternal prenatal care, lower quality nutrition, exposure to lead, less access to books and computers, attendance at schools with less qualified teachers, greater concentrations of low-SES students and significantly less funding than schools serving more affluent students (Anyon, 2005; Berliner, 2009; Kozol, 2005; Rothstein, 2004, 2010). Further evidence of the impact of socioeconomic variables is seen in the fact that interventions to address these factors produce educational benefits. Detailed reviews by Rothstein (2004) and Berliner (2009) highlight extensive evidence that non-school interventions such as increasing family income, ensuring adequate nutrition, provision of prenatal and general health care were associated with increased cognitive ability and/or academic achievement among low-income students.

Rothstein (2004) estimates that out-of-school factors associated with SES (most of which are beyond the control of teachers) account for about 60% of the variance in student achievement outcomes, leaving only 40% that can potentially be accounted for by in-school factors. Thus, it is unrealistic to expect instructional interventions alone to reverse the achievement gap when the bulk of this gap is associated with socioeconomic disparities.

However, the distinction between in-school and out-of-school factors is less clear-cut than implied by the preceding discussion. Some out-of-school factors associated with SES, such as access to print, are also very much affected by in-school policies and interventions. Several research studies have reinforced the fact that students from lower-income communities have significantly less access to books and other forms of print in both their schools and homes than is the case for students from middle-income communities (Duke, 2000; Neuman & Celano, 2001). The fact that low-SES students have significantly less access to print throws light on the consistent relationship between reading engagement and reading achievement observed in the PISA studies. Not only has reading engagement emerged as a highly significant predictor of reading achievement but, across OECD countries, the PISA data show that approximately one-third of the association between reading performance and students' SES was mediated by reading engagement (OECD, 2010a). The implication is that schools can counteract the negative influences of limited access to print outside the school and lessen the negative effects of socioeconomic disadvantage by ensuring that within the school students have access to a rich print environment and become actively engaged with literacy.

Educators can also directly challenge the devaluation of the social capital of low-SES communities by validating students' language, culture and identities within the school.

The link between societal power relations and school experiences of minority group students has been succinctly expressed by Ladson-Billings (1995: 485) with respect to African-American students: 'The problem that African-American students face is the constant devaluation of their culture both in school and in the larger society.' Schools that actively attempt to affirm students' language, culture, and identities are therefore addressing simultaneously both in-school (instructional) and out-of-school causes of underachievement. This perspective is elaborated in the following section.

In summary, SES effects on student achievement are dynamic rather than static and, to some extent, can be mitigated by instructional strategies that address components of SES such as print access/literacy engagement and devaluation of student and community identity.

Societal power relations

Despite the fact that the influence of societal power relations on the educational experiences of subordinated group students is clearly evident in the historical record, current educational policies in OECD countries make virtually no mention of power relations as a relevant variable affecting students' academic achievement. The discourse of equality and social justice initiated in many countries during the 1960s, together with legal inscription of equality rights and non-discrimination, has desensitized many policymakers and educators to the more subtle forms of exclusion and discrimination that continue to operate in societal institutions, including schools.

The intersection of societal power relations and SES in affecting achievement is clearly evident in the social segregation characteristic of communities and schools in the United States and many European contexts. Low-income and socially marginalized communities tend to live in segregated housing contexts and attend schools that have high concentrations of students from similar backgrounds. Attending schools with large concentrations of low-income and minority group students is strongly related to student achievement above and beyond the effect of individual SES (OECD, 2010c).

The structure and content of teacher education programmes represents another example of how societal power relations operate. Most teacher education faculties that prepare teachers to teach a highly diverse student body (e.g. in major cities in North America and Europe) devote minimal attention to the instructional skills required to teach content effectively to immigrant students who are in the process of learning the school language (a catch-up process that frequently requires about five years). It is assumed that teaching language is the job of a specialist language teacher and is thus not directly a concern of the 'mainstream' classroom teacher. The structure of teacher education programmes reflects the educational priorities of the society and thus, in many contexts, it can be inferred that it is not a priority to ensure that teachers and school administrators have the knowledge base required to teach immigrant students effectively.

There is an extensive research base, primarily from the disciplines of sociology and anthropology, that documents how societal power relations influence educational achievement (e.g. Bankston & Zhou, 1995; Bishop & Berryman, 2006; McCarty, 2005; Ogbu, 1978, 1992; Portes & Rumbaut, 2001; Skutnabb-Kangas, 2000). As noted previously, groups that experience long-term educational underachievement have frequently experienced material and symbolic violence at the hands of the dominant societal group over generations. The operation of these power structures is a direct determinant of the current low SES of many of these groups. A direct implication is that in order to reverse this pattern of underachievement, educators, both individually and collectively, must challenge the operation of societal power relations in the classroom interactions they orchestrate with minority or subordinated group students. The intersection of societal power relations and identity negotiation in determining patterns of academic achievement among minority group students is expressed in Figure 1.2.

The framework proposes that relations of power in the wider society, ranging from coercive to collaborative in varying degrees, influence both the ways in which educators define their roles and the types of structures that are established in the educational system. Coercive relations of power refer to the exercise of power by a dominant individual, group, or country to the detriment of a subordinated individual, group or country. For example, school policies that prohibit minority group students from using their home languages (L1) within the school can be seen as expressions of coercive relations of power insofar as they communicate to students that only the dominant language and culture are legitimate within the school and society. Such policies are entirely ideological and without empirical justification with respect to either language learning or academic achievement (see Cummins, 2001 for documentation).

Collaborative relations of power, by contrast, reflect the sense of the term 'power' that refers to 'being enabled', or 'empowered', to achieve more. Within collaborative relations of power, 'power' is not a fixed quantity but is generated through interaction with others. The more empowered one individual or group becomes, the more is generated for others to share. Within this context,

SOCIETAL POWER RELATIONS
influence
the ways in which educators define their role (teacher identity)
and
the structures of schooling (curriculum, funding, assessment, etc.)
which, in turn, influence
the ways in which educators interact
with linguistically – and culturally – diverse students.

These interactions form an
INTERPERSONAL SPACE
within which
learning happens
and
identities are negotiated.

These IDENTITY NEGOTIATIONS
either
reinforce coercive relations of power
or
promote collaborative relations of power.

Figure 1.2 Societal power relations, identity negotiation, and academic achievement (Adapted from *Negotiating identities: Education for empowerment in a diverse society* by J. Cummins, 2001: 20)

empowerment can be defined as *the collaborative creation of power.* Students whose schooling experiences reflect collaborative relations of power participate confidently in instruction as a result of the fact that their sense of identity is being affirmed and extended in their interactions with educators.

Educator role definitions refer to the mindset of expectations, assumptions and goals that educators bring to the task of educating culturally diverse students. Educational structures refer to the organization of schooling in a broad sense that includes policies, programmes, curriculum and assessment. Although these structures will generally reflect the values and priorities of dominant groups in society, they are not by any means fixed or static. As with most other aspects of the way societies are organized and resources distributed, educational structures can be contested by individuals and groups.

Educational structures, together with educator role definitions, determine the patterns of interactions between educators, students and communities. These interactions form an interpersonal space within which the acquisition of knowledge and formation of identity is negotiated. Power is created and shared within this interpersonal space where minds and identities meet. As such, these teacher–student interactions constitute the most immediate determinant of student academic success or failure.

The interactions between educators, students and communities are never neutral; in varying degrees, they either reinforce coercive relations of power or promote collaborative relations of power. In the former case, they contribute to the disempowerment of culturally diverse students and communities; in the latter case, the interactions constitute a process of empowerment that enables educators, students and communities to challenge the operation of coercive power structures.

Negotiation of identity by teachers and students

Parallel to the omission of societal power relations as a factor in accounting for students' underachievement, issues related to students' identity have also been omitted from policy consideration in most contexts. This is somewhat surprising in view of the fact that 'over the past 15 years, there has been an explosion of interest in identity and language learning, and "identity" now features in most encyclopedias and handbooks of language learning and teaching' (Norton & Toohey, 2011: 413). The comprehensive review of this research carried out by Norton and Toohey highlights how language learners negotiate their identities in relation to teachers and their native-speaking peers and frequently resist their positioning within the school system (e.g. as an 'ESL student').

One likely reason why this research has received so little attention from researchers and policy-makers concerned with educational reform is that the construct of 'identity' is difficult to operationalize in quantitative ways. As Norton and Toohey (2011: 426) point out, the 'methods required for investigating the intersection between identity positions and language learning are complex ... [and] methods that rely on static, inherent, and measurable learner "variables" are not consistent with some of the major understandings of these approaches'. Because the construct of identity is conceptualized as 'multiple, changing, and a site of struggle' (p. 414), it cannot be reduced to a quantifiable variable whose influence on achievement can be objectively measured. They note that fieldwork-based studies of identity and language learning include 'ethnographic observation, interviews (including life history interviews), diary studies, journal writing and written responses (narrative or other) to researcher questions' (p. 428).

In addition to these qualitative studies, the role of identity negotiation in the performance of various cognitive tasks can be inferred from quantitative research into the phenomenon of *stereotype threat* (Steele, 1997). Schofield and Bangs (2006: 93), in a review of this phenomenon, define stereotype threat as 'the threat of being judged and found wanting based on negative stereotypes related to one's social category membership'. They point out that stereotype threat can significantly undercut the achievement of immigrant and minority students: 'Stereotype threat can undermine the academic performance of children as young as 5 or 6 years of age, and its effects can be quite large' (p. 93). Thus, deficit perspectives on the abilities of minority group communities in the wider society are frequently communicated directly or indirectly to students in teacher–student interactions. The result is that students internalize these negative attributions which undermine their confidence in their intellectual and academic abilities.

The impact of identity negotiation and its relationship to broader patterns of power relationships can be seen in the research of Bishop and Berryman (2006) that explored patterns of educational engagement among Maori youth in New Zealand. Very different perspectives on causes of students' lack of academic engagement emerged from interviews with educators, the students themselves, and community members. Bishop and Berryman (2006) describe the varying perspectives as follows:

> A large proportion of the teachers we interviewed took a position from which they explained Maori students' lack of educational achievement in deficit terms [i.e. Maori students themselves and their homes]. This gave rise to low expectations of Maori students' ability or a fatalistic attitude in the face of 'the system', creating a downward-spiralling, self-fulfilling prophecy of low Maori student achievement and failure. In terms of agency, this is a helpless position to take, because it means that there is very little any individual teacher can do about the achievement of the Maori students in his or her classroom. (p. 261)
>
> . . ..
>
> In contrast, the students, their whanau *[family]*, and their principals most commonly identified the major influences on Maori students' educational achievement as coming under the broad heading of 'relationships and interactions'. Those who take this position are putting forward explanations based on the power differentials and imbalances between the various participants in the relationships and focusing on how they can and must be managed better. (p. 263)

Bishop and Berryman (2006) highlight the influence of the 'imagery' that teachers hold of Maori children:

> Simply put, if the imagery held of Maori children (or indeed of any children) and the resulting interaction patterns stem from deficits and pathologies, then teachers' principles and practices will reflect this, and the educational crisis for Maori students will be perpetuated. (p. 263)

On the basis of interventions they helped initiate in collaboration with educators, they argue that in order to be effective, instruction must challenge the devaluation of Maori identity in the school and wider society. This type of instruction involves 'the teacher creating a culturally appropriate and responsive learning context, where young people can engage in learning by bringing their prior cultural knowledge and experiences to classroom interactions, which legitimate these, instead of ignoring or rejecting them' (pp. 264–265).

In summary, effective education for minority or subordinated group students will affirm students' identities at school, thereby challenging patterns of coercive power relations in the broader society. The goal is to promote *identities of competence* (Manyak, 2004) among students by enabling them to showcase their linguistic talents, intellectual abilities and creativity. When schools legitimate and expand students' cultural capital in this way, they reduce the impact of SES on students' achievement to the extent that some of this negative impact is mediated through societal power relations.

The framework presented in the next section attempts to articulate the core empirical relationships that have been established regarding the forms of instruction that will most effectively promote academic achievement among linguistically diverse students, many of whom also come from marginalized and low-SES communities. In particular, the framework highlights the roles of literacy engagement and identity affirmation that have been minimally considered in contemporary school improvement initiatives in countries around the world.

A Framework for Implementing Evidence-based Pedagogy in Diverse School Contexts

The Literacy Engagement framework (Figure 1.3) posits print access/ literacy engagement as a direct determinant of literacy attainment. Print access and literacy engagement are two sides of the same coin – without abundant access to books and printed materials in home or school, children are unlikely to engage actively with literacy. This relationship between

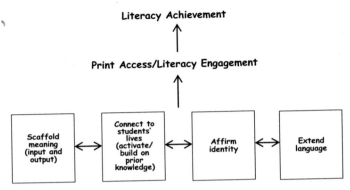

Figure 1.3 An evidence-based framework for promoting literacy achievement among linguistically diverse students

literacy engagement and achievement is strongly supported by the empirical research (e.g. Guthrie, 2004; Krashen, 2004; Lindsay, 2010; OECD, 2004, 2010d). The PISA studies have consistently reported a strong relationship between reading engagement and reading achievement among 15-year-old students in countries around the world. For example, the 2000 PISA study (OECD, 2004) led to the conclusion that 'the level of a student's reading engagement is a better predictor of literacy performance than his or her socioeconomic background, indicating that cultivating a student's interest in reading can help overcome home disadvantages' (OECD, 2004: 8). The authors point out that 'engagement in reading can be a consequence, as well as a cause, of higher reading skill, but the evidence suggests that these two factors are mutually reinforcing' (p. 8). As noted earlier, the more recent PISA studies (OECD, 2010a, 2010d) show that about one-third of the impact of SES on achievement is mediated by reading engagement. In these more recent PISA studies engagement in reading was assessed through measures of time spent reading various materials, enjoyment of reading, and use of various learning strategies.

The importance of print access/literacy engagement has been confirmed by a comprehensive meta-analysis of 108 research studies that concluded: 'Separate meta-analytic procedures performed on just those effects produced by "rigorous" studies (i.e. experimental or quasi-experimental) suggest that children's access to print materials plays a *causal* role in facilitating behavioral, educational, and psychological outcomes in children – especially attitudes toward reading, reading behavior, emergent literacy skills, and reading performance' (Lindsay, 2010: 85).

The framework also specifies four broad instructional dimensions that are critical to enabling all students (and particularly those from marginalized groups) to engage actively with literacy from an early stage of their schooling. Literacy engagement will be enhanced when (a) students' ability to understand and use academic language is scaffolded through specific instructional strategies (e.g. use of visual and graphic organizers, development of learning strategies, enabling students to use their L1 to clarify content [e.g. through discussion, dictionary use, or L1 electronic or text resources]), (b) instruction connects to students' lives by activating their prior knowledge which is often encoded in their L1, (c) instruction affirms students' academic, linguistic and cultural identities by enabling them to showcase their literacy accomplishments in both L1 and L2, and (d) students' knowledge of and control over language is extended across the curriculum through instructional strategies such as encouraging them to compare and contrast L1 and L2.

The distinctions captured in the framework are frequently fused in classroom practice. For example, acknowledging and activating students' prior experience simultaneously affirms the legitimacy of that experience and, by extension, the legitimacy of students' identities. Bilingual students' identity is also affirmed when they are encouraged to use their L1 writing abilities as a stepping stone or scaffold to writing in their L2. Although not highlighted as a separate category, the implementation of bilingual instructional strategies that acknowledge and legitimate students' L1 is an integral component within each of the instructional dimensions.

There is virtually universal consensus among researchers and educators about the relevance of scaffolding instruction, activating prior knowledge, and extending students' awareness of and ability to use academic language. However, there has been only sporadic acknowledgement of the importance of literacy engagement and identity affirmation within educational policies. The role of students' L1 as a cognitive and academic resource has also not been widely acknowledged.

The following sections outline briefly how empirical evidence in relation to the achievement of immigrant and minority group students has been taken up by policy-makers in two educational contexts: the United States and Canada.

Interpretations of Evidence-based Policies in Two International Contexts

The United States

Educational policies designed to promote literacy achievement in US schools over the past decade have been dominated by the provisions of the *No Child Left Behind* (2001) legislation that increased the amount of mandated standardized testing schools were required to administer and instituted punitive sanctions for any school that consistently failed to make 'adequate yearly progress'. These policies have failed to deliver the anticipated outcomes. Significant achievement gaps persist between economic and social groups and more than 50% of American schools are failing to make 'adequate yearly progress' as defined by the provisions of the *No Child Left Behind* legislation.

From the perspective of the Literacy Engagement framework, the failure of educational reform efforts designed to 'leave no child behind' can be attributed to the minimal attention paid to the role of literacy engagement in predicting literacy achievement and the total omission of consideration related to the impact of societal power relations and their reflection in patterns of teacher–student identity negotiation.

Instead, policy discourse in the United States has focused on blaming teachers and teacher unions for the perceived 'fact' that the system is 'broken'. This discourse, most prominently expressed in the 2010 film *Waiting for Superman*, attributes the problems of American education to the influence of 'bad teachers' who cannot be held accountable (and fired) because they are protected by teacher unions. The proposed solutions involve eliminating unions' right to collective bargaining, expanding non-unionized charter schools, and using high-stakes standardized tests to measure not only the progress of students but also the effectiveness of teachers and the teacher education programmes that certified them.

The evidence-free nature of these policies can be seen in the fact that EAL (English as an Additional Language) students have been exempted from testing only in their first year of learning English despite the fact that the empirical evidence shows that even after three years of learning English (in English-only programmes), only 12% of EAL students had acquired sufficient academic English to be re-designated as English-proficient (Parrish *et al.*, 2006).

Opposing the dominant perspective are a large majority of educational researchers (e.g. Berliner, 2009; Darling-Hammond, 2010) who dispute the blanket generalization that American schools are failing and highlight instead the fact that underachievement is concentrated in schools serving low-income and racially/culturally marginalized students. The impact of SES on achievement within the United States is dramatically illustrated in the 2009 PISA data (OECD, 2010a). Students in schools with less than 10% of students eligible for free or reduced-price lunch scored an average of 551 on the reading measure, whereas those in schools with 75% or more students eligible for free or reduced-price lunch scored 446, a difference of more than 100 points. The US mean was 500, slightly higher than the

OECD average of 493. These SES differences in achievement are very significantly larger than in countries such as Finland, Canada and Australia that show much higher levels of overall achievement. Despite the overwhelming negative impact of SES-related variables and the evidence regarding how long it takes EAL students to learn academic English, any attempt to invoke these factors in explaining school performance is met with a 'no excuses' response.

Canada

As noted previously, PISA data suggest that immigrant students in Canada perform relatively well academically in comparison to those in most other countries. The OECD (2010c) summarizes the Canadian profile as follows:

> PISA results suggest that within three years of arrival in Canada, immigrants score an average of 500 on the PISA exam, which is remarkably strong by international standards. For comparison's sake, in the 2006 PISA assessment of reading, Canadian first-generation immigrants scored an average of 520 points, as opposed to less than 490 in the United States and less than 430 in France. Canada is also one of very few countries where there is no gap between its immigrant and native students on the PISA. (By contrast in the United States the gap in reading is 22 points, and in France and Germany it is around 60 points). Second-generation Canadians perform significantly better than first-generation Canadians, suggesting that the pattern is of progress by all students over time. Finally, Canada is one of the few countries where there is no difference in performance between students who do not speak the language of instruction at home and those who do. (OECD, 2010c: 70–71)

The OECD (2010c: 71) attributes the relative success of immigrant students as a group to the fact that they 'have much the same advantages in terms of parental education and socio-economic status as native-born students, and they attend schools that by all measures are relatively equal'. They also point to the fact that immigrants are welcomed as part of Canada's commitment to multiculturalism which 'provides a distinct philosophy that seeks to both respect the importance of native cultures while also incorporating immigrants into a distinctively Canadian identity' (p. 71).

Contributing to the overall positive outcomes with respect to reading achievement within Canadian schools is the fact that, unlike the United States, Canada has largely avoided divisive ideological debates about the teaching of reading. Balanced approaches that emphasize the development of effective decoding skills together with extensive reading of engaging texts both within the school and at home are characteristic of most Canadian school systems. Thus, literacy engagement is more likely to be emphasized in Canadian schools serving low-income schools than is the case in the United States.

Standardized tests are also used sparingly within most provincial systems of education. The OECD (2010c: 75) pointed out with respect to Ontario that

> the ministry drew a sharp contrast between its capacity-building approach to reform and the more punitive versions of accountability used in the United States, and, to a lesser extent, in Britain. They chose to downplay the public reporting of results, and they emphasised that struggling schools would receive additional support and outside expertise rather than be punished or closed.

Despite the overall positive picture of immigrant students' success within the Canadian educational system, some qualifications are in order. First, the generally positive outcomes obscure the fact that there are significant differences among linguistic and cultural minority groups in educational success, with certain groups (e.g. refugee students) showing low levels of school completion (McAndrew, 2009). Also, some significant gaps in provision can be identified. For example, there has been a lack of serious policy consideration at all levels of the educational system (provincial ministries, school boards, university-level teacher education programmes and individual schools) regarding the pedagogical implications of linguistic diversity. Home languages other than English or French are still viewed by many educators as largely irrelevant to children's schooling. Consequently, many schools do not encourage bilingual students to showcase their linguistic accomplishments, thereby missing an important opportunity both for identity affirmation and enabling students to use their L1 as a cognitive tool.

The policy vacuum in relation to linguistic diversity at the level of provincial ministries, school boards, and individual schools is paralleled by the absence of any required courses in most faculties of education that focus specifically on linguistic diversity issues. Thus, it is legitimate to ask 'How well prepared are classroom teachers in elementary and secondary schools to support English-as-an-additional-language (EAL) students during the five or so years they are catching up academically?' In an education context characterized by linguistic diversity and high rates of immigration, it is no longer sufficient to be an excellent Science teacher or Mathematics teacher in a generic sense; excellence must be defined by how well a teacher can teach Science or Mathematics to the students who are in his or her classroom, many of whom may be in the early or intermediate stages of English language acquisition.

In summary, the relatively strong performance of immigrant students in the Canadian context should not obscure the fact that certain groups of students (frequently those from refugee and low-SES backgrounds) *do* experience academic difficulties and there are significant gaps in the extent to which coherent policies have been formulated at all levels of the educational system to address the implications of linguistic diversity for instruction. In particular, there has been little consideration of the importance of *identity affirmation* and only sporadic attention to the fact that there is a knowledge base regarding scaffolding strategies that all teachers and administrators should be familiar with in order to implement effective instruction for students learning the school language.

Conclusion

In conceptualizing the management of linguistic diversity it is important to acknowledge that this process operates not just at the macro level of national or state/provincial policies but also at the micro level of individual schools and classrooms. Macro-level policies in both the Canadian and US contexts (as well as most other jurisdictions) can claim only partial consistency with the empirical evidence. However, at the micro-level of individual schools, educators, individually and collectively, constantly make instructional choices that define their identities as educators. They determine for themselves the social and educational goals they want to achieve with their students. They make choices with respect to the messages they aspire to communicate to students about their abilities and talents. Despite external constraints, they exercise agency with respect to their orientation to students' language and culture, the extent to which they explore pedagogically powerful uses of technology, and the forms of parent and community participation they encourage. The empirically based instructional directions articulated in the Literacy Engagement framework (Figure 1.3) can potentially serve as a catalyst for educators within schools to begin the process of developing and implementing school-based policies that respond explicitly to linguistic diversity. The PISA research together with a range of other studies suggests that enlightened policies have the potential to push back the negative effects on student achievement of SES and coercive relations of power within the wider society.

References

Anyon, J. (2005) What 'counts' as educational policy: Notes towards a new paradigm. *Harvard Educational Review* 75, 65–88.

Bankston, C.L. and Zhou, M. (1995) Effects of minority-language literacy on the academic achievement of Vietnamese youths in New Orleans. *Sociology of Education* 68, 1–17.

Barth, H.J., Heimer, A. and Pfeiffer, I. (2008) Integration through education – promising practices, strategies and initiatives in ten countries. In Bertelsmann Stiftung (ed.) *Immigrant Students Can Succeed: Lessons from around the Globe* (pp. 119–187). Gütersloh: Bertelsmann Stiftung.

Berliner, D.C. (2009) *Poverty and Potential: Out-of-School Factors and School Success.* Boulder and Tempe: Education and the Public Interest Center & Education Policy Research Unit. Retrieved 5 March 2010 from http://epicpolicy.org/publication/poverty-and-potential.

Bishop, R. and Berryman, M. (2006) *Culture Speaks: Cultural Relationships and Classroom Learning.* Wellington: Huia Publishers, Aoteroa New Zealand.

Christensen, G. and Segeritz, M. (2008) An international perspective on student achievement. In Bertelsmann Stiftung (ed.) *Immigrant Students Can Succeed: Lessons from around the Globe* (pp. 11–33). Gütersloh: Bertelsmann Stiftung.

Coulombe, S., Tremblay, J. and Marchand, S. (2004) *International Adult Literacy Survey. Literacy Scores, Human Capital and Growth across fourteen OECD Countries.* Catalogue no. 89-552MIE. Ottawa: Statistics Canada.

Cummins, J. (2001) *Negotiating Identities: Education for Empowerment in a Diverse Society.* 2nd edition. Los Angeles: California Association for Bilingual Education.

Darling-Hammond, L. (2010) *The Flat World and Education. How America's Commitment to Equity will determine our Future.* New York: Teachers College Press.

Duke, N. (2000) For the rich it's richer: Print experiences and environments offered to children in very low and very high-socioeconomic status first-grade classrooms. *American Educational Research Journal* 37 (2), 441–478.

Guthrie, J.T. (2004) Teaching for literacy engagement. *Journal of Literacy Research* 36 (1), 1–30.

Hart, B. and Risley, T.R. (1995) *Meaningful Differences in the Everyday Experience of Young American Children.* Baltimore, MD: Paul H. Brookes Publishing.

Kieffer, M.J. (2011) Before and after third grade: Longitudinal evidence for the shifting role of socioeconomic status in reading growth. *Reading and Writing: An Interdisciplinary Journal.* Springer Science + Business Media B.V. Published online 6 September 2011.

Kozol, J. (2005) *The Shame of the Nation: The Restoration of Apartheid Schooling in America.* New York: Crown.

Krashen, S.D. (2004) *The Power of Reading: Insights from the Research.* 2nd edition. Portsmouth, NH: Heinemann.

Ladson-Billings, G. (1995) Toward a theory of culturally relevant pedagogy. *American Educational Research Journal* 32, 465–491.

Lindsay, J. (2010) *Children's Access to Print Material and Education-related Outcomes: Findings from a Meta-analytic Review.* Naperville, IL: Learning Point Associates.

Little, D. (2010) *The linguistic and educational integration of children and adolescents from migrant backgrounds.* Strasbourg: Council of Europe. Retrieved from http://www.coe.int/t/dg4/linguistic/ListDocs_Geneva2010.asp

Manyak, P.C. (2004) "What did she say?" Translation in a primary-grade English immersion class. *Multicultural Perspectives* 6, 12–18.

McAndrew, M. (2009) *Educational Pathways and Academic Performance of Youth of Immigrant Origin: Comparing Montreal, Toronto and Vancouver.* Report submitted to the Canadian Council on Learning and Citizenship and Immigration Canada. Ottawa: Canadian Council on Learning.

McCarty, T.L. (ed.) (2005) *Language, Literacy, and Power in Schooling.* Mahwah: Lawrence Erlbaum Associates.

Neuman, S.B. and Celano, D. (2001) Access to print in low-income and middle-income communities: An ecological study of four neighbourhoods. *Reading Research Quarterly* 36, 8–26.

No Child Left Behind Act of 2001, Pub. L. No. 107–110 (2001).

Norton, B. and Toohey, K. (2011) Identity, language learning, and social change. *Language Teaching* 44 (4), 412–446.

OECD (2004) *Messages from PISA 2000.* Paris: Organization for Economic Cooperation and Development.

OECD (2006) *Where Immigrant Students Succeed: A Comparative Review of Performance and Engagement in PISA 2003.* OECD briefing note for Germany. Retrieved on 20 December 2007 from www.oecd.org/pisa/pisaproducts/pisa2003/36701527.doc

OECD (2010a) *PISA 2009 Results: Overcoming Social Background – Equity in Learning Opportunities and Outcomes (Volume II).* Paris: OECD. Retrieved from *http://dx.doi. org/10.1787/9789264091504-en*

OECD (2010b) *Closing the Gap for Immigrant Students: Policies, Practice and Performance.* OECD Reviews of Migrant Education. Paris: OECD.

OECD (2010c) *Strong Performers and Successful Reformers in Education: Lessons from PISA for the United States.* Retrieved 27 December 2010 from http://www.oecd.org/datao-ecd/32/50/46623978.pdf

OECD (2010d) *PISA 2009 Results: Learning to Learn – Student Engagement, Strategies and Practices (Volume III).* Paris: OECD. Retrieved 15 December 2010 from http://www.oecd.org/dataoecd/11/17/48852630.pdf

Ogbu, J.U. (1978) *Minority Education and Caste.* New York: Academic Press.

Ogbu, J.U. (1992) Understanding cultural diversity and learning. *Educational Researcher* 21 (8), 5–14 and 24.

Parrish, T., Merickel, A., Perez, M., Linquanti, R., et al. (2006) *Effects of the Implementation of Proposition 227 on the Education of English Learners, K–12: Findings from a Five-year Evaluation (Final Report).* Palo Alto and San Francisco: American Institutes for Research and WestEd.

Portes, A. and Rumbaut, R.G. (2001) *Legacies: The Story of the Immigrant Second Generation.* Berkeley: University of California Press.

Rothstein, R. (2004) *Class and Schools: Using Social, Economic, and Educational Reform to Close the Black-White Achievement Gap.* Washington, DC: Economic Policy Institute.

Rothstein, R. (2010) How to fix our schools. Issue Brief No. 286, Economic Policy Institute. Retrieved 5 January 2011 from http://www.epi.org/publications/entry/ib286

Schofield, J.W. and Bangs, R. (2006) Conclusions and further perspectives. In J.W. Schofield, *Migration Background, Minority-Group Membership and Academic Achievement: Research Evidence from Social, Educational, and Developmental Psychology.* AKI Research Review 5, 93–102. Berlin: Programme on Intercultural Conflicts and Societal Integration (AKI), Social Science Research Center. Retrieved 21 December 2007 from http://www2000.wzb.eu/alt/aki/publications.en.htm

Skutnabb-Kangas, T. (2000) *Linguistic Genocide – Or Worldwide Diversity and Human Rights.* Mawah: Lawrence Erlbaum Associates.

Stanat, P. and Christensen, G. (2006) *Where Immigrant Students Succeed: A Comparative Review of Performance and Engagement in PISA 2003*. Paris: OECD. Retrieved 15 December 2007 from http://www.oecd.org/pisa/pisaproducts/pisa2003/36664934.pdf

Steele, C.M. (1997) A threat in the air: How stereotypes shape intellectual identity and performance. *American Psychologist* 52 (6), 613–629.

US Commission on Civil Rights (1973) *Teachers and Students: Differences in Teacher Interaction with Mexican-American and Anglo Students*. Washington, DC: US Government Printing Office.

United States v. State of Texas (1981) Civil action #5281 (Bilingual Education) Memorandum Opinion.

2 English as an Additional Language: Symbolic Policy and Local Practices

Tracey Costley and Constant Leung

England, along with many other contemporary societies, has long been characterised by ethnic and linguistic diversity. As the title of this book suggests a key challenge to such societies is how to engage with and manage diversity. This chapter examines educational policy as a means of managing diversity and how, in turn, policy shapes and informs local schooling practices. Our specific focus is on English as Additional Language (EAL) students in the context of state-funded education in England, and the professional and institutional processes through which policy is rendered 'on site' by teachers in local schools.

The chapter is divided into three parts. In Part 1, we trace the policy dispositions and social values regarding the teaching of EAL to linguistic minority students. In Part 2 we draw on ethnographic data collected in a case study of an inner-London primary school to provide an account of the ways in which a local school conceptualised and organised EAL provision. We explore the ways in which the learners' needs were construed by the school and how the views of the staff were translated into curriculum arrangements and classroom pedagogy. We present these data to illustrate how national policy positions highlighted in Part 1 can be interpreted in local classroom practice(s). In the final part of the chapter we suggest that a pedagogic and curricular vacuum has been engendered by a 'symbolic policy' on EAL. We suggest that the symbolic nature of policy makes it possible for a school community to share the broad rhetorical commitments to educational values of equality of access to mainstream provision and academic excellence, and at the same time to engage in curriculum and teaching practices that are commensurate with educational segregation on the basis of students' language and cultural backgrounds.

The Teaching of EAL

Over the last 50 years or so England has seen much immigration from New Commonwealth countries, other European Union member countries, as well as from other parts of the world. Education policy has therefore needed to acknowledge and respond to the changing ethnolinguistic profile of schools. The term policy here includes formal statements of government intent and all associated curriculum documents (see Rizvi & Lingard, 2010, Chapter 1 for a discussion on the meanings of education policies). The central government has taken action in a variety of ways. The additional funding made available by the Local Government Act of 1966 is a good example. The Act foregrounded achievement as a goal for all students, and in particular it highlighted ethnolinguistic minority students as being at risk of underachievement owing to insufficient knowledge of English. Grant monies were therefore made available to schools in order to address this disadvantage. These monies were to be used to employ additional staff (including bilingual teaching assistants) to teach English and to support ethnic minority student learning more generally. Organised under different legislative schemes over the years, these monies have continued to be a part of the central grants for schools and local authorities to support the additional provision earmarked for ethnolinguistic minority students (including those from other EU member states). It is important to note that this additional funding has been, since its inception, time-limited and its renewal has been subject to ministerial decision. In other words, it is not part of regular mainstream education funding.

Although the 1966 Act can be viewed as an acknowledgement of the need to recognise and respond to diversity in schools, some of the grant-aided provisions in the ensuing 20 years were considered to be both socially and pedagogically divisive. A prime example was the withdrawal of EAL learners from classrooms in order to develop their English language proficiency (see Leung & Franson, 2001 for a detailed discussion). An investigation by the Commission for Racial Equality (1986) into the provision in a particular local authority found that EAL learners who were being withdrawn from mainstream classrooms for English language lessons suffered both educational and social disadvantage as a result. The Commission called for the practice to end. This report was significant in that the findings and recommendations were accepted by government officials and it prompted an end to withdrawal and separate language teaching units for EAL learners across the country.

The end of separate provision for EAL learners meant that mainstreaming became the *de facto* policy in terms of provision for EAL learners; it was regarded as an educationally principled way of ensuring equality of access and treatment. Mainstreaming in English educational policy means the integration of all students, regardless of language and ethnic backgrounds, into age-appropriate classes. This is a particular interpretation of the notion of equality in terms of uniformity of treatment (Taylor, 1992). A result of this was that withdrawal classes for English language teaching were no longer considered to be educationally appropriate. The implementation of the statutory National Curriculum in 1991 in many ways cemented mainstreaming as an approach to EAL in that 'irrespective of ethnicity, language background, culture, gender, ability, social background, sexuality, or religion' all students should experience a common curriculum (DfEE & QCA, 1999: 12). While the National Curriculum was not intended as an explicit language or EAL policy, it has consolidated the ways in which EAL learners are conceptualised and catered for in the curriculum.

Central to the National Curriculum is the assumption that irrespective of the diverse social, language and ethnic backgrounds of the student population, developmental processes and learning goals are the same for all. This approach, together with the mainstreaming policy for EAL, means that conceptually there is no need for separate and dedicated curriculum space for EAL. Successful learning of the language of schooling (in this case English) is seen as taking place most effectively in the mainstream classroom through exposure to ordinary classroom activities and meaningful language use. Helping students to learn EAL is, therefore, the business of all teachers. Within the current policy context EAL is regarded as a 'diffused curriculum concern' (Leung, 2001: 38) in that there is no distinct EAL curriculum or pedagogy. Whilst this understanding of language learning has underpinned policy for over 20 years, no pedagogic guidance on EAL within the context of curriculum content teaching has been provided; official advice has tended to be framed in terms of 'good practice'. For instance, teachers are asked to use group work to encourage students to engage with learning activities (NCC, 1991). In a sense what the policy has done is to treat additional language learning as a kind of delayed naturalistic first language development. Therefore neither explicit language pedagogy nor a dedicated EAL curriculum is needed. This particular approach to language diversity and language teaching is different from that adopted by other English-speaking education systems. In Australia, Canada and the US, for example, the needs of EAL learners have traditionally been conceptualised more in terms of a specialist subject area (Leung, 2007). Although the current policy in England emphasises equality of entitlement and high levels of achievement for all, student attainments in standardised national assessments have consistently shown a disparity between levels of attainment for EAL learners and their English mother-tongue peers. There is clear evidence that suggests that ethnolinguistic minority students continue to perform less well than their English mother tongue peers (see, for example, Department for Education, 2011; OECD, 2009; and http://www.education.gov.uk/rsgateway/DB/SFR/s000968/sfr33-2010).

At present additional curriculum provision for ethnolinguistic minority students is made available in schools through the Ethnic Minority Achievement Grant (EMAG), and this is an iteration of the additional funding first made available under the 1966 Act. These funds are ear-marked to make, where needed, *additional* support available to schools. Although EMAG policy documents and guidance materials promote the broad goal of reducing the gaps in pupil attainment, they do not provide explicit guidance on teaching programmes or learning objectives. What we do have are general statements of principles and brief case studies of different local practices and uses of the funds (Department for Education and Skills, 2004). As a result the ways in which these funds have been used by Local Authorities and schools have differed considerably. This raises a number of questions about the ways in which the funds are used in schools. A key issue here is: what counts as EMAG provision?

Policy in Practice

The data discussed below are drawn from a case study conducted in 2007 in a London primary school (Costley, 2010). The case study adopted an ethnographic perspective to develop an account of the ways in which EMAG funds were used to develop localised teaching and learning strategies and approaches for EAL students (Green & Bloome, 1997). In keeping with established ethnographic research traditions (Heath *et al.*, 2008) and case study research (Stake, 1995) this particular study involved a sustained engagement with a group of participants at a particular site. In this case it meant spending between 1–4 days a week, for approximately 36 weeks, at a particular school observing lessons and participating in curriculum activities generally and often 'hanging around' at lunch times, break times and being involved in a range of events throughout the school day. These research activities aimed at generating 'thick description' (Geertz, 1973) in the sense that the goal was a detailed and reflexive account of experience/s and interpretations (both of the participants and the researcher), or what Ponterotto (2006: 547) describes as the production of 'thick meaning' for the reader. The ideas and themes discussed in this chapter are informed by the analysis of the following data sets collected during the nine month research period:

- Audio-recordings: approximately 40 hours of classroom audio-recordings with teachers and students in Years 4, 5 and 6 (ages 9, 10 and 11).
- Field notes: details of classes, classroom layout and activities associated with the audio-recorded classes, details of other encounters with staff and students outside lessons.
- Interviews: conducted at various stages in the field work period with teachers and students.
- Lesson materials: students' work, school reports, school policy documents and other school-based artefacts.

In the next three sections we will comment specifically on how this school:

- Organised additional support using EMAG monies.
- Conceptualised the learning needs of a particular group of EAL learners.
- Developed curriculum responses to meet these needs.

Overview of research site and school context

South River is characteristic of many inner-London boroughs in that it is linguistically and culturally diverse, and whilst there are areas of great prosperity there are also areas of significant deprivation. The particular part of South River where Park Tower School is located is characterised by high unemployment, low income jobs and a high density of ageing 1960s social housing. In 2007 when the research was conducted 314 students were registered at Park Tower School, making it a larger than average primary school. Ofsted (Office for Standards in Education, Children's Services and Skills, a government inspection agency) reports from 2003 to 2008 described Park Tower School as having a higher than the national average number of ethnic minority students, over three quarters of whom needed additional support in learning English when they arrived at the school.

The school staff comprised teachers and classroom assistants. The teachers were predominantly of white British heritage with two exceptions, one white South African and one white Australian. All of the classroom assistants were of Black Caribbean heritage except for one who was of white British background. A further five auxiliary staff were employed to support students identified as having Special Educational Needs (SEN) and/or behavioural problems, as well as students in need of reading support. In addition to these staff members, the school used its EMAG grant money to employ one full-time staff member, Maria, to support students from ethnolinguistic minority communities (pseudonyms are used in this chapter). Maria described herself as never having formally learnt English and described her knowledge of English as being 'self-taught'. She trained as a primary teacher in her home country, Portugal, and taught there for several years before moving to England, where she did not have Qualified Teacher Status (QTS). So in effect Maria was employed as an 'unqualified' teacher. This diverse staff profile in terms of specialisms and ethnicities was commended by OFSTED as reflecting the school's commitment to supporting the full range of its learners' needs.

School implementation of EMAG

When she first joined Park Tower School, Maria worked alongside classroom teachers providing 'in-class support' to EAL students who had been identified as being in need of help with reading, writing and general comprehension. She worked with these students in all of their classes to help them understand instructions, follow explanations and complete tasks. In discussing her work during an interview at the start of the research period, Maria said that this form of support was insufficient to address the needs of the targeted students. The feelings she had about the shortcomings of in-class student support were not only based on her experiences as a teacher, but also derived from her own experiences of being a language learner. She made a case to the principal to change the nature of the support offered and argued for withdrawal classes as she felt students' needs would best be met in small groups outside the mainstream classroom. The principal decided that support classes based on a withdrawal model should be trialled in the school. At the time of the research withdrawal classes, organised by Maria, had been taking place for almost four academic years.

The EMAG funding received by the school made it possible for Maria to work full time in supporting a group of 30 'EMAG' students across the school, from Year 1 to Year 6 (ages 5–11). 'EMAG students' were identified largely on their perceived English language levels (their ability to participate in classes both in terms of their oral and written work), their length of time in England and previous schooling experience. The 'EMAG' group was designed to provide support for students arriving at the school with no prior educational experience within the UK. It was decided that given the nature of the students' needs the focus of support would be literacy and they would not attend what can be termed 'mainstream literacy' (i.e. National Curriculum English Literacy) classes; instead they would attend EMAG literacy classes with Maria. In recent years, the term 'literacy' in school education in England has tended to refer to both English language and literacy.

In both primary and secondary schooling in England, literacy is a high-profile subject. It is viewed as a set of skills which underpin all curriculum subjects and which form the basis for students' overall achievement in school. This has been a highly prescriptive area of the National Curriculum (for England). The Primary National Framework (PNF) for Literacy (Department for Education and Skills, 2006), for instance, has 12 learning objectives for literacy (also including Speaking, Listening and Responding, and Drama). For each year group these learning objectives are broken down into specific language learning goals which are assessed in national tests. For example, Year 6 students should (amongst other things) be able to '[e]xpress subtle distinctions of meaning, including hypothesis, speculation and supposition, by constructing sentences in varied ways' (DfES, 2006: 61).

The curriculum and organisation of the EMAG literacy classes at Park Tower School represent a significant departure from the mainstream model of provision (as discussed above) on two levels. First, adopting a withdrawal model for classes goes against the principle of equality (as understood in the prevailing policy) that has underpinned mainstream provision for the last twenty years. Second, given the high status of literacy within the curriculum it is significant that students who are identified as EMAG students are in effect constructed as being students in need of something different from their mainstream non-EMAG counterparts. As the discussion below details, EMAG literacy students did not follow the PNF or any other national literacy curriculum in their EMAG literacy classes. What we have then is a case in which nationally recommended materials and teaching and learning objectives for a core curriculum subject are suspended for a particular group of students. Before moving on further, it is necessary at this point to note that the curriculum at the school (both EMAG and mainstream) had been regularly approved by local advisors and national school inspectors. In effect the organisation and content of the EMAG classes had been officially sanctioned at a local level.

What is EMAG literacy at Park Tower School?

In this section we draw on classroom observation and interview data to provide a glimpse of the content of EMAG literacy classes. To start we provide a copy of the EMAG literacy syllabus as designed by Maria which was displayed in the school. Figure 2.1 is a faithful reproduction of how it was presented at the school. It was part of a larger document giving information to parents on EMAG literacy and the contents of study for EMAG students in these classes.

Maria explained that the syllabus represented the key goals for EMAG literacy classes in relation to the types of activities and outcomes that were desirable and necessary for her group of students, i.e. to develop their ability to read and write. In an interview she gave the following account of her

EMAG literacy syllabus

LITERACY (Developing Readers and Writers)

LITERACY (Beginners Readers and Writers)

EXTENDED WRITING

EXTENDED WRITING and READING

READING JOURNAL

Figure 2.1 EMAG literacy syllabus

conceptualisation of EMAG literacy, and it goes some way to help understand the ideas informing the syllabus. In Maria's account priority is given to teaching her students to read and write independently, to be able to speak (and be understood), and to be able to listen (and understand) with confidence.

Extract 1

Transcription Conventions: **M** = Maria; **R** = researcher; **(.)** = brief pause; **(number)** = duration of pause in seconds; **[word]** = comment on context

01	**M:**	the main target (.) and the first target (.) is to teach them to read independently (.) because
02		they can't do that (.) to write independently a piece of writing
03	**R:**	yeah
04	**M:**	and speak
05	**R:**	yeah
06	**M:**	to make themselves understand while speak and listen (.) obviously because listening is
07		not just in speaking and listening lessons (.) it is in every lesson another thing I do that class
08		teachers don't do because I don't think they need to do that in class (.) is that I do I er (.) make
09		them confident
10	**R:**	yeah
11	**M:**	and very welcome (.) because I think that is the main the main thing for the targeted
12		children especially for the Somali children and the Afro-Caribbean (.) some of them they
13		don't believe they can do (.) can learn and I think there is a lot and that's a job

From Maria's account, developing students' self-confidence and a sense of self-belief is a fundamental characteristic of her work in EMAG literacy. It is also something which is highlighted as differentiating her work from that of the mainstream literacy teachers. In describing what it is that EMAG seeks to do, Extract 1 can be read as a statement of what EMAG students are perceived as not being able to do. During the interview Maria added to the description of EMAG with the following:

Extract 2

```
01   M:    for example I will give a quick example (.) they may work on
02         adjectives and connectives and adverbs and synonyms for
           example
03         and I will just work on adjectives and connectives coz I (.)
           know my group can't
04         take much more than that
```

Maria highlights the pace at which teachers and students work (Lines 03–04) as a key difference between the two types of classes (mainstream and EMAG literacy). The term 'they' in Line 01 refers to the mainstream literacy classes. Maria's comments suggest that at a conceptual level the issue of pace, in relation to acquisition and cognition, impacts upon the types of activities and tasks that EMAG and non-EMAG students are expected to do in their respective literacy classes. Maria felt that the pace at which classroom teachers progressed through learning aims and objectives was too quick for EMAG students, who required more time to understand and to practise. In effect what Maria says is that EMAG students are inherently different to mainstream students in terms of capabilities and needs.

EMAG literacy and curriculum divergence

From classroom observations over the course of the research period clear patterns were discerned in terms of the content and structure of EMAG literacy classes. All EMAG literacy classes, regardless of the year group, would be organised and conducted in a very similar way and were typified by students being engaged in the following tasks and activities:

(1) receiving comments from Maria on either homework or in-class tasks,
(2) drafting short written responses and receiving feedback/corrections,
(3) copying corrected texts,
(4) illustrating texts with pictures.

The types of texts students were asked to produce were also similar in that they took the form of either short answer questions or a short narrative; the students were not required, in any of the classes observed, to produce other types of texts.

The lesson aims and projected learning outcomes for all the EMAG students across the year groups appeared to be broadly similar. Figure 2.2 presents the learning targets which were set by Maria for students in March 2007. In a similar way to the syllabus presented earlier, these lesson aims have been faithfully reproduced from the original document given by Maria. Read together with Maria's comments in Extract 2, these learning targets seem to mirror Maria's contention that EMAG literacy students need a revised and reduced curriculum.

It should also be noted that these targets were not simply targets for March; they framed all EMAG literacy classes that took place in that year. All teachers at Park Tower School were asked to make learning targets and objectives clear and accessible to students in the form of a WILF, which stands for 'What I am Looking For'. These were to be written on whiteboards at the start of each lesson and copied down by students. The WILFs in Figure 2.3 were copied from the whiteboard from Year 4 and Year 6 EMAG literacy classes observed in May.

What is striking about these WILFs is not only their apparent uniformity of goals across the year groups and the length of time spent on them, but also their simplicity when compared to the Primary National Framework which covers a wide range of goals and genres, and is clearly differentiated in terms of levels of attainment. What is also of significance is how the ideas Maria communicated in Extracts 1 and 2 in regard to the speed at which her

EMAG literacy learning targets

Year 5/6 Writing	To write 4 connectives and 3 pieces of punctuation
Year 4 Writing	To write a letter with connectives and 3 different forms of punctuation
Year 3 Writing	To write 4 sentences (capital letters and full stops)
Year 2 Writing	To write a letter which includes 3 sequencing connectives and one form of punctuation

Figure 2.2 EMAG literacy learning targets

Lesson WILFs
Thursday 10th of May
WILF
To write a letter using adjectives, connectives and different punctuation

Tuesday 8th of May
WILF
To write a paragraph using adjectives, connectives and different punctuation

Figure 2.3 Lesson WILFs

students are able to make progress in relation to English play out in classroom practice. What we see in the WILFs is in many ways a reflection of Maria's (and the school's) expectations for these students in terms of their developing proficiencies in English.

In Extract 3 below we see a telling episode in terms of showing how students' English language proficiency was framed in class. Maria complimented a Year 6 student, Faisa, on the work that she had produced and addressed the following comments to the whole class:

Extract 3

01	**M:**	okay look what this girl did look look reading journal here on a Friday with
02		me (.) she went home and look (6) Faisa if it was not English language if it was
03		[showing the students the pages]
04		another language her language she would get a level five or six in the SATs don't you
05		agree with me?

Faisa was considered by Maria to be a very hardworking and 'good' student. Faisa would often be publicly complimented by Maria and used in class as an example of how a 'good' student should work. For example, her handwriting was neat and she always did her homework, she never got into trouble in school and always helped the teacher by being well behaved. In Extract 3 what we see is Faisa's scholarly efforts being acknowledged with the caveat that if she were working in her mother-tongue, or home language, she would be achieving higher marks. In other words, although Faisa works hard and applies herself, her grades are restricted because of her knowledge of English.

English language, then, is signalled as being an 'issue' or a 'problem' that will keep Faisa from getting a high score in the SATs. Of significance to us here is that Maria did not elaborate upon the elements of Faisa's work or English language that were weak or holding her back, and nor was there any discussion of how the EMAG classes would help students such as Faisa improve their work. These types of comments were missing not only from this particular class but from all of the classes observed during the time spent at the school.

A key feature of the EMAG literacy classes that were observed was the lack of explicit English language teaching that took place, even though as Extract 4 suggests the use of English was considered to be an issue for these students. From the classes observed the learning of language did not emerge as a dominant goal or explicit learning activity. Although students were set tasks to do that were language and/or literacy-oriented (as framed by the WILFs) Maria tended to dominate class time by talking to the students about issues relating to achievement and behaviour. Class time therefore was not necessarily spent in the production of texts but in receiving 'advice' and/or 'correction' from Maria.

Extracts 4 and 5, which are taken from an interview with Maria, go some way, we believe, towards explaining the particular style of teaching that characterised the EMAG literacy classes. The extracts are helpful in gaining access to Maria's conceptualisation and understanding of the learning needs of these students:

Extract 4

01	**M:**	Somali Somali children erm very often come as I said before come
02		come from Somali with no previous school
03	**R:**	mmmn
04	**M:**	education (.) parents are not literate themselves they have a different
05		culture and religion but may not be relevant here and they have a
06		different way of live and deal with the children and many other things

Extract 5

01	**M:**	I think they have shock with society with the way we live because er
02		well if you think they come from a country that is a totally different
03		place

Maria's comments here can be read as an expression of concern about how well these students and their families *fit* into the school system. This suggests that Maria's understanding of the students is not necessarily framed in terms of their being English language learners, but of their being in need of learning more about the social environment and social practices of schooling and society more generally.

These comments can be interpreted as a set of assumptions about EMAG students and the types of educational 'issues' these students are likely to have. They in turn inform the ways in which the learning needs of the students are conceptualised. The themes emerging from this study are that EMAG students arrive at school with:

- insufficient prior schooling and as a consequence they are not familiar with what to 'do' in school,
- cultural practices that may be at odds with the dominant local (London) culture,
- different home/school experiences and priorities,
- 'culture shock' and it limiting effect on students' ability to adapt to a new system and rules.

Seen in this light there is an assumed relationship between students' sociocultural and ethnic backgrounds and their perceived performance or achievement in school. The (perceived) practices of the students' homes and communities were regarded as incompatible with school expectations and values. As a result EMAG literacy appears to be charged with the task of adjusting the values and practices of both the students and their parents in order to help them become successful students (and citizens). In this sense EMAG literacy is more than language and is concerned with a larger process of socialisation and integration.

Practice as a Reflection of Policy (or not)

This account of EMAG literacy raises questions as to what language and language learning are considered to be in a particular school and how they are translated into practice. The curriculum provision at Park Tower School is significantly different to that outlined in mainstream national policy. It is an example of how, in the context of a highly centralised and prescriptive curriculum, provision for ethnic and linguistic minority students can run counter to the officially endorsed model. To the extent that this particular curriculum provision has been approved by local and national inspectors, the national policy can be said to be open to interpretation.

As part of a research project commissioned by the Teacher Development Agency a team of researchers looked into EAL provision across the country from November 2008 to April 2009. Their final report (IoE, 2009), which summarises the findings from 10 case studies they conducted, provides an account of diverse and localised interpretations of national policy in relation to EAL. These studies of localised practices of various kinds suggest that variation as opposed to consistency is the norm. As Ball (1997) suggests, policy enactment is never a straightforward process of technical application. Policies pose problems to be addressed and resolved on the ground (Ball, 1997). The construction of EMAG literacy is an example of how Park Tower School has responded to policy, and in many ways it displays the 'ad hocery' that Ball suggests is characteristic of policy responses. It also highlights how 'policies are intimately shaped and influenced by school-specific factors which act as constraints, pressures and enablers of policy enactments' (Ball et al., 2012: 19). This discussion of EMAG literacy is not, then, simply about what one particular school does or does not do, but how particular policy configurations afford or create spaces for particular types of response to take place. The case of Park Tower School suggests that the present policy disposition provides large spaces for interpretation. In this regard it is not the specific practices themselves that we seek to raise questions about but rather the nature of the national policy itself.

At present education policy in England is something of a vacuum in relation to the ways in which the learning needs of EAL students are conceptualised. Mainstreaming has effectively generalised the learning needs of all students to the extent that EAL is not (at the policy level) regarded as a distinct curriculum concern. There is, therefore, no need for a distinct EAL pedagogy. By default this also means that EAL does not exist as an area of specific teacher training, and trainee teachers receive little or no input on the distinctiveness of EAL learners. As a result many teachers enter into multilingual and multiethnic schools and classrooms with little awareness and understanding of the ways in which the learning trajectories of EAL students may differ from those of their monolingual counterparts. The lack of requisite professional knowledge and expertise can cause schools and teachers difficulties. A recent case in California illustrates the potential difficulties well. The American Civil Liberties Union of Southern California recently filed a lawsuit against a school that was felt to be operating unfair and pedagogically unsound teaching arrangements for linguistic minority students (EL Gazette, http://www.elgazettedigital.com/, August 2012 edition). Rizvi and Lingard (2010) draw a distinction between material and symbolic policies. Material policies are those which are given significant funding and have clear and measurable implementation structures. They are policies that are often carefully monitored to ensure that they are being implemented as they represent a state-level commitment to effect change. The effort and resources successive governments in England have put into literacy in the mainstream National Curriculum can be regarded as an example of a material policy (e.g. Department for Education and Skills, 2006). The literacy curriculum seeks to equip students with the skills they need to succeed both at school and in the wider world of work. These aims are carefully, and publicly, monitored by the government through nationalised testing as well as formal inspections. The current National Curriculum policy as a whole can be described as being material in the sense that they represent policy intentions that seek to 'change the behaviours and practices of others so as to steer change in a particular direction' (Rizvi & Lingard, 2010: 24).

Symbolic policies, by contrast, tend not to have the same level of top-down commitment that accompanies material policies. Indeed, symbolic polices tend to be vague in their goals and outcomes, which means that monitoring their relative successes or failures is often difficult. Whereas material policies are likely to produce measurable outcomes, symbolic policies are often deemed a success on account of the fact that they constitute a 'political response to pressure for policy' (Rizvi & Lingard, 2010: 25). In other words, the fact that symbolic policies simply exist is viewed as being evidence of their success. EAL policies can be understood as being symbolic in that they have not been included in regular mainstream curriculum provision. The discussion of EMAG literacy here can be seen as a telling example of symbolic policy in action. The observed practice was a result of a school working with vague guidelines and limited professional training and resources. This case study suggests that further empirical work is needed in schools in order to understand the range of EAL provision being made available in school. Without an adequate knowledge and understanding of how EAL has been localised, it would be very difficult to develop a policy that takes account of the professional development needs of teachers and policy makers.

References

Ball, S.J. (1997) Policy sociology and critical social research: A personal review of recent educational policy and policy research. *British Educational Research Journal* 23 (3), 257–274.

Ball, S.J., Maguire, M. and Braun, A. (2012) *How Schools Do Policy. Policy Enactments in Secondary Schools*. London: Routledge.

Commission for Racial Equality (1986) *Teaching English as a Second Language: Report of a Formal Investigation in Calderdale Local Education Authority*. London: Commission for Racial Equality.

Costley, T. (2010) The social construction of EMAG: from policy to practice. Unpublished PhD thesis, University of London.

Department for Education (2011) *Statistical First Release*. SFR 22/2011. London: Department for Education.

Department for Education and Employment and Qualifications and Curriculum Authority (1999) *The National Curriculum: Handbook for Secondary School Teachers in England*. London: DfEE and QCA.

Department for Education and Skills (2004) *Aiming High: Supporting Effective Use of EMAG*. London: DfES.

Department for Education and Skills (2006) *Primary National Strategy: Primary Framework for literacy and mathematics*. London: DfES.

Department for Education and Skills (2006) 2006-DOC-EN *Pupil Language Data: Guidance for Local Authorities on schools' collection and recording of data on pupils' languages*. Retrieved 2006-06-01, from http://www.standards.dfes.gov.uk/ethnicminorities/resources/laguidance_datacollection_mar06

Geertz, C. (1973). *The Interpretation of Cultures*. New York: Basic Books.

Green, J. and Bloome, D. (1997) Ethnography and ethnographers of and in education: a situated perspective. In J. Flood, S. Heath and D. Lapp (eds) *Handbook of Research on Teaching Literacy through Communicative and Visual Arts* (pp. 181–202). New York, Simon and Shuster Macmillan.

Heath, S.B., Street, B. and Mills, M. (2008) *Ethnogprahy*. New York: Teachers College Press.

Institute of Education (2009) English as an Additional Language (EAL) provision in schools – 10 case studies. London: IoE, University of London.

Leung, C. (2001) English as an Additional Language: Distinct language focus or diffused curriculum concerns? *Language and Education* 15 (1), 33–54.

Leung, C. (2007) Integrating school-aged ESL learners into the mainstream curriculum. In J. Cummins and C. Davison (eds) *The International Handbook of English Language Teaching* (pp. 249–269). New York: Springer.

Leung, C. and Franson, C. (2001) England: ESL in the early days. In B. Mohan, C. Leung and C. Davison (eds) *English as a Second Language in the Mainstream: Teaching, Learning and Identity* (pp. 153–165). Harlow, Essex: Longman.

National Curriculum Council (1991) *Circular Number 11: Linguistic Diversity and the National Curriculum*. York: National Curriculum Council.

OECD (2009) *Programme for International Student Assessment: Assessment framework – key competencies in reading, mathematics and science*. Strasbourg: OECD.

Ponterotto, J.G. (2006) Brief note on the origins, evolution, and meaning of the qualitative research concept of 'thick description'. *The Qualitative Report* 11 (3), 538–549.

Taylor, C. (1992) *Multiculturalism and 'The Politics of Recognition'*. Princeton: Princeton University Press.

Rizvi, F. and Lingard B. (2010) *Globalizing Education Policy*. Abingdon, Oxon: Routledge.

Stake, R.E. (1995) *The Art of Case Study Research*. London: Sage.

3 Germany after the 'PISA Shock': Revisiting National, European and Multicultural Values in Curriculum and Policy Discourses

Daniel Faas

Since the 'PISA shock' in 2001, Germany has embarked on a contentious educational reform debate that, among other things, has led to the evaluation of student competences and educational progress. This chapter mainly draws on interviews with seven education policymakers to discuss the challenges and transformations following the 'PISA shock' as well as their views on how to balance cultural diversity and social cohesion in 'post-PISA' Germany. The interview material is triangulated with history, geography and citizenship curriculum documents. The study found that national, European and multicultural values are important and that interculturalism should become a 'lived reality' in the classroom. But there was disagreement with regard to cultural autonomy between ministry officials on the one hand and curriculum planners as well as educational evaluators on the other. The chapter reveals that despite reform efforts following PISA, Germany still has some way to go to close the gap between ethnic majority and migrant minority students, especially those from Turkish communities. Many of the questions raised in this chapter constitute part of ongoing debates within Germany but also elsewhere in Europe.

Introduction

When the first results of the Programme for International Student Assessment (PISA) were published in December 2001, it came as a shock for Germany to find herself placed 21st among 32 participating Organisation for Economic Co-operation and Development countries (OECD, 2001).[1] Since 2001, education has been an important election topic in Germany, OECD tests have received high coverage in the media, and the term 'PISA' itself has become synonymous for testing and evaluation, including a new television show 'PISA: the Test'. Policymakers, educators and parents across Germany have engaged in a contentious reform debate. This has led to a full-day school programme (Bundesministerium für Bildung und Forschung, 2012), an expansion of the provision of early childhood education which is considered especially important for migrant students in developing their language skills (Laschet, 2009), proposals for making the final year of kindergarten obligatory (see Presse- und Informationsamt der Bundesregierung, 2010), national educational standards, and subsequent curriculum reforms to replace the input orientation with an output-oriented competence-based approach.

It is now more widely accepted in Germany that the outcome of schooling has to be evaluated through assessment of student competences. To this end, Germany has seen the foundation of a new Institute for Educational Progress (IQB), a research institute based at Humboldt University Berlin which, among other tasks, develops standardised tests based on national educational standards, develops the standards further, and also designs various learning tasks illustrating these standards for implementation in the classroom. The first national test, which focused on language competences, found that students aged 14–15 in southern and western federal states score significantly better than their counterparts in northern and eastern federal states (Köller et al., 2010). Girls performed significantly better than boys, and students without a migration background scored significantly better than migrant students across all federal states. Among migrant minorities, Turkish youth had the lowest score, which reflects earlier PISA studies (see OECD, 2004, 2006). Although the gap between non-immigrant and immigrant students is slowly closing, it remains the equivalent of two academic years between German and Turkish migrant students (Klieme et al., 2010).

Educational reform is not an easy task in Germany because, unlike in many other European countries, the school system is federalised and under direct control of regional governments that have autonomy over all matters including curriculum development and structure of the education system. In addition to national tests developed by the IQB, there are regional tests that compare student performance in German, mathematics and foreign languages within a federal state. I return to these issues of autonomy in the discussion of my data. Because of the federalised nature of the German educational system, it is impossible to cover the particularities of all 16 states, which is why this chapter focuses on one state, Baden-Württemberg. This is both my home state and a region where students have consistently obtained higher test results than elsewhere in Germany, with the exception of neighbouring Bavaria. It is a state with a so-called tripartite secondary system comprising vocational-track schools (*Hauptschule*), intermediate schools (*Realschule*) and university-track grammar schools (*Gymnasium*). Migrants are disproportionately concentrated in vocational-track schools, which leads to a socio-ethnically segregated system where, at the same time, students achieve higher overall scores than in the more integrative school systems in the North.

The federalised nature of the German school system presents difficulties of coordinating not just the evaluation of educational progress after PISA, but also the implementation of national, European and multicultural values in regional curricula and policies.[2] The Standing Conference of the Ministers of Education and Cultural Affairs (Kultusministerkonferenz, KMK) is the voluntary assembly of 16 education ministers who meet regularly to issue directives and guidelines that concern matters of interest in all federal states. Several of these directives concern the areas of Europe (e.g. 'Europe at School', Kultusministerkonferenz, 2008) and ethno-cultural diversity (e.g. 'Intercultural Education at School', Kultusministerkonferenz, 1996). The federal state of Baden-Württemberg revises curricula every 10 years. Reflecting macro-political developments (see Faas, 2010), in 1984 the focus was still very much on national values; however it shifted to European values with a reform in 1994 before responding to national educational standards in 2004.

The remainder of this chapter analyses how national, European and multicultural values are intertwined in history, geography and citizenship curricula and in the discourses of education policymakers. This includes a discussion of how to balance notions of cultural diversity and social cohesion such as the balance between advocating mother-tongue education and learning German as an additional language. The second goal is to explore how education policymakers in one federal state (Baden-Württemberg) discussed the challenges and transformations following the 'PISA shock'. The chapter engages with a number of broader issues of importance in Germany. How has the situation for migrant students changed during the past decade in terms of integration? To what extent is there a difference between the views of curriculum developers, legislators and those working in research institutes like the IQB? How are concepts such as 'Europe', 'integration' or 'interculturalism' defined? To what extent does the sovereignty of federal states in cultural matters facilitate or hinder educational reform and progress? How is Baden-Württemberg positioned, broadly speaking, in relation to other federal states? What factors affect integration in the school community and in society? Many of these questions constitute part of ongoing debates not just in Baden-Württemberg, but in Germany and Europe.

Methodology

This study draws on interviews with education officials and contextualises these findings through a critical analysis of geography, history, and citizenship education curricula in Baden-Württemberg. The data were collected in 2007 as part of a larger European project.

The broader study began by reviewing the literature on national, European and multicultural issues in Greece, Germany and England. Thirty semi-structured interviews were conducted with policymakers in Athens (13), Stuttgart and Berlin (7), London (6) and DG Education and Culture in Brussels (4). The six main institutions were compatible in terms of their responsibilities and focus on European and intercultural issues relevant for this project. They included the Department for Children, Schools and Families and the then Qualifications and Curriculum Authority in England; the Ministry of Education, Youth and Sports as well as the State Institute of Education in Baden-Württemberg; and the then Ministry of National Education and Religious Affairs and Pedagogical Institute in Greece. The interview data were interpreted with reference to Greek, German and English curricula for history, geography and citizenship. Two main selection criteria were applied: age and compulsory schooling. This ensured a curriculum analysis of five years of compulsory schooling with students aged between 10 and 15 (for a comparative curriculum analysis, see Faas, 2011a).

In this chapter, I focus on Germany, or Baden Württemberg to be more precise. To analyse the curricula and policy discourses, I developed a conceptual framework linking European and multicultural values. First, *inclusive national* approaches which include a range of migration-related topics combined with a national dimension. Second, *inclusive European* approaches which include a range of migration-related topics combined with a more European dimension. Third, *exclusive Eurocentric* approaches which consist of a strong European ethos and little if any acknowledgement of ethno-cultural diversity. Fourth, *exclusive nationalistic* approaches which consist of a strong national ethos and little if any acknowledgement of diversity. I carried out a content analysis to find out which curriculum units and subunits across the five age groups referred to Europe, diversity and the nation state. In addition, interviews were conducted with two representatives from the Baden-Württemberg Ministry of Education, Youth and Sports (KM); three officials from the State Institute of Education (LfS); and two researchers within the Institute for Educational Progress in Berlin (IQB). The LfS is an autonomous institution of public law established in 2005 as a service provider for quality development in education and schools in Baden-Württemberg. As part of its portfolio KM gives advice to schools, the ministry and the administration on the basis of research experience and practical experience in schools. The identities of all respondents in the study were protected by using pseudonyms.

Cultural Autonomy, Integration and Diversity in Baden-Württemberg

The cultural autonomy of federal states (*Kulturhoheit der Länder*) leads to paradoxical situations and debates in contemporary Germany. For example, Frau Ohlsen, a senior official in the European unit within the Ministry (KM), not only strongly defended educational federalism in Germany but also questioned the legality of current educational activities at German national level and European level within the European Commission. There is little dissent in Germany about matters of cultural autonomy between more conservative-controlled (CDU) federal states and Social Democrat-governed (SPD) states. Frau Ohlsen tried to justify her particularly critical stance by linking the educational autonomy of federal states to broader cultural autonomy including cultural diversity. She pointed toward the fact that Germany is the country with the most opera houses in the world and that this is in part attributable to the cultural richness which is a result of local/regional sovereignty. Consequently, she dismissed the 2008 Green Paper *Migration and Mobility: Challenges and Opportunities for EU Education Systems* (European Commission, 2008) as an EU attempt to impinge on state sovereignty. Frau Ohlsen also rejected the idea of the Federal Minister of Education and Research, Annette Schavan (CDU), to introduce a common textbook for each school subject and year. 'Why should federal states like North-Rhine Westphalia, Baden-Württemberg and Bavaria with 10–17 million people each not have the same rights and autonomy as Austria or the new EU member states that are much smaller?' Throughout our discussion, Frau Ohlsen referred to current legislation and the principle of federalism that she would like to defend, while acknowledging that there are topics worthwhile discussing for the KMK. She warned, however, that standardisation and abandoning educational federalism would always tend towards the lowest common denominator to the disadvantage of successful federal states.

In other words, federal states that currently rank high in PISA, such as Bavaria and Baden-Württemberg, fear they might have to adopt educational measures (such as abandoning the selective tripartite secondary system), which might impact on their ranking and educational quality.

In contrast, the education officials I spoke to in the State Institute of Education in Stuttgart (LfS), and especially in the Institute for Educational Progress in Berlin (IQB), had a less legalistic and more nuanced view of how to handle issues of cultural autonomy. For example, Herr Becker in the curriculum unit of LfS thought that the *Common European Framework of Reference for Languages*[3] provides a good opportunity to evaluate the language competences of ethnic majority and migrant minority students in Europe. However, at the same time, he also pointed to the limits of EU influence, arguing that 'it is important in education to have national, regional and personal interests in curricula and to respect the limits of the EU, the federal government and the KMK in this policy field'. Similarly, Herr Schneider in the School Development Unit of LfS felt that 'there are tensions within the federal state toward Brussels and Berlin. We need to stand up against this patronisation, which is constitutionally not legitimate.'

Under current regulations, each federal state has a core curriculum covering two thirds of curriculum space and time and a school-specific curriculum covering one third. In Baden-Württemberg, European values are particularly integrated into geography and history (Kultusministerium Baden-Württemberg, 2004). The geography curriculum is a good example of what I call an inclusive European curricular approach. About one third of geography teaching units deal with national topics (e.g. cities and industrial areas in Baden-Württemberg, mountains in south-western Germany) and European topics (e.g. European integration, the continent of Europe, socio-economic processes in Europe) as well as intercultural and global topics (e.g. culture zones including the Muslim world, living in one world, India and China). The introductory notes of the geography curriculum refer to the importance of a local, national, European and global perspective, thereby promoting the creation not just of European citizens but 'self-reflective, ethically responsible world citizens' (Kultusministerium Baden-Württemberg, 2004). At the same time, one of the stated goals of this subject is to awaken students to the value of, and understanding for, other peoples and cultures. Herr Schneider at LfS attributed this inclusive European orientation to the economy, saying that 'Europe and diversity are central values in geography because of the early participation of Germany in the European Economic Community'.

The history curriculum in Baden-Württemberg works slightly differently in that it reflects more the country's 'Europeanised national identity' (Faas,

2010). There is a more or less equal balance between national and European content, with topics including Charlemagne, the Enlightenment in Europe and Germany after World War Two. The introductory notes refer to the 'importance of developing a European identity when dealing with the different historical epochs' (Kultusministerium Baden-Württemberg, 2004) as well as the need to promote tolerance and values of a pluralistic democratic society. Students are required to learn about the importance of antiquity for the development of European civilization and culture and, in doing so, are taught that the notion of a European identity has a long history. They also discuss the processes of European integration from the 1957 Treaties of Rome to the 2002 launch of the Euro as a single currency. Despite this national-European emphasis, there are topics that address multicultural values; for example, there is one topic area on past and present migration, ranging from the migrations (*Völkerwanderung*) between the third and sixth centuries and emigration from central Europe, through World War Two expulsions, to present-day integration problems and refugee movements.

In comparison, European and multicultural issues seem to have a surprisingly low priority in citizenship education, where students discuss democratic elections, democratic forms of government, political parties, Germany's basic law (*Grundgesetz*), and the meaning of the freedom of the press. Herr Schneider at LfS commented that 'this perceived ethnocentricity in citizenship education reflects the view of our society as the prototype of a pretty good democracy and we teach our students based on that experience what democracy means today'. There are indeed also topics dealing with diversity in citizenship. For example, in the 'living together of different cultures' unit, students are familiarised with the ways in which increasing mobility results in cultural encounters and exchanges and explore how to develop respect and understanding for other cultures.

When I asked my respondents about the extent to which national, European and multicultural values and issues should be or are currently intertwined in Baden-Württemberg, there was consensus that all are important for curriculum and education policy development. Herr Schneider at LfS argued that 'intellectually, we have not yet succeeded in bringing together the historically more dominant national and European issues in Germany with multiculturalism'. Herr Thiel from the quality assurance unit of LfS, by contrast, thought that European and intercultural perspectives are mutually inclusive: 'Europe can only become a reality when it is lived via a local, cultural, intercultural dimension.' This notion of 'living' Europe and interculturalism was further underscored in several discussions I had in which respondents argued that it is less important to legislate for integration and interculturalism in the curriculum than to live it.

'The changing emotional aspect is far more important with regard to integration – that is something that can only develop through the lived multicultural reality of the classroom.' Herr Unger from IQB was convinced that languages have a vital role to play in this process and that national thinking is a thing of the past. 'National values are passé. For me, a young child experiences the local community first and starts picking up intercultural aspects there. One can develop this into a super-competence in school but it is always a lived experience.'

Arguably, one area in need of development as part of this 'lived' interculturalism is the further recruitment of teachers with a migrant background in Baden-Württemberg and in Germany at large. Although 30% of young people aged 5 to 15 now have a migration background in Germany, only 1 or 2% of teachers have a migration background (according to estimates in 2006 from a teachers' organization, the *Verband Bildung und Erziehung*; see Eckinger, 2006). According to Herr Peters from the integration unit of the Ministry, 'it would be highly desirable to have more teachers with a migration background to act as role models in schools; unfortunately, this is not the case yet except in Islamic religious education', a new subject currently being piloted in schools. There were only isolated views such as that by Herr Thiel from LfS, who felt that 'it is part of living in Germany to experience new things instead of always expecting that the person I am dealing with to share my cultural and religious background'. This despite compelling research evidence of the positive impact of teachers with a migrant background on migrant students. Nationally, there are two foundations, Zeit Foundation and Hertie Foundation, which have programmes that aim to recruit more students with a migration background into teacher training.

Although interviewees agreed that national, European and intercultural values are important for students, there was somewhat less consensus with regard to the role of schools in this process. Some, like Frau Ohlsen, felt that 'you cannot be integrated into a society if you cannot speak the language, and that's why it is absolutely right that we demand that migrant students learn German in the first place'. In a similar vein, Herr Schneider in the school development unit of LfS favoured German language learning over mother-tongue education when he said: 'I think it is wrong for the State to enter into financial contributions toward mother-tongue teaching so long as migrant students have deficits in German. We need to streamline our resources better.' Having said that, he dismissed assimilation and thought that Turkish and other migrant students will learn their heritage language from their parents. In contrast, Herr Peters from the integration unit in the Ministry felt it right for the State to support consulates in providing mother-tongue teaching.

The extent to which the education system in Baden-Württemberg favours learning German over heritage languages is closely intertwined with integration. Herr Becker from the curriculum development unit at LfS argued that language is the main integration factor and that all should have German as a lingua franca in schools: 'How we get there is up for debate and there are those who say we should begin with the heritage language. But it is a *conditio sine qua non* that we end up with German as a lingua franca to operate successfully in society.' Others had an issue with this hype surrounding integration and instead preferred to talk about 'participation'. Both Frau Ohlsen and especially Herr Schneider felt that integration means quasi-assimilation. 'For me', he said, 'it is important that everyone is enabled to and wants to participate in society. We do not need to assimilate migrants but they should have the opportunity to become active citizens. The German language is an important factor in this regard.'

Language competence for both ethnic majority and migrant minority students was generally seen as being important among the education stakeholders I talked to. There were yet again conflicting views as regards the evaluation of these competences, with Frau Ohlsen from the European unit of the Ministry strongly advocating local autonomy. This was diametrically opposed to Herr Unger and Frau Altmann at IQB in Berlin, who felt that the *Common European Framework of Reference for Languages* was already a quasi-European educational standard. Frau Altmann observed that the current curricula across the 16 federal states are coming 'closer and closer to resembling and reflecting the agreed national educational standards. By default, within the next 5 to 10 years, Germany will see a covert standardisation and harmonisation of curricula.' Yet there are still enormous differences between federal states. Although all federal states take part in national evaluations every six years, each runs a different regional evaluation of the implementation of educational standards. In Baden-Württemberg, monitoring consists of yearly self-evaluations in mathematics, German and foreign languages (Year 3 and Year 8, students aged 8–9 and 14–15 respectively) plus external school evaluations conducted by representatives of LfS every five years. In the words of Herr Thiel from the quality assurance unit at LfS, 'we are not approaching this like England or other German federal states in terms of inspections. We observe a school development approach without being able to cut school budgets and fire teachers if schools are not doing well in these external evaluations.'

More school autonomy and mandatory evaluations are however not the only response to (migrant student) underachievement in Germany. The 'PISA shock' has also triggered several other debates, including the role of parents. Frau Ohlsen from the Ministry of Education, Youth and Sports, who talked extensively about the PISA results, argued that Finland and Sweden have many more political refugees than Germany. 'In Germany [...] we have economic migrants from Turkey, Italy and so forth that have a lower socio-economic background.' Moreover, Frau Ohlsen reflected on the relative educational success of Greek and Spanish migrant students compared to the difficulties Turkish and Italian migrant students have encountered. 'Greek parents are more demanding; Italian parents have lower aspirations. We carried out a study in 1999–2000 and found that it is really very difficult to motivate Italian parents, for instance.' She added that 'if mothers refuse to learn German, as is the case among many of our Turks, then it is very difficult to convince their children that it is necessary to become proficient in German'. Similarly, Herr Peters from the integration unit within the Ministry felt that there is only so much the government can do, and that educational success and integration are a two-way process. He pointed toward the seven million euro Baden-Württemberg was spending additionally in 2007–2008 (up from 4.4 million in 2004–2005) to support a programme of language development in kindergarten and primary schools.

Esser (2006) and Portes and Rumbaut (2001) took more or less opposite views regarding the impact of parental background on educational performance. Parental background also featured in the discussions I had with education officials as did the role of the vocational-track *Hauptschulen*, which have by far the largest share of migrant students of any type of school in Baden-Württemberg and Germany more generally. There was consensus, however, that Baden-Württemberg endorses a tripartite education system not least because 'you cannot simply abolish one type of school' and because 'federal states with comprehensive school systems didn't get anywhere near the performances of those with selective systems'. Instead, rehearsing the discourses of his Minister, Herr Peters in the integration unit favoured internal reforms in the sense that *Hauptschule* students not enrolled in the additional *Werkrealschule* branch in Years 8–9 (aged 13–15)[4] will now get the same number of contact hours to enhance their more vocational general competences. With falling student numbers and negative publicity toward the *Hauptschule* (in 2009–2010, 24% of fourth graders chose a *Hauptschule*, 34% a *Realschule* and 40% a *Gymnasium* compared to 37%, 30% and 31% respectively in 1994), it remains to be seen whether and how long it takes before the *Werkrealschule* will eventually replace the *Hauptschule*.

Instead of such structural debates, Herr Thiel from the quality assurance unit at LfS thought that individual monitoring of students is key to improving educational performance, especially of migrant students. 'What we don't have at present is a programme to follow a cohort of students and note how they develop, where they go to, what becomes of the students, what individual pathways are taken.' Such an approach, he asserted, would be far more important than collecting ethnic statistics or carrying out group-specific analyses of PISA and other student evaluation data. 'It is much more important to know something about the cultural background of a student and how much support he or she receives from parents than dividing students into those with and those without a migration background.' In a similar vein, Herr Peters in the integration unit at LfS argued that balancing national, European and multicultural values includes 'telling the individual student that he or she is accepted in society, that he or she is an important part of our society, and that intercultural values are inextricably linked with our new curriculum design and understanding'.

Conclusions

I have argued in this chapter that German federal states engaged in a comprehensive reform in the aftermath of the 'PISA shock'. This also included a re-evaluation of the interface between national, European and intercultural values in education and in society at large. There was consensus that all three dimensions and sets of values are important and that interculturalism should become more of a 'lived reality' rather than a top-down policy. In July 2010, the Federal Minister of Education and Research, Annette Schavan, reaffirmed in an interview with a leading German news magazine that Germany is an immigration country and that migrants are an important and enriching part of society. She also called for more teachers with a migration background. These comments coincided with the 2010 World Cup and the generally upbeat feeling surrounding the fact that, for the first time in the country's history, half the squad had a migration background which, in the eyes of many, is one example of successful integration despite the fact of continuing educational gaps between ethnic majority and migrant students. Since 2006, football has arguably led to a reinvention of German national identity along more multicultural lines, visible in the streets of most major cities, with migrants displaying two national flags so long as their team is in the competition and the German flag in the later stages of both the 2006 and 2010 World Cup.

In contrast, there was disagreement among interviewees with regard to issues of cultural autonomy. Officials in the Ministry were generally following party political and legal conventions, whereas those in the autonomous State Institute of Education, and especially in the Institute for Educational Progress, were far more open to the idea of standardisation and harmonisation of educational content and structures. German language learning was seen as the main factor affecting integration in schools and society, but the picture was more blurred regarding support for mother-tongue teaching. There was conflict even between Ministry officials, with Frau Ohlsen privileging German and Herr Peters arguing in favour of balancing host and heritage language and continuing financial support for mother-tongue teaching. Another important factor affecting integration that was identified was parental background. It became clear that debates over cultural autonomy at times hindered educational progress in the sense that the German education system is very complex to grasp, even for insiders like Frau Altmann, and that a great deal of effort is spent on overlapping regional and national evaluations rather than freeing capacity to further uncover the situation of those lagging behind in education. There is, for instance, neither long-term monitoring of individual students, as requested by Herr Thiel, nor a break-down by nationality in the regional self-evaluation tests, where migrants are treated as a homogenous group. There are also at present no national educational standards and evaluations in the social sciences.

Although Germany has already improved its PISA ranking, the situation of those from socio-economically disadvantaged backgrounds and those with a migration background still demands further effort. For example, the unemployment rate for migrants is nearly twice as high as for Germans, around 12 and 6%, respectively. At the same time, slightly more migrant students are now attending intermediate instead of vocational-track schools. To counterbalance this, so-called intercultural mediators are now being engaged with the aim of connecting educational institutions and parents. Teachers are often still not trained for multi-ethnic classrooms. In 2009, the Technical University of Munich established a new faculty for teacher training in the natural sciences with a gender focus, but this programme does not have any particular relevance for the education of migrant students.

A decade after the 'PISA shock', curricula such as history and geography intertwine national, European and intercultural values in various ways, and education stakeholders consider these values important both for curriculum planning and as part of a 'lived reality' in classrooms. To fully grasp the complexity of contemporary curricula, it is important to intertwine all educational dimensions instead of looking separately at national and European or national and migration-related issues. A federal state like Baden-Württemberg is no longer promoting just national or European values, as was the case in curricula of the 1980s and 1990s, but is responding to the reality of contemporary multi-ethnic classrooms. Yet still more needs to be done to close the current gap between ethnic majority and migrant minority students, especially Turks, for instance through promoting early language learning.

Notes

(1) These OECD studies are conducted every three years amongst 15-year-old students and assess young people's performance in reading, mathematics and science. In addition, Germany has analysed the PISA results by region which will now be replaced by the IQB-generated national tests.

(2) There has been considerable debate as to whether and how national, European and multicultural values can be developed in students through subjects such as history (see Davies, 2000; Salmons, 2003) and citizenship (see Maitles & Deuchar, 2006; Osler, 1999). For more on this, please also see the discussions in Faas (2011b).

(3) The *Common European Framework of Reference for Languages* (Council of Europe, 2001) is used to describe achievements of learners of foreign languages across Europe.

(4) The *Werkrealschule* branch within the vocational *Hauptschule* is a top-up students can opt to enrol in with the aim of obtaining a qualification similar to that of the intermediate school (*Realschule*). Since 2010–2011, the Ministry has created separate *Werkrealschulen* which are thought to gradually replace the *Hauptschulen*.

References

Bundesministerium für Bildung und Forschung (2012) *Deutschland braucht mehr und bessere schulische Ganztagsangebote.* Available online at: http://www.ganztagsschulen. org/108.php (accessed 7 March 2012).

Davies, I. (ed.) (2000) *Teaching the Holocaust: Educational Dimensions, Principles and Practice.* London: Continuum.

Eckinger, L. (2006) Migranten für den Lehrerberuf gewinnen! Statement zum Weltlehrertag 2006 [Attract migrants to the teaching profession! Statement for World Teachers' Day 2006]. Available online at: http://vbe.de/807.html (accessed 1 March 2012).

Esser, H. (2006) *Migration, Sprache und Integration.* Frankfurt: Campus.

European Commission (2008) *Migration and Mobility: Challenges and Opportunities for EU Education Systems.* Available online at: http://ec.europa.eu/education/school21/ com423_en.pdf (accessed 6 March 2012).

Faas, D. (2010) *Negotiating Political Identities: Multiethnic Schools and Youth in Europe.* Aldershot: Ashgate.

Faas, D. (2011a) The nation, Europe and migration: A comparison of geography, history and citizenship education curricula in Greece, Germany and England. *Journal of Curriculum Studies* 43 (4), 471–492.

Faas, D. (2011b) A civic rebalancing of British multiculturalism? An analysis of geography, history and citizenship education curricula and policies. *Educational Review* 63 (2), 143–158.

Klieme, E., Artelt, C., Hartig, J., Jude, N., Köller, O., Prenzel, M., Schneider, W. and Stanat, P. (eds.) (2010) *PISA 2009: Bilanz nach einem Jahrzehnt.* Münster: Waxmann.

Köller, O., Knigge, M. and Tesch, B. (eds.) (2010) *Sprachliche Kompetenzen im Ländervergleich: Befunde des ersten Ländervergleichs zur Überprüfung der Bildungsstandards für den Mittleren Schulabschluss in den Fächern Deutsch, Englisch und Französisch.* Berlin: Institut für Qualitätsentwicklung im Bildungswesen.

Kultusministerium Baden-Württemberg (2004) *Bildungsplan 2004.* Available online at: http:// www.bildung-staerkt-menschen.de/service/downloads/Bildungsplaene (accessed 3 March 2012).

Kultusministerkonferenz (1996) *Interkulturelle Bildung und Erziehung in der Schule: Beschluss der Kultusministerkonferenz vom 25.10.1996*. Bonn: Sekretariat der Ständigen Konferenz der Kultusminister der Länder in der Bundesrepublik Deutschland.

Kultusministerkonferenz (2008) *Europabildung in der Schule: Beschluss der Kultusministerkonferenz vom 08.06.1978 in der Fassung vom 05.05.2008*. Bonn: Sekretariat der Ständigen Konferenz der Kultusminister der Länder in der Bundesrepublik Deutschland.

Laschet, A. (2009) *Die Aufsteigerrepublik: Zuwander als Chance*. Berlin: Kiepenheuer and Witsch.

Maitles, H. and Deuchar, R. (2006) 'We don't learn democracy, we live it!': Consulting the pupil voice in Scottish schools. *Education, Citizenship and Social Justice* 1 (3): 249–266.

OECD (Organisation for Economic Cooperation and Development) (2001) *Knowledge and Skills for Life: First Results from PISA 2000*. Paris: OECD.

OECD (2004) *Knowledge and Skills for Life: First Results from PISA 2003*. Paris: OECD.

OECD (2006) *Where Immigrant Students Succeed: A Comparative Review of Performance and Engagement in PISA 2003*. Paris: OECD.

Osler, A. (1999) Citizenship, democracy and political literacy. *Multicultural Teaching* 18 (1): 12–15.

Portes, A. and Rumbaut, R. (2001) *Legacies: The Story of the Immigrant Second Generation*. Berkeley: University of California Press.

Presse- und Informationsamt der Bundesregierung (2010) *Pressemitteilung Nr. 247*. Available online at: http://www.bundesregierung.de/Content/DE/Pressemitteilungen/BPA/2010/07/2010-07-07-ib-bericht.html (accessed 3 March 2012).

Salmons, P. (2003) Teaching or preaching? The Holocaust and intercultural education in the UK. *Intercultural Education* 14 (2): 139–149.

4 Teaching English to Immigrant Students in Irish Post-primary Schools

Rachael Fionda

This chapter presents research findings from a small-scale empirical exploration of language support for EAL (English as an Additional Language) students in Irish post-primary schools. The research began by analysing Department of Education and Skills (DES) provision of teaching allocation for English language support. A survey of ten schools revealed that many of them struggled to devise programmes that developed students' English language proficiency while at the same time drawing them into curriculum subject content knowledge. Other research carried out in Ireland suggests that the needs of EAL students are not being met (Keogh & Whyte, 2003; OECD, 2009: 9). The research presented in this chapter complements the work of the Trinity Immigration Initiative's (TII) English Language Support Programme (ELSP), which carried out a more extensive survey of English language support in post-primary schools (Lyons & Little, 2009).

The research was undertaken from a broadly Gramscian perspective (Gramsci, 1971) which describes how dominant cultural ideology can be maintained and reproduced in education systems, which in turn maintains the disadvantage of minority cultural groups. One key argument concerns the 'gap' between the kind of knowledge presented by the school system, coupled with the culture of school in general, and the knowledge and experience of marginalised students (Bernstein, 1997; Bourdieu, 1997). The findings reported in this chapter link research on educational disadvantage to the context-specific needs of diversity in Irish post–primary education.

Introduction

The aim of my research was to identify characteristics of good practice appropriate to the Irish post-primary English language support context. My investigation addressed the following questions: Do the main actors (the DES, schools and teachers) facilitate the provision of language support programmes which:

- Address the demands of the curriculum and the linguistic challenges of school?
- Build on students' prior experience?
- Develop proficiency in the language of instruction (English)?
- Develop content knowledge in the mainstream subjects?

To find out what the varied landscape of English language support in Irish post-primary schools looked like, I developed a two-phase empirical plan to explore provision and practice.

Phase 1 was a preliminary exploration undertaken in ten schools. I interviewed principals, EAL coordinators, EAL and mainstream teachers about their EAL students and their English language support programmes. The data collected showed that provision varied widely from school to school. Most of the schools were struggling to open up access to education for their EAL students and very few schools in my sample appeared to have established successful language support programmes. Nevertheless, some identifiable characteristics of a successful language support programme did emerge from the data.

Phase 2 consisted of three case studies. In the course of the school year 2008–2009 I collected data that enabled me to compare how the schools had developed their language support programmes, how effective those programmes were (as far as could be observed), and what happened in the classrooms. I analysed the data under the following headings: leadership, flexibility, curriculum, teachers and pedagogy (Blair & Bourne, 1998; Keogh & Whyte, 2003; Lyons & Little, 2009; Nowlan, 2008).

The conclusion of my research established a framework of characteristics which contribute to successful English language support and educational provision for migrant students in the Irish post-primary school setting. In brief, the empirical research gathered data which built a trustworthy picture of how Ireland is meeting the challenges of diversity in schools, what opportunities exist for sharing good practice, and where there is a need for further investigation.

Hegemony and 'Gaps'

My interpretation of Gramsci's theory of hegemony (Gramsci, 1971) focuses on its relevance to education, and links power relationships to the transmission and accessibility of knowledge. My understanding of hegemony in this context owes much to Tosi (1988: 91):

> [T]he organization of consent through invisible cultural dominance rather than visible political power. Thus Gramsci's approach and the current concern of sociologists of education converge in their common attempt to interpret the role of educational change in order to understand the mechanism of control which is exercised through social and cultural reorganisation.

A common thread of argument is the recognition that students who are raised in an environment similar to the school environment have an unquestionable advantage in achieving success within that school system:

> In a whole series of families, especially in the intellectual strata, the children find in their family life a preparation, a prolongation and a completion of school life; they 'breathe in', as the expression goes, a whole quantity of notions and attitudes which facilitate the educational process properly speaking. They already know and develop their knowledge of literary language.... (Gramsci, 1971: 31)

Lyons and Little (2009), Nowlan (2008) and Devine (2005) recognise that Ireland's EAL students face significant obstacles in accessing education: social, cultural and religious barriers, as well as linguistic ones. The EAL student often brings many resources to the classroom, including a rich experience of language and culture. These are not recognised by the national curriculum in Ireland, which reflects the environment and experience of white, Catholic, middle-class, Irish-born students (Devine, 2005; Nowlan, 2008).

My research also drew on Bourdieu's theory of cultural capital, 'the set of constraints, inscribed in the very reality of the world, which governs its functioning in a durable way, determining the chances of success for practices' (Bourdieu, 1997: 46). In order to succeed in school a student must draw upon experiences, social ties and economic resources – their 'cultural capital'. Where the culture of the dominant group is promoted, educational differences and failure are often misrecognised as resulting from a lack of academic talent, when in reality they stem from 'gaps', i.e. class differences or cultural diversity (Bourdieu & Passeron, 1979: 22–23).

My study looked at classroom practice and considered underlying assumptions which may help or hinder the acquisition of language and knowledge. Freire's Critical Pedagogy (1972: 46) explains the concept of 'banking education' as simply depositing knowledge into the mind of the student, and thereby establishing an unequal power relationship, with the 'giver' of the knowledge in a position of higher status. Freire argues that banking education both forms and maintains the 'gap' (1972: 54). Diametrically opposed to banking education is Freire's proposal of 'problem-posing' education, which emphasises intention and consciousness in the process of engaging cognitive interaction: 'In problem-posing education, people develop their power to perceive critically *the way they exist* in the world *with which* and *in which* they find themselves' (Freire, 1972: 56; emphasis in original). Much of the literature specific to Ireland claims that this disempowerment is a reflection of the habitus of the individual educators (Nowlan, 2008), of institution-wide and national policy and legislation (Kuhling & Keohane, 2007; Lentin & McVeigh, 2006) and of the society in which the educational institution is set.

Official Policy

In 1999 the DES responded to the challenge of an increasingly diverse school population by making funding available for the provision of English language support (Nowlan, 2008: 253). Guidelines were issued in 2007 in a circular entitled 'Meeting the needs of pupils for whom English is a second language' (DES, 2007). The circular insists that mainstream teachers are responsible for EAL students in their classes, though many mainstream teachers appear not to inform themselves about matters related to EAL (DES, 2007, 2009). The DES provides schools with a per capita teaching allowance so that they can organise two years of English language support for each qualifying student, the expectation being that this will take place in small groups apart from mainstream classes (Ó Riagáin, 2013). In 2009 the economic recession and extensive budget cuts caused Circular 0053/2007 to be replaced by Circular 0015/2009. I completed my research just after the end of the school year 2009–2010, when the impact of this new circular was only just beginning to be felt. Its provisions may be summarised as follows:

- Schools were limited to a maximum of two EAL teachers.
- Each school was required to have its own EAL policy.
- The DES recommended that the post-primary assessment kit developed by Integrate Ireland Language and Training should be used to monitor EAL students' progress.

- Schools with between 14 and 30 students entitled to English language support received one additional teaching post, whereas schools with between 31 and 90 such students received two posts.
- It was open to schools with more than 90 EAL students to apply for funding to provide additional teaching hours.

Academic Language and Learner Autonomy

The task of acquiring the language of education is complex. Students are required to master the varieties of academic English specific to the different curriculum subjects, and as they progress through post-primary school the use of academic English tends to become increasingly abstract (Collier, 1989: 512). At the same time, students must engage with the subject knowledge transmitted by the language: 'We cannot make a clear distinction between the content and the form of the curriculum, or treat the subject matter as the end and the communication as no more than a means. The two are insepa-rable' (Barnes, 1976: 14).

Pedagogical approaches that develop learner autonomy can help to bridge the gap between EAL students' prior knowledge and the knowledge their school expects them to acquire: 'By definition, the autonomous learner tends to integrate whatever he or she learns in the formal context of the classroom with what he or she has already become as a result of developmental and experiential learning' (Little, 1995: 175). EAL students need to become autonomous learners of content knowledge and of the L2 (English in this context), meaning that there are two discrete dimensions to learner auton-omy in the EAL context – pedagogical and communicative (1995: 176). As Little (1995: 176–177) notes:

> In formal educational contexts learners do not automatically accept responsibility for their learning – teachers must help them to do so; and they will not necessarily find it easy to reflect critically on the learning process – teachers must first provide them with appropriate tools and with opportunities to practise using them.

Teachers, Provision and Pedagogy

Teachers are generally reported as saying that they are 'struggling to meet the needs of their bilingual [EAL] students in a context of limited train-ing and resources' (Nowlan, 2008: 253); whereas Kearney (2008: 111; see also

Kearney, this volume) has shown that many teachers have a negative attitude towards EAL students. Pre-service teacher education in Ireland does not include a compulsory module on language awareness or on teaching students from migrant backgrounds. However, teachers who have completed the post-graduate teaching qualification report that some non-compulsory courses are available. The OECD has noted that training for EAL and mainstream teachers is a key challenge for Ireland (OECD, 2009: 40–41).

The two-year limit imposed on EAL support is controversial in light of recent changes in provision (DES, 2007, 2009). The suggested B1 cut-off-point[1] seems reasonable: once students have achieved level B1 in reading, writing, listening and speaking they should be able to develop their English language proficiency further by participating fully in the mainstream. It is necessary to point out, however, that B1 skills do not allow students to access mainstream education to the same degree as their native speaker peers or to do well in exams. They still need English language support, but it must be provided in the mainstream classroom by mainstream subject teachers.

Research agrees that provision for immigrant students still has a long way to go before it corresponds to stated national policy (Lyons & Little, 2009; Nowlan, 2008; Smyth et al., 2009). Provision is frequently unsystematic and practice is inconsistent, which often results in the unintentional disempowerment of EAL students. Quite simply, 'Language support practices vary widely and do not reflect international best practice' (Nowlan, 2008: 253). Lyons and Little (2009: 80) agree, describing English language support as 'poorly coordinated' and 'downright haphazard' in many cases.

Phase 1 of My Investigation

Phase 1 of my research had two main aims:

- to describe the EAL programmes of 10 Dublin post-primary schools;
- to generate questions for further investigation, which provided the foundation for Phase 2.

The report that Lyons and Little published in 2009 described provision in 87 post-primary schools and identified 12 key challenges for EAL in the areas of language support: coordination and provision, teacher training, the over-representation of EAL students in resource-poor schools, classroom issues, school management structures, teacher attitudes, parent/home issues, intercultural education, lack of ICT facilities, extramural administration, exemption from Irish, and general frustration. My own research took this report as its starting point. In Phase 1 I used a semi-structured interview format (Bryman, 2004) as I wanted to guide the participants, while giving them the option of elaborating on their answers to provide insights which might not be elicited by strict guidelines. Analysis of Phase 1 data involved identifying trends in the participants' answers, and the data obtained were collated to identify the trends across the EAL programmes of the survey schools. Presentation of the trends served two ends; first as an initial description of EAL in the survey schools, and second as the basis of the Phase 2 plan.

Three significant findings emerged from the survey. One was that the status of English language support appeared to be undermined by school organisation and practice, and that these structures and practices go unquestioned. Many English language support teachers were not qualified to teach any language as an L2, and many were not qualified to teach at all, which is indicative of the low status of English language support in many schools. I also found that in many cases EAL funding was not used for language support but was allocated to other departments in the school. Secondly, there was an evident separation between language learning and mainstream content knowledge learning, contrary to theories that the two are inseparable (e.g. Barnes, 1976: 14). This was evident both in the lack of communication between EAL and mainstream teachers and in the inadequate methodology deployed in the English language support classroom. Enabling EAL students to learn means removing the obstacles to mainstream access (Devine, 2005; Lyons & Little, 2009; Nowlan, 2008), whereas structures within the survey schools appeared to be driving English language support further away from mainstream learning. The third significant finding was a lack of flexibility in the use of allocated funding, in accommodating EAL students who arrived during the school year or who needed extended English language support, and in teaching methods which didn't include the kind of student-centred approaches which draw on EAL students' linguistic and cultural capital (Bourdieu, 1997). Where English language support was provided the survey schools appeared to favour a 'one-size-fits-all' approach to programme design, allowing for little flexibility on how allocation was shared among students according to need and not allowing for changes to be made throughout the school year.

Phase 2 of My Investigation

Phase 2 explored policy and practice in three schools (Table 4.1) by focusing on four issues – leadership and ethos, flexibility, curriculum, teachers and pedagogy – and collecting data with a view to triangulation. The elicitation

Table 4.1 Participating schools

School	Total number of students	Total number of migrant students	Total number of students in English language support programme
Parkend	640	50	Not known
Linthorpe	450	20	4
Southbank	780	130	80

tools made it possible to give a comprehensive account of the schools' EAL programmes. I began each case study by interviewing a contact person in order to negotiate the best terms and procedures for my visits. The case study involved three visits to each school, with each visit lasting approximately three days. During each visit I followed EAL students and EAL teachers; I also had more limited contact with other school personnel and parents. My contact with the participants involved, for example, English language proficiency testing, interviews, observation of classroom practice, and examining existing class work and assessments. The data obtained from Phase 2 suggested principles to guide best practice in a whole-school approach to English language support. To preserve anonymity, the schools are given pseudonyms in the account that follows.

Case study 1: Parkend School

Table 4.2 summarizes the policy stance, desired outcome, assumptions, mainstream provision and pedagogy characteristic of Parkend School. EAL students comprised up to 7% of the student population at Parkend School,

Table 4.2 School 1 – Parkend

Policy stance	Equal entitlement and access to mainstream curriculum for all; required language – English; ESL students' needs must be identified
Desired outcome	Monolingual competence in English; laissez-faire on minority bi/multilingualism
Assumptions	Maximum exposure and effort in English; L1 seen as a barrier to L2
Mainstream provision	English-medium curriculum; no dedicated English language (L2) curriculum provision; no ESL-oriented assessment; no ESL teacher specialism required; tendency to be staffed by teachers with free periods; ESL becomes homework supervision
Pedagogy	TEFL approach; special needs education-approach; beyond early stage - mainstreaming

although not all were eligible for English language support. Students appeared to be overrepresented in the lower ability bands owing to the streaming system; 43% of migrant students were placed in the lowest streams.

Teachers on Parkend School's EAL programme were fully qualified, and many of them had experience of teaching special educational needs students because of the relatively high number of students in this category at the school. There didn't appear to be a 'main' EAL teacher, and because of the nature of the EAL timetable (where all students exempt from Irish participated in the allocated language support teaching period), teachers didn't necessarily organise and prepare a language support lesson for the students. Rather, they provided homework supervision or 'learning support'.

No distinction was made between EAL and Learning Support, and EAL periods were viewed as simply a 'free period', an idea which was further reinforced by the presence of English L1 students who were exempt from Irish. Consequently, because the EAL lessons I observed were in fact simple 'free periods' or 'homework sessions', there was no obvious structure to record and analyse.

One could claim that there was no EAL programme in place at Parkend School, which in itself reveals much about the implementation of the DES guidelines and the EAL structure as interpreted by this school.

Case study 2: Linthorpe School

Table 4.3 summarizes the policy stance, desired outcome, assumptions, mainstream provision and pedagogy characteristic of Linthorpe School. EAL students formed approximately 4% of Linthorpe School's student population.

Table 4.3 School 2 – Linthorpe

Policy stance	Equal entitlement and access to mainstream curriculum for all; required language – English; recognise difference; encourage Christian values
Desired outcome	Monolingual competence in English; laissez-faire on minority bi/multilingualism
Assumptions	Maximum exposure and effort in English
Mainstream provision	English-medium curriculum; no dedicated English language (L2) curriculum provision; no ESL-oriented assessment; no ESL teacher specialism required; tendency to be staffed by unqualified teachers
Pedagogy	TEFL approach; Special Needs education approach; beyond early stage, mainstreaming

Although only four students were actively receiving English language support, I identified 20 EAL students in the school altogether, five of whom were officially entitled to support. EAL staff indicated that the four students in receipt of language support happened to have space on their timetable when the EAL teacher was available. The other students were not free at this time and so didn't benefit from language support.

Both English language support teachers were unqualified. Although they had CELTA (Certificate in Teaching English to Teachers of Other Languages) qualifications, this short course is not appropriate to EAL and mainstream curriculum-based pedagogies. What is more, the teachers were frequently asked to cancel the language support sessions should they be needed to provide cover for a mainstream subject lesson.

The Learning Support department at Linthorpe was responsible for the organisation of EAL lessons, as school management interpreted EAL policy as falling under its remit. The Learning Support teachers were dedicated but apprehensive about how best to provide for the EAL students. Efforts aimed at creating an inclusive school environment included a few instances of classroom/school displays, designed to reflect the diversity of the student body, and the creation of a multi-cultural club.

Linthorpe School's use of unqualified teachers may have been holding the students' overall progress back as curriculum subject knowledge was replaced by an EFL grammar course book. Though several members of staff did attempt to address the needs of EAL students, such attempts appeared to be failing owing to lack of expertise in the area. Students missed out on timetabled English language support either because their own timetable didn't allow for attendance or because a language support lesson was cancelled to provide cover for a mainstream subject.

Case study 3: Southbank School

Table 4.4 summarizes the policy stance, desired outcome, assumptions, mainstream provision and pedagogy characteristic of Southbank School. Almost 20% of students at Southbank School (approximately 130) came from a country other than Ireland. Each summer, when the school received its allocation for the EAL students entitled to English language support (around 60 students in 2008–2009), other students who were no longer officially entitled but still in need of support were included in the language support programme.

Twelve teachers contributed to the English language support programme, five more than the previous year owing to an increase in hours. However, the majority of the language support classes (over 80%) were taught by eight teachers, all chosen for their interest in the area and their capacity to teach

Table 4.4 School 3 – Southbank

Policy stance	High achievement for all; equal entitlement and access to mainstream curriculum for all; required language – English; L1 acknowledged
Desired outcome	Competence in English; L1 acknowledged; literacy standards developed
Assumptions	Maximum exposure and effort in English; pupils' L1 as learning aid; intensive specialist teaching at early stage; links between English language support and mainstream
Mainstream provision	English-medium curriculum; dedicated English language (L2) curriculum programme; ESL-oriented assessment; tendency to be staffed by specialist ESL teachers
Pedagogy	Learner autonomy approach, student-centeredness; dialogic learning strategies; adapted use of English in mainstream curriculum activities; eventual full mainstreaming; focus on literacy

an L2. The EAL coordinator informed the principal which teachers would be suitable to provide language support, and the principal endeavoured to slot in gaps for these teachers against Irish classes, so that the EAL teachers could be available when the students needed them.

Southbank's English language support programme was based on a clearly articulated policy, the goals of which were to facilitate students' acquisition of English and cultural knowledge, as well as to include EAL students no longer officially entitled to support. The programme was responsible for providing access to the curriculum, extracurricular activities and social opportunities. According to the policy, the English language support programme should take account of the multicultural nature of the school's population and of society in general, value students' prior experience and culture of origin, encourage learner autonomy, and promote a positive relationship between the student and the school. Features of the school's commitment to an inclusive environment included the provision of materials and translations available to parents and students (in Polish), the notice board in the staffroom displaying comprehensive information about the language support programme, and the availability of books from a wide range of cultural backgrounds.

The successful English language support programme at Southbank School was characterised by, among other things: a supportive principal, a defined language support policy, a flexible language support timetable which was frequently revised, an EAL coordinator who had developed expertise in the area, and a student-centred/learner autonomy pedagogical approach in mainstream and EAL classrooms.

Discussion

Gaps in the system

The arrival of thousands of English L2 students in Irish schools challenged policy makers, schools and individual teachers to develop structures which would allow critical reanalysis of existing, habitual and 'common sense' structures. However, the haphazard implementation of English language support means that some schools have established programmes which do little to bridge the gap; indeed, some practice may even widen the gap. There is a great disparity between stated policy, practice in schools, and the outcomes achieved by EAL programmes.

I have presented arguments and theories which emphasised that students' prior knowledge plays an essential role in the language learning process; valuing a student's prior experience (in this case L1) is essential in order to provide adequate education for EAL students in Ireland. Bernstein (1971) discussed the continuity between the home and school environment for the middle-classes, which gives their children a head start and unfairly excludes students from outside the (native) middle-glass group.

Southbank School shows what can be achieved with existing provision, while also achieving policy aims of equality, and at the same time brings to light further areas for improvement both in terms of what a school can do and in terms of how official policy can help. Because the school's English language support programme was enthusiastically supported by the principal, its significance and remit could be promoted across the whole school, giving it visibility and ensuring funding for resources. The programme's teachers were qualified and interested in teaching EAL, and their availability to do so was facilitated by the principal. The creation of an EAL coordinator role was crucial to the programme's effectiveness because it ensured that the programme was coherent, a policy was developed, no student was forgotten, students who needed it were provided with support beyond the two-year limit, funding and training could be researched and sought, and so on. The principal's support meant that the language support programme could maintain flexibility throughout the year, accommodating students' needs rather than having to adhere to a fixed structure. The way Southbank School developed and ran its language support programme reflected an underlying pedagogical approach which aimed to bridge the gap between migrant students and Irish schools, and compensate for shortfalls in policy and practice. A student-centred approach seemed to be characteristic of the school as a whole, which meant that language support students could employ strategies they learnt in language support to their mainstream classes and vice versa.

When I reviewed the communicative demands of school in general, my findings led me to acknowledge that the gaps between academic language and the genres of language many (if not most) students are accustomed to can present significant obstacles to learning for *all* students, not just EAL students. Thus, the role of the teacher in communicating knowledge to students, and as a consequence introducing them to academic language at a pace which is tailored to their needs, seems an inherent and obvious part of every teacher's duty. The specific variety of language used in schools, however, is reproduced by culturally dominant structures and is a variety which many students (both EAL and non-EAL) do not have access to. This creates a bias in the education system which benefits those who belong to culturally dominant groups.

Practice that benefits migrant students is not above and beyond what is normally expected of teachers, so why do schools and teachers persist in practice which doesn't bridge the gaps between school and the students who really need it? Wacquant (1998: 216) has observed that, although education has the potential to act as an equaliser in society, as long as educational capital depends on the cultural experience, social ties and economic resources that each student has access to, many students will miss out. Gramsci's theory of hegemony (1971) describes how culture is reproduced, and it appears that the school system's failure generally to adopt the practices implemented at Southbank School is indicative of this reproduction.

Several features of policy and provision in the Irish context obstruct the development of good practice – for example, the fact that allocation of funds annually makes retention of teachers uncertain from one year to the next, and the bureaucratic complexities of applying for an extension of support in individual cases. Such structures present challenges also in Southbank School.

The gaps which maintain inequality in the school system are highlighted by the presence of migrant students. Southbank School developed a framework which built on the school's student-centred ethos and which enjoyed a large degree of success in terms of drawing migrant students into the curriculum. Other schools could adopt such a framework, but hegemony may explain why policy, schools and individual educators hold back from a more critical approach to pedagogy which could subvert cultural reproduction and promote educational equality. In order for this to happen, existing educational structures would need a comprehensive overhaul. True equality in education means providing more resources to address the needs of vulnerable students. In Ireland many educators recognise that the needs of EAL students are not being met, although there is widespread confusion in deciding which programme design would best promote EAL students' access to mainstream education.

Conclusion

The outcome of my study is a broad generalisation, identifying processes which can counteract the observed inequality in EAL educational provision and contribute to models of good practice adapted to the Irish post-primary context. What Bassey describes as educational research corresponds to the aims of my own investigation: 'Educational research is critical enquiry aimed at informing educational judgements and decisions in order to improve educational action' (1999: 39). An empirical exploration of this context tends to uncover pedagogy, policy and practice that result in unfavourable outcomes not only for the EAL student but also for the Irish-born student from lower socio-economic backgrounds.

The finding that a student-centred, learner autonomy approach helps to bridge the gap between migrant students and what the educational system expects from them suggests that such approaches should be more widely used in schools anyway. English language support should be viewed as a place where students are given tools which support their participation in the mainstream classroom. Policy can facilitate such approaches by recognising the need for a long-term commitment to EAL students, beyond a two-year allocation of English language support, and by making the bureaucratic processes by which schools apply for additional funding more straightforward. There is a fundamental inconsistency between official policy, practice in schools, and the outcomes achieved by the majority of EAL programmes. For EAL students these outcomes translate, quite simply, into an inequality in their access to education.

In conclusion, EAL students are, in many cases, not being offered a system which helps them to access education, while developing proficiency in the language of instruction. Schools and teachers (mainstream and EAL) share responsibility for English language support, as confirmed by DES policy (DES, 2007). But as Lyons and Little argue: 'Until the DES forges a more flexible policy that takes account of international findings, large numbers of newcomer students in our post-primary schools will continue to be at serious risk of educational failure' (2009, Executive summary).

Note

(1)   In the summer of 2000 the DES charged Integrate Ireland Language and Training (IILT), a not-for-profit campus company of Trinity College Dublin, with the task of developing English Language Proficiency Benchmarks (IILT, 2003) to guide schools in the provision of English language support. The Benchmarks are an adaptation of the first three proficiency levels of the *Common European Framework of Reference for Languages* (Council of Europe, 2001) – A1, A2 and B1.

References

Barnes, D. (1976) *From Communication to Curriculum*. Harmondsworth: Penguin.

Bassey, M. (1999) *Case Study Research in Educational Settings*. Buckingham: Open University.

Bernstein, B. (1971) *Class, Codes and Control, Volume 1*. London: Routledge.

Bernstein, B. (1997) Class and pedagogies: Visible and invisible. In A. Halsey, H. Lauder, P. Brown and A. Stuart-Wells (eds) *Education: Culture, Economy and Society* (pp. 59–79). Oxford: Oxford University Press.

Blair, M. and Bourne, J. (1998) *Making the Difference: Teaching and Learning Strategies in Successful Multi-Ethnic Schools*. London: Open University.

Bourdieu, P. (1997) The forms of capital. In A. Halsey, H. Lauder, P. Brown and A. Stuart-Wells (eds) *Education: Culture, Economy, Society* (pp. 46–58). Oxford: Oxford University Press.

Bourdieu, P. and Passeron, J. (1979) *The Inheritors: French Students and their Relation to Culture*. Chicago: University of Chicago Press.

Bryman, A. (2004) *Social Research Methods*. Oxford: OUP.

Collier, V.P. (1989) How long? A synthesis of research on academic achievement in a second language. *TESOL Quarterly* 23 (3), 509–531.

Council of Europe (2001) *Common European Framework of Reference for Languages: Learning, Teaching, Assessment*. Cambridge: Cambridge University Press.

DES (2007) *Circular 0053/2007 – Meeting the Needs of Pupils for Whom English is a Second Language*. Dublin: Department of Education and Science.

DES (2009) *Circular 0015/2009 – Meeting the Needs of Pupils Learning English as an Additional Language (EAL)*. Dublin: Department of Education and Skills.

Devine, D. (2005) Welcome to the Celtic Tiger? Teacher responses to immigration and increasing ethnic diversity in Irish schools. *International Studies in Sociology of Education* 15 (1), 49–70.

Freire, P. (1972) *Pedagogy of the Oppressed*. London: Penguin.

Gramsci, A. (1971) *Selections from the Prison Notebooks*. London: Lawrence and Wishart.

IILT (2003) *English Language Proficiency Benchmarks for non-English-speaking students at post-primary level*. Dublin: Integrate Ireland Language and Training.

Kearney, F. (2008) Inclusion or Invasion? How Post-Primary Teachers View Newcomer Students. Unpublished Master of Studies thesis, School of Education, University of Dublin, Trinity College.

Keogh, A. and Whyte, J. (2003) *Getting on: The Experiences of Immigrant Students in Second Level Schools Linked to the Trinity Access Programmes*. Dublin: Trinity College, Children's Research Centre.

Kuhling, C. and Keohane, K. (2007) *Cosmopolitan Ireland*. London: Pluto Press.

Lentin, R. and McVeigh, R. (2006) *After Optimism: Ireland, Racism and Globalisation*, Dublin: Metro Éireann Publications.

Little, D. (1995) Learning as dialogue: The dependence of learner autonomy on teacher autonomy. *System* 23 (2), 157–181.

Lyons, Z. and Little, D. (2009) *English Language Support in Irish Post-Primary Schools: Policy, Challenges and Deficits*. Dublin: Trinity College, Trinity Immigration Initiative.

Nowlan, E. (2008) Underneath the Band-Aid: Supporting bilingual students in Irish schools. *Irish Educational Studies* 27 (3), 253–266.

OECD (2009) *OECD Reviews of Migrant Education – Ireland*. Paris: OECD.

Ó Riagáin, P. (2013) The linguistic challenge of multi-cultural Ireland: Managing language diversity in Irish schools. In J. Ulin, H. Edwards and S. O'Brien (eds) *Race and Immigration in the New Ireland* (pp.107–129). South Bend: University of Notre Dame Press.

Smyth, E., Darmody, M., Mcginnity, F. and Byrne, D. (2009) *Adapting to Diversity: Irish Schools and Newcomer Students*. Dublin: Economic and Social Research Institute.

Tosi, A. (1988) The jewel in the crown of the modern prince: The new approach to bilingualism in multicultural education in England. In J. Cummins and T. Skutnabb-Kangas (eds) *Minority Education: From Shame to Struggle* (pp. 70–102). Clevedon: Multilingual Matters.

Wacquant, L. (1998) Pierre Bourdieu. In R. Stones (ed.) *Key Sociological Thinkers* (pp. 215–229). New York: New York University Press.

5 Inclusion or Invasion? How Irish Post-primary Teachers View Newcomer Students in the Mainstream Classroom

Fiona Kearney[1]

This chapter presents the findings of a study that explored the attitudes of Irish post-primary teachers to the inclusion of newcomer students in mainstream classes. The study examines how teacher attitudes are mediated by ideological and structural factors such as personal experience and school context and argues for the importance of training and support in moderating teacher resistance to inclusion. The impetus for the study was the unprecedented wave of inward migration that Ireland has experienced during the last decade. The scale and speed of this development have had the single most overwhelming impact on the working lives of teachers in the history of the state. The current study was undertaken as an initial step in an evolving process: in due course the impact of the new student cohort on the hitherto mono-cultural post-primary classroom is likely to prompt large-scale investigation of how Ireland approaches intercultural and inclusive educational practice. The study comprised a written survey of the attitudes of 66 mainstream teachers to newcomer inclusion. This was followed up by semi-structured interviews with 10 respondents. The aim of the study was to explore teacher attitudes towards newcomer inclusion in the mainstream classroom, identifying the factors influencing those attitudes and determining teacher perception of how newcomer inclusion might best be achieved.

Introduction: Sample and Methodology

The study was conducted among mainstream curriculum subject teachers employed in five post-primary schools in Dublin West. This area was chosen because the proportion of recent immigrants living there was almost 22%, double the national average, making it unique in Irish experience (CSO, 2006).

Five schools participated in the study and 66 teachers completed the survey questionnaire. One school was a single-sex fee-paying Voluntary Secondary school (34 teachers), one a single-sex free Voluntary Secondary school (7 teachers), two were co-educational Community Colleges (15 teachers), and one was a co-educational Community school (10 teachers). Two of the schools were Roman Catholic in ethos. While the remaining three schools were nominally multi-denominational, all had a Roman Catholic majority in their student population. Enrolment of newcomer students varied among the participating schools, ranging from 5% (low-incidence) to 42% (rapid-influx). The schools selected represented a diversity of management structures, socio-economic intake and ethnic student background.

The sample included both newly-appointed and long-serving teachers, with 20% teaching for five years or less and 39% teaching for 20 years or more. Gender data were not collected. Sixty-three teachers reported that their schools currently had newcomer students and 59 taught newcomer students in their mainstream classes. As the study was intended to elicit teacher attitudes towards newcomers as a distinct group, race and nationality were excluded as variables. Accordingly, the newcomer cohort remained undifferentiated in survey and interview questions. As the process of immigration becomes embedded in future decades, the specificity of race and nationality as distinct variables might profitably be incorporated into a larger-scale study.

The study used a mixed method research design (Creswell, 2003) employing both quantitative and qualitative methods. Triangulation was considered the optimal research design for the study because of its capacity to use 'different kinds of measurements to verify or rule out certain conclusions' (Miles & Huberman, 1994: 267). Given that the study would be the first Irish enquiry of its kind, it was hoped that the combination of tools would facilitate cross-checking and verification of data across both quantitative and qualitative instruments, ultimately enhancing validity of the research data. More specifically, the triangulated method appeared most likely to yield a substantial accumulation of survey data as well as a fine-grained exploration of the research issues and questions. Overall, it was hoped that the completed study might provide a reliable body of data on which further research might be based.

The research instruments chosen were the questionnaire (Appendix A) and the semi-structured interview (Appendix B). The questionnaire was designed to elicit survey responses to 30 questions, using a combination of question constructs – category, rating and ranking statements – from the Likert Rating Scale (Likert, 1932). The questions were targeted at teacher experience of and attitudes towards newcomer inclusion in the mainstream classroom, including perceptions of how newcomer inclusion might be advanced. Owing to the small-scale qualitative nature of the survey a total of 100 questionnaires were distributed. This was considered the minimum figure for viability purposes. As noted above, survey data were collected from 66 subject teachers in both rapid-influx and low-incidence communities. This response rate was achieved after no more than two reminders. Respondents ranged across diverse career phases, subject areas and teaching levels.

The second instrument used was the semi-structured interview. It was envisaged at the outset that no more than 10% of the sample would progress to the qualitative stage of interview. The fact that 10 of the 66 respondents volunteered for interview in their survey responses was considered highly successful. Gender was not a determinant in this survey as already reported. The interview method was chosen to generate qualitative data, including detailed explanations of the survey findings. The specific questions chosen for interview follow-up were those structured to expose assumptions underlying respondents' attitudes to ethnic integration and the efficacy of training to teach newcomer students.

Key Survey Findings on Teachers' Attitudes to Newcomers' Inclusion in Mainstream

The main topics addressed in the questionnaire were: teachers' perspectives on teaching newcomer students; teacher perceptions of the challenges and issues arising from teaching newcomer students as well as the reciprocal benefits; and teachers' views of the adequacy of training received (Q-data). The interview questions explored the questionnaire responses in more depth (interview data). For the purposes of clarification for this article all data in respect of Q-data will be expressed in percentage terms and all interview data will be expressed in terms of number of interviewees. Both datasets will be discussed at the same time.

General support for the principle of newcomer inclusion was undermined by an overwhelming resistance (70% of questionnaire respondents) to the practicalities of incorporating newcomers within mainstream classes. This resistance was not equally distributed over the five schools surveyed, with more positive, optimistic beliefs and attitudes expressed by respondents in the fee-paying and free Voluntary Secondary schools. The level of resistance conveyed was mediated by a complex pattern of attitude development, personal experience and school context. Key variables ranged from subject specificity and newcomer English language deficiency to structural and organisational concerns, including staff shortages, additional workloads and inflexible timetables.

Key variables: Newcomer language deficit and subject specificity

Although resistance to newcomer inclusion was multi-factorial, English language deficiency emerged as the strongest determinant of teacher attitude. Four interviewees claimed that lack of English constituted the main obstacle to newcomer integration, while six interviewees and 39% of survey respondents gave this as the main reason for their reluctance to accept newcomers.

> 'The students who arrive with little or no English are a problem. You ignore them for a while within your class.' (Interviewee 2)

> 'From the outset you are wasting your time.' (Interviewee 3)

In line with findings by Biggs (1999) and Asmar (2005), most respondents construed newcomer students as problems. Six interviewees said they needed to devote individual time to newcomer students, with five needing to do so in every class. With respondents citing the need to spend more lesson time on explanations for newcomers (46%) as well as more time on class preparation (27%), the findings confirm Devine's conclusion (2005: 58) that teachers adopt deficit perspectives when framing the language needs of newcomer students. The results also indicate that resistance to newcomer inclusion may be dictated by more pragmatic than ideological concerns. When the subject-specific variable is taken into account, this becomes even more apparent. While Maths teachers, in particular, expressed positive views towards newcomers:

> 'As a Maths teacher I find that a lot of newcomer students are very good mathematically and I welcome their inclusion within my class groups' (Interviewee 9)

such optimism was not shared by teachers of language-dependent subjects such as English and History, where newcomers' lack of conceptual language formed the crucial determinant of teacher attitude:

'They [newcomer students] have huge difficulties with dealing with the likes of *Macbeth*. Also the poetry is a problem trying to teach them.' (Interviewee 3)

The significance of the subject-specific variable validates Stodolsky and Grossman's claim (1995: 228) that subject matter influences pedagogic practice. It also suggests that the determinant of respondent attitude is twofold: increasing demands on teacher input and standards of newcomer performance. Although newcomers' relative success in Maths-related subjects may be attributable as much to prior attainment levels in their countries of origin as to lack of text-dependence, such success clearly makes teachers' lives easier. Conversely, teacher frustration at increased workloads on foot of newcomer language deficits is entirely predictable.

Respondents also identified parental language deficits as a source of communication problems, with home–school encounters often reliant on translation by the newcomer or siblings:

'When you need to speak to parents of newcomer students about, say, a behavioural issue of their child, it's often the case that you will be speaking to an older sibling because the parents' English is so poor. I feel what I have to say is not the business of the older sibling. It is for the parents.' (Interviewee 10)

The consequent ethical dilemma became more acute when potentially divisive issues arose. Eight of the 10 interviewees reported that African parents used corporal punishment to discipline their children and admitted that this knowledge influenced their reluctance to report discipline issues to parents:

'Africans beat their children. You know that if you send for the parents and the dad says that he is going to beat the child, you have to intervene.' (Interviewee 3)

Given that the newcomer cohort remained undifferentiated in terms of race, religion and nationality and that the respondents had all been educated within the majority Christian tradition, detailed knowledge of different African cultures would not have been available to them. Nevertheless, the ease with which they resorted to racial stereotype subverted their professed support for inclusion and illustrates how issues such as corporal punishment are likely to become the fault lines of intercultural tensions as the process of immigration becomes embedded.

Deficit perspectives also exposed the underlying conviction that newcomer needs should be subordinated to those of the indigenous cohort:

'I do dislike the disruption that the newcomer students' arrival creates, particularly coming to a class that has already done 3 years of ...' (Interviewee 4)

'Teachers are spending more time in having to give newcomer students their attention in order to provide them with an education.' (Interviewee 7)

'I feel that particularly in exam years, everyone is entitled to education and, in spending a lot of time with a newcomer student, then the rest suffer ... They are drawing on resources.' (Interviewee 10)

The equation of investment in newcomer needs with resource depletion for indigenous students is already well documented by, among others, Devine (2005) and Nowlan (2008). It is, however, impossible to determine whether respondents' expressions of frustration and resentment are exclusively newcomer-specific, as the scale and speed of the newcomer cohort's arrival in the mainstream classroom are unprecedented in the Irish experience. For this reason, initiatives on the integration of Traveller or Special Needs students do not provide a valid basis for comparison.

Moreover, the fact that respondents failed to identify options for inclusion other than English language acquisition by newcomers indicates a tacit acceptance of the status quo. Alternatives such as translating course content into newcomers' native languages were not raised and the correlation of fluency in English with academic competence remained the dominant assumption. If, as Horenczyk and Tatar (2002: 436) argue, teachers' approaches and behaviours toward culturally diverse populations reflect the norms and values of 'the larger society and of the educational settings in which the interactions take place', the findings of this study suggest that intercultural considerations remain outside the conceptual sphere of the respondents.

Structural factors

Taking into account that 53% of all post-primary schools in Ireland are owned and managed directly by religious communities or private organisations, it is not surprising that rapid immigration has pushed the issue of school patronage to the forefront of the Irish political agenda. Lynch et al. (2004: 3) argue that 'the religious control of schools in a predominantly state-funded system presents serious challenges to the pursuit of equality by particular minorities in education'. The current study provides clear examples of how school patronage perpetuates the social exclusion of newcomer students, with two interviewees reporting that newcomers' non-participation in Religious Education classes and rituals resulted in staff hostility towards them:

> 'There would be an issue around attendance of religious classes – the school has to make alternative arrangements for newcomer students at the times of the school's Masses and R.E. . . . There was an issue last year where a parent covered over the cross on the school jumper. It caused a lot of bad feeling amongst the staff towards newcomer students.' (Interviewee 2)

> 'I think sometimes within this school that minority religions are being given more emphasis than the Roman Catholic and other main religions. That's not fair.' (Interviewee 10)

As the socio-cultural background of all respondents (and most Irish teachers) is white, middle-class and Christian, these defensive responses are hardly surprising. More significantly, however, the affront occasioned by newcomers' refusal to conform to the majority religious practice reveals the extent to which an assimilationist perspective intensifies conformist pressures on newcomers. This is just one instance of emerging intercultural dilemmas that are likely to gain momentum in the future. How these issues will be addressed will reveal the limits of intercultural commitment in Ireland.

The structure of Irish post-primary school management systems constitutes a further barrier to newcomer inclusion. The traditional top-down hierarchical model of school governance militates against rapid change and, with school leadership the key determinant of school ethos and teacher attitudes alike (Levine & Lezotte, 2001; Stanovich & Jordan, 1998), innovation at a structural level within schools is stifled. In particular, teachers have little individual capacity to alter arrangements in the interests of diverse learners, such as deviating from the standard 30–40 min lesson length, if this is required to secure better learning outcomes. Aguado and del Olmo (2003) have shown that such teacher disempowerment correlates highly with disparaging attitudes toward students, whereas Gillborn (1995) has established that teacher disengagement is most detrimental in the case of newcomer students. The current study builds on these findings, with school context emerging as a key signifier of teacher attitudes towards newcomers. Respondents in low-incidence, fee-paying schools reported more positive attitudes towards newcomers than those in rapid-influx, high-exposure schools. This suggests that teacher attitude is largely dictated by the work demands associated with large numbers of new students, irrespective of the specific composition of the new cohort.

Additionally, the fact that the most positive attitudes towards newcomers were espoused by respondents in fee-paying schools indicates that the more likely bias informing respondent attitudes is one of class rather than colour, race or nationality. As the intake of fee-paying schools is largely dictated by levels of parental income – what Walsh and Donnelly (2006: 1, 26) term 'education by chequebook' – newcomers in such schools are likely to have benefited from prior private tuition and are less likely to require additional teacher input. Moreover, as fee-paying schools are characterised by restricted intake policies, often excluding Special Needs students and those from deprived backgrounds, fewer demands are likely to be made on teachers in such schools. Furthermore, as Thrupp points out (1999: 142), the disproportionate levels of high-achieving students in fee-paying schools clearly help to raise the mean achievement level, thereby boosting the academic reputation of the teacher cohort. It is not surprising, therefore, that these factors have such a strong impact on teacher attitude to newcomers encountered in such optimal settings:

> '[Newcomers] have a positive impact within classes because they are very good role models for the rest and very high work ethics, . . . bring to the class differences and multiculturalism and offer a different perspective on things and a wonderful variety for the indigenous Irish students.' (Interviewee 2)

Overall, the fact that these newcomers come from professional or middle-class backgrounds, are sufficiently affluent and low in numbers to 'fit in' and not challenge the status quo, suggests that conformist impulses are also influencing teacher responses.

At this early stage in the immigration process, the significant increase in student diversity has not yet been matched by the structural changes in school organisation, curriculum and pedagogic strategies that commitment to inclusive practice will require. The presumed norms on which future policy will be constructed will test whether the Irish education sector opts for a strategy of newcomer absorption within existing parameters or one of radical change in the interests of genuine inclusion.

Dismantling Teacher Resistance to Inclusion: The Case for In-service Provision

Given the significant impact of teachers' attitudes on newcomers' academic success, the most encouraging finding in this study was the extent of respondent enthusiasm for training in newcomer-specific strategies.

Twenty-seven percent of respondents and five interviewees favoured the incorporation of intercultural studies in teacher training programmes. In addition, eight interviewees recommended that a modular approach be developed and delivered in consultation with subject teacher associations. Respondents were adamant that in-service be delivered primarily by practising teachers with direct experience of newcomers. This suggests a commitment among respondents to active engagement with the mechanics of inclusive education rather than a grudging passivity in the face of unwelcome change.

Earlier studies on culturally relevant pedagogy (Dickens-Smith, 1995; Wilczenski, 1993) have established the beneficial effects of quality training on teacher attitudes to inclusion. Additionally, Spangenberg-Urbschat and Pritchard (1994) have shown that the absence of such initiatives leads teachers to marginalise newcomers. Response data in the current study support these findings:

> 'I have to spend more time with them. I have to give a lot more differentiated handouts and I have no training in differentiated learning in a realistic way with students whose first language is not English. It puts more pressure on me.' (Interviewee 7)

The finding that 92% of survey respondents and nine interviewees reported no training whatsoever in teaching newcomers, exceeds Walker et al.'s 2004 study of 87%. Cochran-Smith (2004: 16–17) notes that few programmes contain the intellectual content to support teachers' learning about racism, diversity and social justice in relation to education. Even where course provision does exist, it is often, according to Sugrue (2003: 206) 'of short duration without subsequent follow-up or support at school level'. Taken in conjunction with extant research, the findings of this study, therefore, bode ill for current and future inclusive practice.

Considering that 35% of respondents and three interviewees expressed feelings of inadequacy at their inability to deliver a newcomer-appropriate curriculum, the correlation between lack of training and teacher self-efficacy emerged as a significant finding in the study. It also confirmed the existence of what Hargreaves (cit. Woods & Carlyle, 2002: 174) terms the 'guilt trap' of teaching:

> 'You feel a failure trying to teach a Leaving Certificate syllabus to students who have no understanding of English.' (Interviewee 3)

> 'As an individual teacher I feel inept in coping with students who have low levels of English language competency. My philosophy is that those

newcomer students who come into me at Leaving Certificate with no English, it will be their children who will succeed, not them. It means that they are condemned to poor jobs.' (Interviewee 5)

'I don't know how to help them or, do I have the time to help them, so I feel guilty about that as well.' (Interviewee 6)

Additionally, 70% of respondents and seven interviewees claimed that inadequate institutional support had proved detrimental to teacher morale:

'I feel that there is no expertise at a Department of Education and Science level to deliver training on newcomer students. Suppose I was to ring up the Geography Support Service tomorrow morning and ask for advice on how to include newcomer students in the mainstream Geography classes. I bet no-one would be able to help me.' (Interviewee 5)

The small-scale nature of this study made it impossible to determine whether respondents' enthusiasm for newcomer-specific training was dictated more by concerns to safeguard their own professional capacity than to maximise the educational outcomes of the students. However, the fact that respondents failed to interrogate the ideological basis upon which training programmes might be developed, suggests that teachers have yet to engage with extant discourses on multiplicity, identity and transactional power in the educational context. More specifically, the preference for absorption as the primary tool for addressing newcomer requirements, which was discernible throughout the data, indicates that the needs of newcomer students are construed as subordinate to those of the indigenous cohort. Redressing this balance will be fundamental to any future programmes on newcomer inclusion, the efficacy of which will need to be tested in future research.

Conclusion: The 21st Century School – Gatekeeper of Elitism or Trailblazer for Inclusion?

Despite the timbre of the rhetoric in official strategy documents, the ideological basis of Irish government policy towards newcomer students remains assimilationist rather than inclusive. The designation of immigrants as 'non-nationals' in all official documentation up to 2005 is illustrative of the exclusionary ideology underpinning official discourse on immigration. Although the term 'non-national' has been replaced by 'newcomer student', this too has assimilationist overtones, designating the immigrant student as a stranger who must merge into the dominant culture. The determination to mould newcomers to pre-existing structures constitutes what Kendall (cit. Walker *et al.*, 2004: 147) terms 'cultural racism', a 'way of thinking, speaking and responding that becomes so pervasive in the mainstream culture that it is almost invisible'. Current Irish educational policy is underpinned by mono-cultural assumptions that privilege the status quo and favour absorption rather than inclusion of immigrants. These assumptions dictate school curricula and have direct implications for teacher perception and practice with minority ethnic students. Both Valdes (2001) and Youngs and Youngs (2001) have established that teachers' perceptions not only affect newcomer students' academic performance but also their adjustment to school, classroom and classmates.

To date, the state's response to newcomer students' inclusion has been confined to language-oriented support, with language support teachers appointed on a temporary basis, which precludes capacity-building of teacher expertise. Additionally, the widespread perception among teachers that training on inclusion is not available runs counter to the DES's directive that full training on inclusion of ethnically and culturally diverse learners is available through the Advisory Council of English Language Schools (ACELS).[2] ACELS course content, however, is focused on general English language learning and teaching rather than curriculum-specific requirements. The accessibility and relevance of such training to post-primary teachers calls into question state commitment to the principle of inclusion.

This study set out to compile preliminary data on the attitudes of post-primary teachers to newcomer students and to offer some initial insights into teachers' perceptions of the challenges posed by increasing ethnic diversity in school. Despite strong levels of reluctance to accept such students into the mainstream classroom, the existence of widespread enthusiasm among respondents for newcomer-specific training indicates a willingness to engage with inclusive practice. However, while there was little evidence of overt racism in the response data, it was possible to discern a privileging of indigenous cultural dominance in survey extension questions and interview responses. More generally, widespread assimilationist perspectives suffused the terminology used by respondents, illustrating how language operates as the most significant ideological conduit in shaping teacher attitudes to immigrants.

Since this study was completed, in December 2007, Ireland has experienced the worst economic depression in its history. Although immigration has now dwindled, the newcomer cohort will continue to grow, as existing migrants become embedded in Irish society. The coming years will reveal whether, with pressure intensifying on diminishing resources, state commitment to newcomer inclusion is genuine or not. It is obvious that the advancement of inclusion will require a comprehensive programme of newcomer-specific training both at pre-service and in-service levels. To be effective, professional development must embed interculturalism within critical pedagogy. Practical support measures including extra teachers, reduced teaching workloads, more classroom support staff, interpreters and cultural mediators will also be required if the needs of the pluralist classroom are to be met.

Devine (2005) has shown how teachers' concepts of different immigrant groups cannot be divorced from their own positioning as white, Catholic middle-class professionals. Not surprisingly, this means that they develop feelings of affiliation and sensitivity to those who most appropriate to this norm. It is therefore inevitable that teachers bring to their classrooms a series of internalised discourses on ethnicity, immigration and identity that both reflect and are influenced by the norms and values prevalent in the wider society. From the evidence of this study, it is clear that dismantling the traditional hegemonic practices of teaching will be fundamental to eradicating the mismatch between the homogeneity of the teaching cohort and the heterogeneity of the newcomer population.

All of these measures, however, will not be enough to make inclusion happen. Race, as Devine (2005) observes, is central to the dynamics of inclusion and exclusion. Until the subterranean assumptions underlying existing educational policy and individual school practice are addressed, little progress will be made. At a political level, a commitment to interrogate institutional and conceptual racism will be required, accompanied by a willingness to identify and eradicate it. Without this radical approach, the inclusion project is likely to remain little more than a pious aspiration.

Notes

(1) The views and opinions expressed in this article are the personal views and opinions of the author.
(2) ACELS was established in 1969 under the auspices of the DES to control standards in EFL schools through an inspection/recognition scheme. Its remit also includes recognition of teacher training (TEFL) courses and the development of materials and examinations for overseas students. It has been involved in setting up an ELT qualifications register for English language professionals in Ireland.

References

Aguado, T. and del Olmo, M. (2003) *INTER Guide: A practical guide to implement intercultural education at schools.* Online document: http:www.migration-boell.de/web/integration/47 1480.asp (accessed 24 April 2008).

Asmar, C. (2005) Internationalising students: Reassessing diasporic and local student difference. *Studies in Higher Education* 30 (3), 291–309.

Biggs, J. (1999) *Teaching for Quality Learning at University.* Buckingham: Society for Research into Higher Education and Open University Press.

Cochran-Smith, M. (2004) *Walking the Road: Diversity and Social Justice in Teacher Education.* New York and London: Teachers College Press.

Creswell, J.W. (2003) *Research Design: Qualitative, Quantitative, and Mixed Methods Approaches* (2nd edn). London: Sage.

CSO (2006) *Census Interactive Tables for Census 2006.* Dublin: Central Statistics Office.

Devine, D. (2005) Welcome to the Celtic Tiger? Teacher responses to immigration and increasing ethnic diversity in Irish schools. *International Studies in Sociology of Education* 15 (1), 49–70.

Dickens-Smith, M. (1995) The effect of inclusion training on teacher attitude towards inclusion. *Educational Leadership* 42 (4), 35–38.

Gillborn, D. (1995) *Racism and Anti-racism in Real Schools.* Buckingham: Open University Press.

Horenczyk, G. and Tatar, M. (2002) Teachers' attitudes towards multiculturalism and their perceptions of the school organisational culture. *Teacher and Teacher Education* 18 (1), 435–445.

Levine, D. and Lezotte, L. (2001) Effective schools research. In J. Banks and C. Banks (eds) *Handbook of Research on Multicultural Education* (pp. 525–547). San Francisco: Jossey-Bass.

Likert, R. (1932) *A Technique for the Measurement of Attitudes.* New York: Columbia University Press.

Lynch, K., Lodge, A., Kenny, M., Hanafin, J., Clarke, M., Barry, E., Malone, R. and Shevlin, M. (2004) Introduction. In A. Lodge and K. Lynch (eds) *Diversity at School* (pp. 1–6). Dublin: Institute of Public Administration (for the Equality Authority).

Miles, M.B. and Huberman, A.M. (1994) *An Expanded Sourcebook – Qualitative Data Analysis* (2nd edn). Thousand Oaks: Sage.

Nowlan, E. (2008) Underneath the Band-Aid: supporting bilingual students in Irish schools. *Irish Educational Studies* 27 (3), 253–266.

Spangenberg-Urbschat, K. and Pritchard, R. (1994) *Kids Come in All Languages: Reading Instruction for ESL Students.* Newark, DE: International Reading Association.

Stanovich, P.J. and Jordan, A. (1998) Canadian teachers' and principals' beliefs about inclusive education as predictors of effective teaching in heterogeneous classrooms. *Elementary School Journal* 98 (1), 221–238.

Stodolsky, S. and Grossman, P.L. (1995) The impact of subject matter on curricular activity: An analysis of five academic subjects. *American Educational Research Journal* 32 (2), 227–251.

Sugrue, C. (2003) Teacher education in Ireland. In B. Moon, L. Vlasceanu and L.C. Barrows (eds) *Studies on Higher Education: Institutional Approaches to Teacher Education within Higher Education in Europe: Current Models and New Developments* (pp. 190–216). Bucharest: UNESCO, CEPES.

Thrupp, M. (1999) *Schools Making a Difference. Let's be Realistic! School Mix, School Effectiveness and the Social Limits of Reform.* Buckingham: Open University Press.

Valdes, G. (2001) *Learning and Not Learning English: Latino Students in American Schools.* New York: Teachers College Press.

Walker, A., Shafer, J. and Iiams, M. (2004) 'Not in my classroom': Teacher attitudes towards English Language Learners in the mainstream classroom. *NABE Journal of Research and Practice* 2 (1), 130–160.

Walsh, J. and Donnelly, K. (2006, December 4) Revealed: The great schools' class divide. *Irish Independent,* pp. 1, 26.

Wilczenski, F.L. (1993) Changes in attitudes towards mainstreaming among undergraduate education students. *Educational Research Quarterly* 17 (1), 5–17.

Woods, P. and Carlyle, D. (2002) Teacher identities under stress: The emotions of separation and renewal. *International Studies in Sociology of Education* 12 (1), 169–189.

Youngs, C. and Youngs, G. (2001) Predictors of mainstream teachers' attitudes toward ESL students. *TESOL Quarterly* 35 (1), 97–118.

Appendix A: Questionnaire

Please tick box For Office Use only □□□
Section A : Your Background

1. Please indicate your employment status (tick ✓ as appropriate)

Permanent	
Temporary Whole time	
Eligible Part-time	
Part-time	

2. Please indicate (tick ✓) the number of years you have been teaching

0–5 years	
6–10 years	
11–20 years	
Over 20 years	

3. Please name the subjects you teach and up to what level? (tick ✓)

	Subject	Junior Cert.		Leaving Cert.		Leaving Cert. Applied
		Higher	Ordinary	Higher	Ordinary	
1.						
2.						
3.						
4.						
5.						

Section B : Your School

4. Please indicate (tick ✓) the type of school in which you teach.

1. Community College	
2. Community School	
3. Comprehensive School	
4. Fee-paying Voluntary Secondary School	
5. Free Voluntary Secondary School	
6. Vocational School	

5.   Please indicate which of the following programmes are available in your school: (Tick 'Yes' or 'No' as appropriate).

	Yes	No
Junior Certificate Schools' Programme		
Leaving Certificate Applied		
Leaving Certificate Vocational Programme		
Transition Year Programme		
FETAC (NCVA) Foundation Level Courses		
Other, please specify..............		

6.   Does your school currently have newcomer students?
     Yes ☐   No ☐   Don't know ☐

Section C: Your experience of teaching newcomer students

7.   Which of the following do you consider most appropriate to describe newcomer students. Please tick ✓

Description	
a) Students from the Accession EU countries	
b) Refugees and Asylum seekers	
c) Children of international economic migrants	
d) International students whose first language is neither English nor Irish	
e) Non-nationals	
f) Other international students whose first language is English	
g) Other	

8.   What is the average class size you teach?
     30–35 ☐   25–30 ☐   20–25 ☐   Other ☐
9.   Are there currently newcomer students in your classes?
     Yes ☐   No ☐   Don't know ☐
10. If yes, how many such students do you teach?

	Per class	In total
Number		

11. Were you given any choice about taking newcomer students into your class groups?

     Yes ☐   No ☐
12. Are there issues relating to the inclusion of newcomers which make you reluctant to take them into your class?
     Yes ☐   No ☐
13. If yes, what are the issues? Please be as honest as possible when giving your reasons

     ....
     ....
     ....

14. Did you receive any information about your newcomer students before they came to your class? (e.g. Special needs, level of language competency, background, health etc.)

     Yes ☐   No ☐
15. If yes, was the information provided sufficient to help you teach them?
     Yes ☐   No ☐   Not sure ☐
16. If you did not receive background information but required it, who would you be most likely to approach?

	Most likely 4	Likely 3	Unlikely 2	Least likely 1
Principal	4	3	2	1
Deputy Principal	4	3	2	1
Language Support Teacher	4	3	2	1
Parents	4	3	2	1

Year Head	4	3	2	1
Class Tutor	4	3	2	1
School student Counselor	4	3	2	1
Individual subject teachers	4	3	2	1
No-one	4	3	2	1
Other	4	3	2	1

17. Did you receive any specific training before you were asked to teach newcomer students?   Yes ☐   No☐

18. If yes, what form did this training take?

Training/assistance provided	Yes/No
(a) English language learning methodologies and approaches .	
(b) Resources available e.g. textbooks, curriculum materials, websites.	
(c) IILT (Integrate Ireland Language and Training) courses in English language teaching + their Portfolios.	
(d) Assessment needs of newcomer students.	
(e) Strategies to support newcomer learners.	
(f) Subject specific training for newcomer learners.	
(m) Examples of best practice models in other schools of ethnic and linguistic diversity.	
(n) Training in cultural norms of other countries e.g. lack of eye contact (cultural mediation).	
(o) Other – please specify:	

19. Which of the above, if any, did you find the most helpful?

20. Did you receive specific training to teach newcomer students in your original teacher training?
Yes ☐   No ☐

21. If yes, what form did it take?
Elective module ☐ Mandatory exam subject ☐

22. Was it useful to you?
Yes ☐   No ☐

23. If 'no' what, in your opinion was missing?

24. Have you found it necessary to spend more class time on a 1-1 basis with your newcomer students than with your Irish students? (please tick ✓)
Yes ☐   No ☐   Depends on the student ☐

25. Has the presence of newcomer students made teaching your classes:
a) Easier ☐ **b)** More difficult ☐ **c)** No difference ☐

26. The following statements concern the impact that teaching newcomer students has had on you. In each case, please ring the response that best reflects your feelings.

	Strongly agree	Agree	Unsure	Disagree	Strongly disagree
I sometimes feel a sense of personal inadequacy	5	4	3	2	1
I feel resentful towards these students because they need me to do more for them.	5	4	3	2	1
Teaching them causes me a lot of stress because some have a poor educational history and weak literacy skills.	5	4	3	2	1
I find teaching newcomer students very rewarding	5	4	3	2	1
Teaching them has increased my workload	5	4	3	2	1
Their presence has enhanced my classroom practice because it has encouraged me to develop new teaching strategies.	5	4	3	2	1

I have gained insights into other cultures and nationalities	5	4	3	2	1

27. The following statements contain commonly held opinions on newcomer students in Irish schools. In each case, please ring the response that most closely reflects your own perspective. The statements range across the categories of: *Skills and capacities, cultural views, resources* and *parental involvement.*

	Strongly Agree	Agree	Unsure	Disagree	Strongly Disagree
Skills and capacities					
They are compromising the education of Irish students	5	4	3	2	1
They lower academic performance levels in the school	5	4	3	2	1
They are difficult to manage in terms of challenging behaviour	5	4	3	2	1
Cultural views					
They show a total lack of respect towards female members of staff	5	4	3	2	1
They choose not to conform to school norms and expectations	5	4	3	2	1
They self-segregate into their own ethnic groups, choosing not to interact with indigenous peers	5	4	3	2	1

There's a lot of animosity between newcomers and Irish students.	5	4	3	2	1
Resources					
They are drawing hugely on the resources of the school to the detriment of others	5	4	3	2	1
Parental involvement					
Parents of newcomer students do not care about their children's schooling or education in general	5	4	3	2	1
They have different cultural perspectives to punishment than we do, e.g. excessive use of corporal punishment to enforce discipline.	5	4	3	2	1
They do not participate in school activities despite encouragement.	5	4	3	2	1

Section D: The benefit of your experience – suggestions for the future

28. In terms of further supports that may assist teachers in the inclusion of newcomer students within the Post-primary setting, how would you rate the benefits of the following provisions?

Supports	Very useful 4	Useful 3	Unsure 2	Not Useful 1
Peer support programmes/ Buddy systems to assist newcomer students acclimatise to school environment.	4	3	2	1

Provision of information on a range of curriculum and extra-curricular activities available in schools, translated into different languages.	4	3	2	1
Establishment of induction/reception programmes for new students to introduce them to school and the unspoken norms in Ireland.	4	3	2	1
Basic Admissions policy & Code of discipline available in different languages	4	3	2	1
Periodic Standardised testing to assess the level of English language proficiency of students at particular points of time.	4	3	2	1
Culturally specific Home School Liaison officers e.g. East European, West African to understand cultural values of newcomer students and advise schools.	4	3	2	1

29. Overall, how would you rate your skill in teaching newcomer students? Please circle a number , 5 = excellent, 4 = good, 3 = adequate, 2 = fair, 1 = poor.

Excellent	Good	Adequate	Fair	Poor
5	4	3	2	1

30. Arising from your experience of teaching newcomer students, what future training and support do you think is required?

Thank you for taking the time to complete this questionnaire.

Is there anything else you would like to add? Please use this space to elaborate on any answers given or include any suggestions for future improvements.

If you would be willing to have a short discussion at a mutually convenient time about the implications of including newcomer students in the mainstream classroom, please provide contact details below.

Appendix B: Interview Schedule

The main questions of the interview schedule are set out below. Supplementary questions probed the interviewees' ideological assumptions and included those related to newcomers' English language deficiency, inadequate professional training and the perceived abandonment by the Department of Education and Skills (DES).

ISSUE OF RELUCTANCE

RESPONSE TO QUESTION 11 – *Were you given any choice about taking newcomer students into your class groups?* (If ticked 'NO' as given no choice)
*   How did you feel about not having been offered a choice?

RESPONSE TO QUESTION 13 – *If there are issues related to newcomer students' inclusion which make you reluctant, what are the issues?*
*   In your opinion what issues make you reluctant to their inclusion in mainstream?

RESPONSE TO QUESTIONS 14 + 16 –*'Did you receive any information about your newcomer students before they came to class?'* If ticked 'NO' and tied in with no 16' *If you did not receive background information, who would you most likely approach?*
*   Where do you source information on newcomer students? Why did you choose this source?

ISSUE OF TRAINING AVAILABLE AND RECEIVED

RESPONSE TO QUESTION 18: *If you received specific training before teaching newcomer students, what form did it take?*
*   What are your feelings around the current level of provision and in-service in respect of newcomer students?

RESPONSE TO QUESTIONS 20–23: *Did you receive specific training to teach newcomer students in your original teacher training?*
- Did the initial teacher training prepare you for teaching newcomer students? Why/why not?

ISSUE OF RELUCTANCE

RESPONSE TO QUESTION 24: *Have you found it necessary to spend more class time on a 1-1 basis with newcomer students than Irish students?* If ticked 'YES'
- How do you feel about devoting this time?

RESPONSE TO QUESTION 25: *Has the presence of newcomer students made teaching your classes: easier, more difficult, no difference?*
- How has their inclusion made your teaching easier/more difficult?

RESPONSE TO QUESTION 26: Statements *concerning the impact that teaching of newcomer students has had on you.*
- In what ways does their inclusion cause you a sense of inadequacy/stress/reward?

RESPONSE TO QUESTION 27: Statements *re. commonly held opinions on newcomer students in Irish schools*

Skills and capacities
- In your opinion, how are newcomer students compromising the education of Irish students?

Cultural views
- Do you think that newcomer students and Irish students respond differently to school norms and expectations? Why?
- Could your school do anything to advance inter-culturalism?

Parental involvement
- In your opinion how have parents of newcomer students demonstrated their lack of interest in their child's education in general?
- Have you experienced differences in parental perspectives to punishment contrary to those upheld within Irish society? If so, in what form? How has this made you feel? How can this issue be best dealt with?
- How does the lack of newcomer parents' involvement in school activities influence your attitudes towards newcomer students?

ISSUE OF TEACHERS' PERSPECTIVES OF FUTURE TRAINING – WHAT IS REQUIRED

RESPONSE TO QUESTION 30: *Arising from your experience of teaching newcomer students, what future training and support is required?*

- In your opinion, what elements are needed in future teaching training and in-service to equip teachers to effectively include newcomer students in mainstream classes?

6 The Linguistic Challenges of Immigration: The Irish Higher Education Sector's Response

Bríd Ní Chonaill

This chapter focuses on a small-scale exploratory study that I conducted in the higher education sector in Ireland. It provides an overview of the English language support provided to migrants in higher education during the academic year 2009–2010. Telephone interviews were used to gather information from the 27 designated institutions of the HEA (Higher Education Authority) which comprised the data set. In quantitative terms the study found that 10 of the 27 institutions offer language classes or support, in a variety of forms, to non-native speakers of English, which migrants have an opportunity to attend. The qualitative analysis raised issues around the need for language support despite the entry requirements in place, the deficit in terms of academic English which can contribute to migrants underachieving at third level, and the question of where responsibility lies for bringing migrants' English language proficiency to the necessary level – with the migrant, the institution or the state? The question of how such support is funded is pertinent, particularly in times of recession; so too is deciding how best to timetable provision to ensure student attendance. In conclusion, the study found that given the HEA's aim to promote equality of opportunity in higher education, the question of language support for migrants, and indeed all non-native speakers of English, needs to be addressed in order to address their underachievement in both higher education and the labour market.

Overview

This chapter reports on a small-scale exploratory study that I conducted in the higher education sector in Ireland in 2010. The aim of this research was to describe and analyse the different types of English language support available to migrants in this sector during the course of the academic year 2009–2010. I start by outlining the rationale behind the choice of topic, before discussing the promotion of equality in higher education. Having described the methodology used for the research, I discuss data gathered both quantitatively and qualitatively. Finally, I draw some conclusions, in light of the findings, regarding English language support provision for migrants in the higher education sector in Ireland.

Background and Rationale of the Study

Over the 10 years that I have worked at Institute of Technology Blanchardstown (ITB), I have witnessed changes in the student population, which increasingly reflects the diversity of the local population. Its immediate catchment area, Dublin 15, constitutes the fastest growing urban area in Ireland, with foreign nationals constituting a key contributing factor to demographic growth. Non-Irish nationals account for almost 21% of people resident in Dublin 15, which is double the national average of 10.5% (Ryan, 2009). In October 2009 I interviewed 12 non-Irish students at ITB to inform the design of a project that I was working on, which focused on the transition from second to third level as experienced by migrants. In keeping with the literature (Linehan & Hogan, 2008; Warner, 2006), four of the interviewees identified language as a barrier and agreed that 'support would be good' (Participant 3: Uganda). It must be noted that migrants are very diverse in linguistic terms: they are not all non-native speakers of English, and amongst those who are, their proficiency varies considerably. As English language classes were not offered at ITB in the academic year 2009–2010, their comments prompted me to carry out this study, exploring what type of English language support other higher education institutions were offering to migrants among their student body. As at the time ITB had only one 'international student' – i.e. a student usually resident outside of Ireland who comes here on a student visa to study on a fee-paying basis (Warner, 2006: 8) – my focus was on 'migrants', understood as persons moving from one country to another on a temporary or a permanent basis. I use the term 'migrant' in my description of the research, while recognising that it is a social construction and a catch-all term that encompasses great diversity.

The Promotion of Equality in the Higher Education Sector

Education systems tend to reproduce existing inequalities in society at large and these inequalities are also very evident in higher education (Linehan & Hogan, 2008). In the case of Ireland, equality has gained importance in legislative terms since the late 1990s. The Equal Status Act 2000 prohibits educational establishments from discriminating on nine grounds, including race. In addition, in the higher education sector, equality features both in the Qualifications (Education and Training) Act 1999, which is relevant to the Institutes of Technology (IoTs) and the further education sector, and the Universities Act 1997 (Linehan & Hogan, 2008: 5).

The promotion of equality of opportunity in the higher education sector has been one of the core functions of the Higher Education Authority (HEA) since its establishment in 1971 (HEA, 2008: 14). Its National Office for Equity of Access to Higher Education monitors the advancement of under-represented, target groups with a view to increasing their access to higher education. Although the current National Plan for Equity of Access to Higher Education 2008–2013 does recognise the 'need to have special regard to the needs of recent immigrants' (HEA, 2008: 11), it does not include specific action points relating to ethnicity. This is attributable to the dearth of official educational data at the time of the plan's development. This lack is currently being addressed through the Equal Access Data Collection. As the National Office notes, their understanding of the concept 'access' includes retention and successful completion, as well as entry to higher education (HEA, 2008: 14), in keeping with the definition used by the European Access Network (www.ean-edu.org/) – not just equality of access but equality of outcome.

Methodology

The aim of the research was to gain insight into what type of English language support was available for migrants in higher education in Ireland. It set out to provide a snapshot of the sector at a certain period in time – the information collected is valid for the academic year 2009–2010. The participants were the 27 designated institutions of the HEA. Interviews were conducted with all 27, which include the seven universities, the 13 Institutes of Technology and Dublin Institute of Technology, the Royal College of Surgeons, the National College of Art and Design, the Royal

Irish Academy, Mater Dei Institute of Education, St Patrick's College of Education, Mary Immaculate College, and St Angela's College. As I wanted to produce a national picture, given time constraints and distance from the various third-level institutions, telephone interviews were used. Fielding and Thomas (2001: 131) describe the telephone interview as a 'particularly successful' technique for gathering 'factual information as compared to matters of attitude and affect'. My first point of contact was generally the head of the International Office, and then I was frequently redirected to either academic staff, the Registrar's Office, a Language Centre, the Access Office or a learning and support unit – it varied from institution to institution. Disadvantages of the method were the speed at which notes had to be taken but I had a limited number of specific questions in my interview schedule so I wrote in shorthand everything that the interviewees said. In order to improve reliability I employed the technique of 'reflecting back' (May, 2001: 133), where necessary, to allow myself as well as the interviewee the chance to correct and/or modify my account. In a large number of cases, I sought respondent validation (Bryman, 2004: 274) by sending follow-up emails to confirm that the information I had recorded was accurate, or if a query arose.

As noted earlier, my initial group of interest was the migrant population. However, after the first interview, I quickly had to readjust my questions to cover a broader student population, including international and Erasmus students. Administrative classifications such as these run the risk of reproducing 'homogeneous fixed categories of difference' (Gunaratnam, 2003: 28). However, given their current usage in the higher education sector, these labels have implications for non-Irish students as regards fees or access to language support. Furthermore, an issue that had not been considered, namely the question of credits being allocated, was raised in the second interview, and included in subsequent interviews. Once the aim and purpose of the research was outlined to interviewees, they were asked three focused but open-ended questions about what English language classes or support were available for non-native speakers, who benefited from them, and any issues surrounding them. My definition of support, in keeping with the way we operate at ITB, is a facility, a service or some measure designed to help students. They do not pay directly for such support, though they may pay indirectly through their annual student contribution. My focus was on full-time students.

Transcription was carried out, where possible, straight after the telephone conversation, and then the data from transcriptions were coded. Content analysis was carried out manually, with extracts relevant to particular themes being brought together and a grid created (Fielding & Thomas,

2001: 138). The codes were compared, contrasted and critiqued in the context of the HEA's aim to promote equality of opportunity, briefly outlined above. To ensure confidentiality, I have assigned a numerical code to each of the institutions involved: the universities are coded Univ 1–7; the Institutes of Technology and Dublin Institute of Technology, IT 1–14; and the seven other higher education institutes are coded HEI 1–7. The data were analysed both quantitatively and qualitatively.

Results

Results in quantitative terms

First, from a quantitative point of view, 18 of the 27 higher education institutions (67%) reported that they offered English language support/classes of some sort. In the remaining nine institutions (33%), interviewees said that there was no 'need' for such support either as a result of the student profile or because of entry requirements in terms of English language proficiency. This is explored in more detail below.

The support that was offered included English language classes or support for Erasmus and international as well as migrant students, but in the present discussion I focus exclusively on the latter category. Ten higher education institutions (37%) reported that they offered classes or support to any non-native speaker of English, which migrants have an opportunity to attend.

I found that language classes/support were offered in a wide variety of forms: as an elective module on a programme (IT6, Univ2), as weekly English language classes (2 hours) (IT6, Univ7, IT4, IT8, IT13 and if demand is sufficient, Univ6), in clinic format (an Academic English/writing centre drop-in, IT3: student support in English language, IT2), as a pre-sessional course (IT13), and in the form of students being allowed attend classes for teachers training in ESOL (English for Speakers of Other Languages) (Univ1). I have not included support provided through Access Offices (whose mission is to increase levels of participation of underrepresented groups) within the data, given the difficulty of comparing it across the sector and the fact that it only concerned specific arrangements for individual students.

Qualitative analysis of the data

Moving to the qualitative data, a number of issues were raised during the telephone interviews, which will now be analysed in light of the framework outlined above.

'Not up to us to be providing' – A current topic among third-level providers, according to Egan and Dunbar (2008: 63), is 'whether students should be informed that all lectures, notes, tutorials, texts, exams etc. will be in English and that proficiency in this language is the student's personal responsibility, or whether they should seek to provide far more support, either through additional tutoring or through additional languages'. The data gathered echo this debate: 'What level of responsibility do we have? I think it's down to the students – it's not up to us to be providing' (IT5). 'Is it our job to do remedial? How much has to be shoved onto higher education?' (IT3). This leads us in two directions – first of all an examination of the entry requirements for access to higher education in Ireland, and secondly, the provision of English for migrants in Irish society at large.

Entry requirements – As was noted earlier, a number of colleges which did not provide support cited entry requirements as a justification. For example, two interviewees spoke of 'very specific language exams' or a 'test' given at the start of the year (IT14 and HEI7); 'we have a requirement of IELTS [International English Language Testing System – the test of English most widely used in higher education], at least 6.5 and not less than 6 for writing for all students for whom English is not their first language' (HEI6); 'it's college policy to have a certain level of English to be admitted' (Univ3). Egan and Dunbar (2008: 63) raise the issue of some colleges 'reluctantly considering the introduction of more stringent entry testing, including written tests and/or interviews in order to assess the applicant's ability to engage with the course'. In the case of IT9, such a test was introduced in 2010 to assess the suitability of mature students for a course, one of the reasons being to gain a better indication of the applicants' level of proficiency in English.

Lack of uniformity across the sector as regards entry requirements – In their analysis of access to higher education, Coghlan *et al.* (2005: 15) identified a particular problem with access to colleges, namely the 'different requirements of proof of level of knowledge of English' that the various colleges have. This lack of uniformity and consistency across the sector, also highlighted by Warner (2006) among others, was visible in the data gathered. Entry requirements for non-native speakers of English vary from college to college, and indeed within colleges there are divergences: in the case of IT10 an IELTS score of 5.5 is required for Engineering and Science and of 6 for Business and Humanities. There is a similar situation in IT11, while HEI6 requires an IELTS score of 6.5 (not less than 6 for writing). As noted above, potential students in HEI7 sit a test at the start of the year, some institutions have designed a placement test themselves (IT12), whereas in others mature students are interviewed (for example, IT3). There is thus great variation from college to college. One interviewee asked, 'Should we be testing people before they come in?' (IT2), while another asked 'What test and for whom?' (Univ2), alluding to problems in the whole area of testing.

Support required despite entry requirements – Of course, even when entry requirements are in place, students within the system may still require support. Interviewees raised this issue a number of times: students can come in with an 'imbalance on scores: strong oral and weak written' (IT10); 'students get coached – you sometimes find gaps – we give them on-going English language support' (IT11); 'they have to have a certain level when they come in – but because of academic language need more support' (Univ1); 'All students have met scores for entry requirements. Sometimes their skills in reality do not reflect the score' (Univ5). While these remarks were made primarily in relation to international students, the principle remains the same: students can meet the entry requirements and still require further support within the institution to achieve their potential. As Coakley (2009: 5) argues, 'migrants are not the same as their Irish-born counterparts and require an extra and multi-faceted layer of support if they are to progress in Ireland'. It is for this reason that Warner argued for the 'need for assistance with academic English and with understanding the contents of lectures once students have entered higher education' (2006: 46). This is echoed by Dunbar who recommends, in relation to education, that we 'provide additional resources for students who may be experiencing difficulties related to their understanding of the language' (2008: 77). As was mentioned earlier, for the HEA access involves not just entry but also retention and successful completion of higher education. The issue is not just to remove barriers but, as Warner (2006: 36) argues, to adopt a 'proactive approach with policies aimed specifically at this group to overcome the problems caused by language' and other factors. A 'genuine commitment to do so', hand in hand with 'sufficient resources', is required to make it happen (Warner, 2006: 36). We will return to the question of resources shortly.

Students enter higher education through a variety of routes, primarily upon completion of the state examination, the Leaving Certificate, at the end of second level, but also as mature students, or with a FETAC qualification (from the further education and training sector). As regards entry requirements, interviewees in six institutions raised the question of students coming through these 'domestic routes', as opposed to those who enter from abroad: 'we had an issue recently in an academic department, students coming in through domestic routes – worried about the level of English language proficiency' (Univ1); 'we have noticed that there are students who came to Ireland some years ago and sat and passed the Leaving

Cert in spite of having a lower intermediate level in English. These students are not achieving their full potential and would require support if the budget permits next year' (IT3). In the case of IT9, if non-native speakers of English come through the Irish Leaving Certificate or FETAC route, they do not need to prove their proficiency in English. One of the minimum entry requirements is to pass Leaving Certificate English. When questioned on the level of English necessary to meet this, a language support teacher in a local secondary school explained that 'you could pass ordinary level English on an A2 level – students spend six years in school and they learn off quotes' (Thompson, 2010, personal communication). This is far below the B2 level of the Council of Europe's (2001) *Common European Framework of Reference for Languages*. The B2 level is equated to an IELTS score of between 5.5 and 6.5 (IELTS, n.d.), which, as discussed earlier, the third level institutions require at entry level.

Considering the bigger picture beyond third level – This of course must be set in the context of the bigger picture of Irish society. General research has identified a deficit at second level. The Irish state provides two years of language support to non-native speakers of English so that they can access the mainstream classroom. However, for migrant students to successfully transfer to upper second level and higher education, they require 'longer support to achieve mastery of academic English' (Taguma *et al.*, 2009: 9), which has implications for third level. Several participants in Warner's 2006 study felt that 'the problem of language proficiency could not be solved at third level, highlighting the need for a systematic, nationwide policy on teaching English as a second language at secondary school level' (Warner, 2006: 45). There is undoubtedly a deficit, particularly in the case of students who enter the education system later, and it will be an issue in the future, perhaps particularly in the case of the IoTs, where the points required for entry are frequently lower than they are for comparable courses in the universities. We have seen an increase in mature students across the sector, particularly in current recessionary times, and research has shown that the English of adult learners, unlike younger learners, will fossilise without instruction (Long, 2003). There is a problem within higher education of migrant students underachieving, and this shortfall can follow them throughout the course of their studies. Hence equality of opportunity is not being realized in terms of certain students progressing to postgraduate studies or indeed accessing the labour market.

The question of where the responsibility lies leads us to the issue of integration, commonly defined as a two-way process. Is it solely up to the migrant to bring his/her English language proficiency up to an acceptable level? What about the responsibility of institutions to raise awareness among lecturers of barriers to equality of opportunity such as the institutional racism that Fitzgibbon (2003: 50) spoke of? He gives as an example:

> the accent or speed of delivery of a lecturer may make it nigh on impossible for a student to understand, unless their first language is English. While such behaviours may seem innocuous to those on whom they have no effect, they continuously impact on others, and can result in very high levels of frustration and stress.

Finally, what responsibility lies with the state? In wider Irish society there has been an orientation towards the provision of ESOL education, the most significant provider being the VECs (Vocational Educational Committees). The voluntary sector also contributes to ESOL provision. However, O'Mahony and McMahon (2008 : 29), in their analysis of the sector, conclude that 'overall the need for ESOL training is as yet only being met in an incoherent and inchoate manner' in Ireland. They condemn the lack of a national strategy in the area, a deficit identified by others, including Coakley, who calls for it to be 'properly supported' (2009: 5). As one of the VEC ESOL providers points out, 'ESOL is not concerned about higher education' (Rose, 2010; personal communication), hence even if adult learners attend ESOL classes, a gap still remains in terms of preparation for higher education. Furthermore, among his key recommendations, Dunbar (2008: 74) argues that 'standards and guidelines for English proficiency classes at all levels are needed, including a national accreditation system for qualified providers and adequate funding to deliver a programme to agreed standards'. As outlined above, it is clear there are huge gaps at the national level in this area.

Funding – Given Ireland's current economic situation and an already underfunded third-level sector, the question of funding merits discussion. Funding for the English language support/classes provided by tertiary institutions derived from a variety of sources – in the case of IT6, the International Office funded the classes that were offered to all non-native speakers of English; many other initiatives were funded as SIF (Strategic Innovation Fund) or Dormant Accounts projects (IT2). In its National Plan for Equity of Access to Higher Education 2008–2013, the HEA points out that in many institutions the 'demand for access-related services' is increasing faster than 'their resources permit' (HEA, 2008: 36). A number of Access Offices personnel (IT10, IT7) referred to a lack of resources to address the issue. In the case of Univ1, individual faculties pay for students, but one faculty was mentioned as now having no money. If participation is to be broadened, in keeping with the mission outlined in the introduction, then supports also need to be broadened: 'if you widen participation you have to widen supports' (IT3).

Lack of expertise in the area – In addition to lack of resources, a few interviewees raised the issue of lack of specialist expertise in the area of English for Academic Purposes. While one director of a Language Centre raised it as an issue nationally – 'we don't have teachers trained for English for Academic Purposes' (Univ2), another institute which 'has cases this year' of students with language difficulties, spoke of a lack of expertise at local level: 'we haven't got into the area of ESL [English as a Second Language], it's not our speciality' (IT14). Furthermore, quite a number of institutions that provide support in academic writing echoed this, for example: 'it's not geared towards language support' (IT14). Although 'the support is there for their writing' (Univ5), those who require writing support almost inevitably require support with English in general.

Student take-up – In instances where language support was being offered, a number of institutes spoke of poor take-up amongst students – 'I can tell you they don't go ... people who really need to go don't' (IT6). In the case of Univ4 and Univ6, this was echoed, specifically with reference to international students – 'it has been difficult to get them to come. We have tried a number of times – mornings, lunchtimes, the turnout was not great. We tried different times – there is a problem after 6, after 6 p.m. the students work' (Univ4). This quotation underlines how the timing of classes was one factor linked to the low take-up, reaffirmed by another interviewee who spoke of the 'need to have it timetabled better' (IT13). There is an argument that if classes are to be on offer more care should be taken with their timetabling, as opposed to being 'tagged on' (IT7), to quote one Access Officer, at the very end of the day or indeed the week. Another possibility is to offer classes in block format as a pre-sessional course and, in a bid to incentivise student attendance, make it obligatory. In one International Office manager's experience, the language support must be 'compulsory' (Univ5) in order to maximise student take up, while a Language Centre director felt that 'it should be accredited in some way' (Univ6). Such a view may well be what led to the three examples cited in the data of credited classes – in IT4, IT6 and Univ2 these classes constitute an elective module that is offered to migrant students on certain programmes. In an era where we are looking at EBMs (Educational Broadening Modules), accrediting the classes or offering English language classes as an elective merits consideration. It is an issue that could be considered relevant not only to non-native speakers of English, but to the wider student population – the Language Centre director cited above expressed the view, with which I would concur, that 'all Irish students should have a module in English' (Univ6). Indeed, I would go so far as to say *all* students.

Conclusion

This small-scale study was exploratory in nature. It provides a snapshot of the English language support provided to migrants in higher education institutions in Ireland. It found that if the HEA's aim is to promote equality of opportunity in higher education, the question of language support for migrant students, and indeed all non-native speaker students, needs to be addressed. The deficit that remains in terms of students progressing to post-graduate study, and beyond that to employment, was highlighted. Indeed, an ESRI study found that language skills are positively linked to earnings: migrants from non-English speaking backgrounds are subjected to an occupational gap, whereas this is not the case for those from English-speaking backgrounds (O'Connell & McGinnity, 2008).

This is an issue that will not disappear in the future, particularly given the different routes through which students enter higher education. There is a need for further research – for example focusing on initiatives already running and the students who attend them – in order to ensure the best returns on investment. A large number of interviewees were interested to learn what was happening elsewhere in higher education institutions around the country. There is also a need to look to the international sphere to identify best practice in other countries, such as the UK and North America, who have longer experience in the teaching of academic English (for example Bazerman *et al.*, 2005; Ganobcik-Williams, 2006).

Finally, in terms of integration, official definitions do not see the migrant as the sole bearer of responsibility for developing his/her proficiency in English. It is true that more needs to be done externally, in terms of language support at primary and post-primary levels and ESOL in adult education, but a shortfall will still remain. If the higher education sector is truly going to pursue equality of opportunity and avoid creating a migrant educational underclass in the future, it needs to consider its own responsibility for providing English language support.

References

Bazerman, C., Little, J., Bethel, L., Chavkin, T., Fouquette, D. and Garufis, J. (2005) *Reference Guide to Writing Across the Curriculum*. West Lafayette: Parlor Press.

Bryman, A. (2004) *Social Research Methods* (2nd edn). Oxford: Oxford University Press.

Coakley, L. (2009) The challenges and obstacles facing refugees, persons with leave to remain and persons granted subsidiary protection, as they seek to access post-second level education in Ireland. Position paper. Dublin: Refugee Information Service (RIS).

Coghlan, D., Fagan, H., Munck, R., O'Brien, A. and Warner, R. (2005) *International Students and Professionals in Ireland: An Analysis of Access to Higher Education and Recognition of Professional Qualifications*. Dublin: Integrating Ireland.

Council of Europe (2001) *Common European Framework of Reference for Languages: Learning, teaching, assessment*. Cambridge: Cambridge University Press.

Dunbar, P. (2008) *Nasc Research Report: Evaluating the Barriers in Employment and Education for Migrants in Cork*. Cork: Nasc.

Egan, A. and Dunbar, P. (2008) Primary research: Views from key service providers. In P. Dunbar (ed.) *Nasc Research Report: Evaluating the Barriers in Employment and Education for Migrants in Cork*. Cork: Nasc.

Fielding, N. and Thomas, H. (2001) Qualitative interviewing. In N. Gilbert (ed.) *Researching Social Life* (pp. 123–144). London: Sage.

Fitzgibbon, M. (2003) Towards a multi-cultural campus? In R. Lentin (ed.) *Working and Teaching in a Multicultural University*: Dublin: MPhil in Ethnic and Racial Studies, Department of Sociology TCD in association with the Higher Education Authority Equality Unit.

Ganobcik-Williams, L. (ed.) (2006) *Teaching Academic Writing in UK Higher Education. Theories, Practices and Models*. New York: Palgrave Macmillan.

Gunaratnam, Y. (2003) *Researching Race and Ethnicity Methods, Knowledge and Power*. London, Thousand Oaks, New Delhi: Sage.

HEA (Higher Education Authority) (2008) *National Plan for Equity of Access to Higher Education*. Dublin: HEA.

IELTS (n.d.) *Common European Framework* [online] Available at: http://www.ielts.org/researchers/common_european_framework.aspx (accessed 29 August 2012).

Linehan, M and Hogan, E. (eds) (2008) *Migrants and Higher Education in Ireland*. Cork: Education in Employment.

Long, M.H. (2003) Stabilization and fossilization in interlanguage development. In C.J. Doughty and M.H. Long (eds) *The Handbook of Second Language Acquisition* (pp. 487–535). Oxford: Blackwell.

May, T. (2001) *Social Research: Issues, Methods and Process*. Buckingham: Open University Press.

O'Connell, P.J. and McGinnity, F. (2008) *Immigrants at Work. Ethnicity and Nationality in the Irish Labour Market*. Dublin: Equality Authority and ESRI.

O'Mahony, P. and McMahon, L. (2008) *Towards a National ESOL Strategy – Lessons from a Survey of ESOL Provision in the VEC Sector*. Dublin: Irish Vocational Education Association.

Ryan, C. (2009) *Socioeconomic Profile of Dublin 15*. Online document: http://www.bap.ie/dloads/Dublin-15_Socio-Economic_Area_Profile_2009.pdf

Taguma, M., Kim, M., Wurzburg, G. and Kelly, F. (2009) *OECD Reviews of Migrant Education: Ireland*. Paris: OECD.

Warner, R. (2006) *Barriers to Access to Further and Higher Education for Non-EU Nationals Resident in Ireland*. Dublin: Pobal.

Part 2

7 Investigating the Development of Immigrant Pupils' English L2 Oral Skills in Irish Primary Schools

Bronagh Ćatibušić

This chapter reports on research into English L2 acquisition among immigrant pupils in Irish primary schools. Focusing on the development of oral skills, it compares empirical evidence of L2 development with the summary of L2 learning outcomes provided by the *English Language Proficiency Benchmarks for non-English-speaking pupils at primary level* (IILT, 2003), officially sanctioned guidelines for the provision of English language support that are based on the first three proficiency levels of the *Common European Framework of Reference for Languages* (Council of Europe, 2001). The research took the form of a longitudinal study of 18 ESL pupils' acquisition of English L2 over a 10-month period in three primary schools and involved the mixed-methods form-function analysis of about 80 hours of recorded classroom talk. The results show that a clear relation exists between the learning outcomes defined by the Benchmarks and actual patterns of L2 acquisition evident among the participating pupils. Bearing in mind the diversity of the participants and the range of possible internal and external influences on the acquisition of English L2 oral skills, the Benchmarks may thus be said to offer a flexible 'map' of L2 proficiency development appropriate to the individual language learning needs of ESL pupils in Irish primary schools.

Introduction

Background

Over the last two decades, Ireland has experienced sustained immigration for the first time in its recent history. This demographic change has had profound implications for education: approximately 10% of primary school children in Ireland now come from immigrant backgrounds and the majority of them are native speakers of languages other than English or Irish, the two official languages of schooling (DES/OMI, 2010). As most of these children are enrolled in English-medium schools, responding to the needs of pupils learning English as a second language (ESL) has emerged as a prominent issue. In the late 1990s, the Department of Education and Science/Skills (DES) put in place a programme to provide English language support for ESL pupils. Through this programme, ESL pupils are entitled to two years of English language support, from the time they start school in Ireland. This support is provided by designated English language support teachers and generally delivered through regular (daily) withdrawal classes of limited duration (usually 20 to 30 minutes). The delivery of English language support is, however, at the discretion of individual schools and may also be organised in the mainstream environment (e.g. through team-teaching). It should be emphasised, though, that even if withdrawal lessons are the norm, ESL pupils spend over 80% of their time in the mainstream classroom throughout their English language support allocation. This means that ESL pupils must be enabled from the beginning of their education in Ireland to access mainstream learning and integrate socially with their peers.

The establishment of the English language support programme necessitated the development of resources and the provision of in-service teacher training. The DES delegated responsibility for these tasks to Integrate Ireland Language and Training (IILT), a not-for-profit campus company of Trinity College Dublin that was already providing intensive English language programmes for adult immigrants with refugee status. IILT was required to develop guidelines that teachers could use as a 'map' to plan their English language support lessons and monitor the progress of ESL pupils over their support period. These guidelines must be appropriate to English L2 proficiency development among children across the age-range of primary schooling in Ireland (4 to 12 years), while covering key aspects of the Irish primary school curriculum. They were conceived as a 'curriculum within the curriculum' (Little, 2010) which would give ESL pupils access to mainstream learning from the beginning of their English L2 development. The guidelines also had to reflect features of everyday social and classroom interaction in the primary school. Finally, they had to be user-friendly so that teachers could apply them with ease to their own teaching contexts.

Development of English Language Proficiency Benchmarks

The guidelines were published as *English Language Benchmarks for non-English-speaking pupils at primary level* (IILT, 2003): a series of learning outcomes, expressed as functional 'can do' descriptors, which outline English L2 proficiency development from its earliest stages to a level appropriate for ESL pupils' unassisted integration into mainstream education. The Benchmarks are a 'map' of English L2 development, which can be applied in a manner that acknowledges 'individual pathways of learning' (IILT, 2003: 4) among ESL pupils and embeds their English language support firmly within the requirements of the Irish primary school curriculum.

The Benchmarks are based on the *Common European Framework of Reference for Languages* (CEFR; Council of Europe, 2001), for two reasons. First, the CEFR's 'action-oriented' approach (Council of Europe, 2001: 9) is relevant to ESL pupils acquiring English in an L2-dominant educational environment since it views language learning and language use as inseparable and describes proficiency in terms of the accomplishment of communicative tasks. This emphasis on the communicative use of language is essential if ESL pupils are to participate in mainstream classroom activities and to integrate socially within the school community. The CEFR's functional description of L2 development also suggests a task-based pedagogy in which language learning activities reflect real-life situations. In the case of the Benchmarks, the language learning 'tasks' suggested by Benchmarks descriptors are directly related to everyday classroom activities so as to support mainstream learning from the outset of ESL pupils' L2 development.

Secondly, it was thought that by using the CEFR as a model it would be possible to create a cycle of learning, teaching and assessment that would meet ESL pupils' language learning needs but also support more autonomous learning in the mainstream classroom by encouraging the growth of reflective awareness. Resources developed from the Benchmarks include a version of the European Language Portfolio (IILT, 2004), which enables ESL pupils to self-assess their own progress using checklists of Benchmarks-linked 'I can' descriptors, and the *Primary School Assessment Kit* (Little *et al.*, 2007), which allows teachers to assess specific linguistic aspects of pupils' English L2 proficiency. It was hoped that the Benchmarks and these accompanying resources would help teachers to inform their teaching by monitoring closely the development of their ESL pupils' English L2 proficiency.

Structure of the Benchmarks

How do the Benchmarks support this kind of L2 development? The structure of the Benchmarks is fundamental, particularly the way in which aspects of the CEFR have been adapted to meet the specific needs of ESL pupils in Irish primary schools. The Benchmarks cover only the three lower 'common reference levels' of the CEFR: A1, A2 and B1. This restriction exists for several reasons. First, English language support is limited to a two-year period from the child's entry into the Irish education system. Its objective is to support ESL pupils' L2 development from the earliest stages to a point at which they can participate fully and independently in mainstream classroom activities. The CEFR describes the language learner at level B1 as an 'independent user' of his/her L2 (Council of Europe, 2001: 23). It thus seemed appropriate to set the achievement of Level B1 learning goals as the exit point for English language support; and within the limitations of a two-year support period, it also seemed realistic. Another reason for restricting the span of the Benchmarks to the three lower Common Reference Levels was that the type of language use described by the CEFR at the higher proficiency levels generally presupposes cognitive and social experience beyond the 'relatively limited behavioural capacities of younger learners' (Little, 2004: 5).

Whereas the CEFR describes language use across four domains: personal, public, occupational and educational (Council of Europe, 2001: 45), the Benchmarks focus on the personal and educational domains, specifying language learning outcomes appropriate to informal communication with peers and to everyday classroom interaction. They thus include language use associated with what Cummins (1979, 2000) refers to as BICS (basic interpersonal communication skills) as well as the types of language use required for effective engagement with the Irish Primary School Curriculum (NCCA, 1999), which entail the development of CALP (cognitive academic language proficiency), essential for educational success in L2-dominant immersion education (Cummins, 2000).

Like the CEFR, the Benchmarks use positively-worded 'can-do' statements to describe language learning outcomes at the successive proficiency levels. Part 1 of the Benchmarks comprises two scales: the Global Benchmarks of Communicative Proficiency (see Appendix) provide a functional overview of the communicative activities that ESL pupils can accomplish at each of the three proficiency levels in listening, reading, spoken interaction, spoken production and writing; while the Global Scales of Underlying Linguistic Competence describe aspects of L2 lexical, grammatical, phonological and orthographic proficiency at each level. Part 2 comprises 13 'Units of Work': scales that restate the Global Benchmarks in relation to 13 recurrent themes of the primary curriculum. They range from 'interpersonal' themes such as 'Myself' to more 'academic' themes such as 'Caring for my locality', so their descriptors represent learning outcomes associated with the development of both L2 BICS and L2 CALP. It is worth noting that, although the Units of Work are functional in their orientation, their descriptors also highlight aspects of developing L2 pragmatic and sociolinguistic competence. The Units of Work are intended to be used alongside the Global Benchmarks to support the L2 development of ESL pupils in an individual and multi-dimensional manner.

The Need for Empirical Research

Since the Benchmarks were first introduced as guidelines for English language support, informal feedback from teachers has tended to confirm that they describe L2 proficiency development in a way that reflects the general trajectory of ESL pupils' English L2 acquisition. However, it was deemed necessary to undertake an empirical investigation of the relation, if any, between the learning outcomes expressed in the Benchmarks descriptors and patterns of English L2 acquisition among ESL pupils. Considering L2 use as potential evidence of L2 acquisition (and regarding language use as essential to language learning; cf. Council of Europe, 2001: 9), it was decided to examine actual L2 use by ESL pupils in their English language support lessons and to compare this with the Benchmarks descriptors. Some findings of this research are presented in this chapter, focussing on the relation between ESL pupils' acquisition of L2 oral skills and the Benchmarks' description of developing English L2 proficiency.

Data Collection and Methods of Analysis

A longitudinal study was conducted over a 10-month period (September 2007 to June 2008) to collect evidence of ESL pupils' L2 acquisition for comparison with the Benchmarks descriptors. Eighteen ESL pupils participated in the study, which involved the weekly audio-recording of English language support lessons in three primary schools. The 18 pupils came from 10 different national backgrounds and spoke at least 10 different languages at home. These were reported by the teachers as: Polish (5 children), Romanian (3), Serbian (2), Urdu (2), Cantonese, Croatian, Latvian, Lithuanian, Malayalam and Portuguese (1 each). The pupils' ages ranged from 4 to 10 years, although most were under 8 years old and in junior primary classes during the research period. The study included pupils in both the first and the second year of their English language support allocation. Approximately 80 hours of classroom interaction were recorded and transcribed; evidence of pupils' L2 literacy development was also collected and analysed. The audio recordings captured everyday learning activities and conversations in the classroom. They thus involved language use typical of primary school children and could be considered 'naturally occurring samples of L2 use', which according to Ellis and Barkhuizen (2005: 364) 'provide the best evidence' of L2 acquisition.

Owing to the volume of recordings, a broad style of transcription was adopted. However, this was sufficiently detailed to support thorough investigation of pupils' L2 grammatical and lexical development. These two aspects of linguistic competence were selected as the main focus of analysis for several reasons. First, research ranging from the morpheme studies of the 1970s and their more recent meta-analysis (e.g. DeKeyser, 2005) to theories of processability (Pienemann, 2003, 2005), has shown L2 grammatical development to be a major indicator of L2 acquisition patterns. Secondly, analysis of L2 lexical development is essential to any investigation of formal features of L2 acquisition. Thirdly, analysis of the grammatical and lexical indicators of pupils' L2 acquisition evident in the recordings could be compared directly to the descriptors for 'vocabulary control' and 'grammatical accuracy' in the Benchmarks' Global Scales of Linguistic Competence, to establish whether or not these accurately reflect ESL pupils' development of L2 linguistic competence. Although the principal focus of the study was grammatical and lexical development, pupils' phonological and orthographic competence was also investigated as far as was practically possible.

As well as examining formal features of pupils' L2 use in the recorded English language support lessons, it was necessary to examine the evidence of L2 acquisition from a functional perspective, which could account for the development of L2 pragmatic and sociolinguistic competence. In this way the children's L2 use could be compared to the functional 'can do' descriptors in the Global Benchmarks of Communicative Proficiency and the 13 Units of Work. A form-function analysis (informed by evidence of vocabulary development) thus appeared the most effective and appropriate means of analysing the transcribed data in order to compare pupils' actual L2 use with the Benchmarks descriptors. Given the extent of the recordings, this analysis was capable of revealing considerable detail about L2 acquisition and, in particular, the development of ESL pupils' L2 oral skills.

It was also necessary to consider likely influences on pupils' recorded L2 use, relating both to individual variation and to features of the learning environment. Owing to limitations of time, it was not possible to examine all such influences; in any case, for practical reasons the study could only be conducted within English language support lessons, so wider social factors could not be considered. However, some potential influences could be considered, including learner-internal factors such as age, home language background and language learning style, and learner-external factors, particularly features of classroom talk.

Regarding the latter, the audio-recordings showed that classroom interaction patterns (e.g. the ratio of teacher talk to pupil talk, the extent and nature of group-work) appeared to impact on pupils' L2 use. As this could affect the capacity of the recorded data to serve as an indicator of L2 acquisition, it was necessary to analyse interactional features of pupils' oral L2 use in some depth. Applying the techniques of Conversation Analysis (informed by, e.g. Schegloff (2007) and ten Have (2007)), the transcribed oral data were analysed to identify pragmatic features of each turn-at-talk and the interactional behaviour of both participating pupils and teachers in the recorded lessons (while accepting that broad transcriptions offer less detail than those typically associated with Conversation Analysis). This investigation of possible interaction-related influences on ESL pupils' L2 use was designed to further inform the form-function analysis.

Results

Analysis of L2 oral data

Initially, 135 recorded lessons were analysed. Using the 'turn-at-talk' as the unit of analysis, each oral turn produced by the 18 participating ESL pupils was coded for its formal features and its links (if any) to Benchmarks descriptors – most turns appeared to relate to at least one specific descriptor from either the Units of Work or the Global Benchmarks of Communicative Proficiency. All cases which were impossible to link to descriptors were noted and suggestions were made regarding the possible revision of the Benchmarks to account for these instances of L2 use. Interactional features of each pupil turn (and turns produced by teachers) were also coded. A second, more detailed phase of analysis was then carried out for 80 of the 135 recorded lessons. This reduction was necessary for practical reasons and involved the selection of lessons at roughly regular intervals across the study period; on average the lessons analysed accounted for 67% of pupils' total participation in the study. The aim of this phase of analysis was to create individual profiles for each of the 18 ESL pupils, outlining features of their L2 acquisition and investigating whether these related to the Benchmarks, and if so, how.

After that, the individual findings included in each of the 18 profiles could be brought together to determine the nature of any relation between the Benchmarks and the overall evidence of ESL pupils' L2 acquisition.

In this phase of analysis, the 80 selected lessons were coded in further detail, with the addition of linguistic sub-codes to indicate the types of errors or omissions made by pupils in their L2 use. This was important as error-types can offer valuable information with regard to, e.g. stage of L2 grammatical development, cross-linguistic influence, and particular challenges faced by ESL pupils in their acquisition of English L2. Coded turns which involved oral production within literacy-focused activities (e.g. reading aloud or classroom talk based on direct reference to a written text) were then separated for analysis together with other evidence of L2 literacy development (e.g. samples of pupils' L2 writing). The remaining turns served as the basis of the form-function analysis. Altogether 7455 pupil turns were included in this analysis. Oral turns that could not be considered spontaneous and meaningful instances of L2 use – e.g. direct repetition of another speaker or minimum confirmations produced without evidence of comprehension – were excluded from the analysis. Turns that could not be linked to specific Benchmarks descriptors were also removed at this stage of the analysis, although their implications for possible revision of the Benchmarks were noted, as pointed out above. Evidence of pupils' L2 acquisition derived from these oral turns was then analysed using mixed methods: qualitative description of the pupils' L2 proficiency development and quantitative analysis of the distribution of analysed turns across Benchmarks proficiency levels A1, A2 and B1 (proficiency levels associated with each spontaneous oral turn were identified with reference to the Benchmarks-linked functional codes applied to these turns).

The formal analysis focused on features of linguistic competence which, from the data, appeared to be evident in the oral L2 use of ESL pupils during their period of English language support. Fourteen possible indicators of L2 acquisition were identified: 10 grammatical indicators – use of nouns, verbs, pronouns, articles, prepositions and auxiliaries, the ratio of verbs to nouns used (as a basic measure of structural complexity), negative formation, question formation and clause linkage; and four lexical indicators: semantic range, lexical diversity (a ratio based on the number of lexical types per turn), verb lexemes and additional lexico-grammatical indicators (the lexical description of 'function words' which were not included in the analysis of L2 grammatical development, e.g. adjectives, adverbs and possession markers). Verb lexemes were chosen as a focus since the data showed these to be less affected by lesson-related factors than, e.g. noun lexemes. These 14 indicators were all analysed qualitatively for each pupil, their production over the study period was described, and prominent error patterns were noted. Seven of the

Table 7.1 Overview of analytical methods with respect to L2 linguistic indicators

Indicator of L2 acquisition	Method of analysis	
	Qualitative	Quantitative
1 Nouns	✓	✓
2 Verbs	✓	✓
3 Pronouns	✓	✓
4 Articles	✓	✓
5 Prepositions	✓	✓
6 Auxiliaries	✓	✓
7 Verb-to-noun ratio	✓	✓
8 Negative formation	✓	✗
9 Question formation	✓	✗
10 Clause linkage	✓	✗
11 Semantic range	✓	✗
12 Lexical diversity	✓	✓
13 Verb lexemes	✓	✓
14 Additional lexico-grammatical indicators	✓	✗

grammatical and two of the lexical indicators were also analysed quantitatively (using the SPSS Version 16 program for grammatical indicators and the Wordsmith Tools program for lexical analysis). An overview of the indicators analysed and their means of analysis is provided in Table 7.1.

The results of these analyses were presented for each of the 18 participants in his/her 'pupil profile'. These profiles also included additional qualitative description of each pupil's L2 literacy development derived from evidence of L2 reading and/or writing recorded and collected during the study period. Possible internal and external influences on L2 acquisition which could be investigated within the parameters of this research were also evaluated.

The bigger picture

Cumulative analysis of the individual pupil profiles was carried out to determine whether any relation existed between the empirical evidence of the 18 participants' L2 acquisition based on their oral L2 use and the Benchmarks descriptors for spoken interaction and spoken production. To compare evidence relating to the Benchmarks' indication of pupils' L2 proficiency and the linguistic evidence of pupils' L2 acquisition obtained from the 7455 analysable spoken turns across the sample group, the 80 lessons selected for the form-function analysis were grouped in terms of 'proficiency proportion bands'. For each pupil in each of his/her selected lessons, this involved expressing the ratio of turns coded at the pupil's highest recorded L2 proficiency in a given lesson to the total number of analysable turns he/she produced in that lesson. For example, if a pupil produced a total of 50 turns in a lesson, 42 of which were linked to level A1 Benchmarks descriptors, and 8 of which were linked to level A2, his/her proficiency proportion for that lesson would be 16% A2 (0.16 A2). Findings for the 14 linguistic indicators analysed were then compared across lessons which had similar proportions of turns in the same 'proficiency band'. These bands covered the three proficiency levels at intervals of 10%: from 'turns at level A1 only', followed by '1–10% of turns at level A2' etc., up to '91–100% of turns at level B1'. Grouping lessons in this way allowed cumulative results to be derived regarding pupils' L2 proficiency development over time. It also allowed results obtained from the analysis of linguistic indicators of L2 acquisition for each of the 18 pupils to be brought together and compared to the Benchmarks descriptors.

The structure of the cumulative analysis was similar to that of the individual analysis carried out for the individual pupil profiles. First, overall results for L2 proficiency development over time were quantitatively derived. This was done by mapping the proportion of analysed L2 oral turns recorded for each of the three proficiency levels covered by the Benchmarks (A1, A2, B1) to the duration of pupils' English language support expressed in months. By calculating support time thus (in terms of the 10-month primary school year), it was possible to compare the L2 proficiency development of pupils in both their first and second years of English language support. The results of this analysis (Figure 7.1) showed that during pupils' first year of English language support, turns linked to A1-level Benchmarks were dominant. However, the proportion of A2-level turns increased quite steadily over this first year and into the second. From month 12 onwards, evidence of B1 proficiency appeared in the analysed turns. This proportion increased until B1 emerged as the dominant proficiency level from month 18 onwards – close to the end of the typical two-year allocation of English language support.

Although, as Figure 7.1 shows, there was considerably more data available for pupils in the first year of their English language support allocation, the trends apparent in oral L2 development for second-year pupils demonstrate continuing proficiency development across the support period: from A1-dominant to B1-dominant L2 use. If we take this as a reasonable indication of ESL pupils' typical English L2 development, it suggests that the Benchmarks offer an accurate prediction of the trajectory of oral L2 proficiency growth over the two-year allocation of English language support.

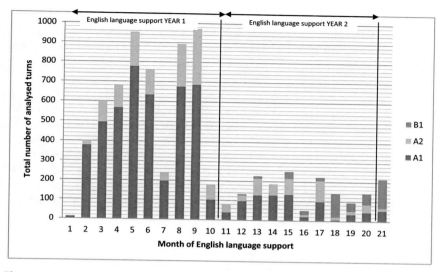

Figure 7.1 Proficiency levels associated with analysed turns across the recorded duration of pupils' English language support

However, to examine this apparent relation in greater detail, it was necessary to undertake a cumulative analysis of each of the 14 linguistic indicators of L2 acquisition. Overall results were obtained for each indicator using the same methods, both qualitative and quantitative, as those outlined for the pupil profiles in Table 7.1. Final analysis of these grammatical and lexical indicators was based on the grouping of lessons in which pupils demonstrated similar levels of L2 proficiency (using the 'proficiency proportion bands' explained above). Qualitative analysis was carried out, describing features of acquisition for the 14 analysed indicators derived from all 18 pupil profiles. For each indicator, this description was referenced to the highest 'proficiency proportion band' associated with the lessons selected for each pupil. Additional comments were made, however, about the development of pupils' L2 oral proficiency over time. From these descriptions, the development of each indicator across the proficiency levels A1, A2 and B1 was then summarised.

Results for the 18 ESL pupils across the seven grammatical and two lexical indicators that were quantitatively analysed were also compared statistically. To do this, statistical means were calculated across each proficiency proportion band for frequency and (where relevant) accuracy of use of the seven grammatical indicators. Mean results for lexical diversity and verb lexeme range across each band were also derived. Mean results were used to ensure greater comparability of data (recorded in a wide variety of lesson contexts) and to allow for differences in the number of analysable spoken turns available in each lesson. It was then possible, using the SPSS program (Version 16.0), to compare these mean results across the proficiency proportion bands in order to investigate the distribution patterns and accuracy rates associated with each of the quantitatively analysed indicators. In this way, these linguistic indicators of L2 acquisition could be tracked across the entire sample of 7455 analysable spoken turns produced by the 18 participating ESL pupils; and any emerging patterns could be compared to Benchmarks-linked progression in L2 proficiency, from L2 use associated solely with Level A1 to that associated, almost fully, with Level B1. Overall quantitative and qualitative results for each of these indicators could then be presented and discussed, both in graphic and in summary form, as shown for grammatical and lexical features of verb use in Figures 7.2 and 7.3 and in Table 7.2. Results, particularly

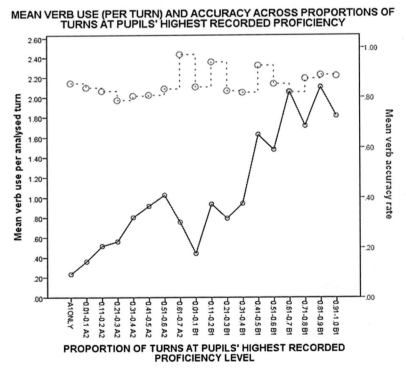

Figure 7.2 Graphic representation of overall results for verb use and accuracy across the Benchmarks proficiency levels

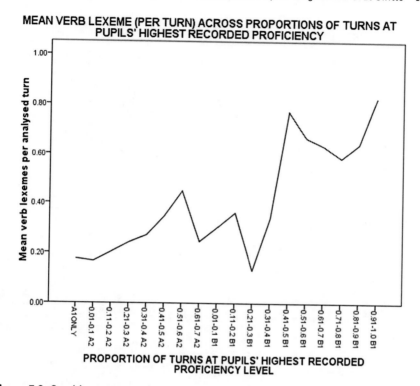

Figure 7.3 Graphic representation of overall results for mean verb lexemes per analysed turn across L2 proficiency ratios

for lexical indicators, could be affected by factors such as lesson-related influences and data shortage in certain 'proficiency proportion bands'. However, overall results show a generally clear progression in the development of indicators of L2 acquisition from level A1 to level B1.

The patterns of development evident in Figure 7.2 and Table 7.2 were typical of those emerging from the cumulative analysis of the 14 grammatical and lexical indicators of L2 acquisition investigated. When development in relation to the indicators was compared to the Benchmarks-linked proficiency levels associated with the analysed spoken turns, it appeared that pupils' L2 grammatical and lexical development corresponded to the progression suggested by the Benchmarks. The Global Scales of Underlying Linguistic Competence for 'vocabulary control' and 'grammatical accuracy' are presented in Table 7.3.

The qualitative descriptions for each of the linguistic indicators analysed also confirmed that the thematic range of the Benchmarks (expressed in the

Table 7.2 Summary of the relation between grammatical and lexical evidence of L2 verb acquisition and the Benchmarks proficiency levels

Indicator	A1-linked L2 use (Max. ratio: 100% A1)[1]	A2-linked L2 use emerging (Max. ratio: 1-30% A2)	A2-linked L2 use increasing (Max. ratio: 31-70% A2)[2]	B1-linked L2 use increasing (Max. ratio: 61-100% B1)
Grammatical features of verb use	Limited, often inaccurate verb use – non-inflected stem verbs and copula (present tense: 'to be') only. Typical errors: no inflection in required contexts.	Limited, but increasing, verb use. Generally non-inflected stem verbs and copula in present tense. Attempts at progressive ('-ing') form, and irregular past tense, isolated production of past participle. Typical errors: non-inflection (3rd person '-s'), tense and aspect choice.	Increasing verb use, accuracy increasing subject to fluctuation. Production generally of non-inflected verbs and copula, but progressive and past forms emerging (usually irregular, some regular). Occasional appropriate use of present and past participles. Typical errors: non-inflection (3rd person '-s'), tense and aspect choice.	Wide range of more accurate verb use. Generally appropriate production of present and past tense forms (irregular and regular). Generally accurate marking of aspect and use of participles. Typical errors (infrequent): occasional over-generalisation of regular ('-ed') ending to irregular past forms, slight confusion of past/perfect forms.
Verb lexemes	Verb use across very limited lexical range (e.g. 'be', 'have', 'look', 'like').	Verb use limited in lexical range, although evidence of diversification (e.g. 'go', 'want', 'eat', 'run', 'write').	Verb use increasing in lexical range, verbs becoming more specific (e.g. 'allow', 'crunch', 'kick', 'grow', 'paint').	Wide range of verb lexemes used to express specific concepts (e.g. 'become', 'collect', 'tickle', 'celebrate', 'measure').

1. 'Max. ratio' refers to the highest proficiency proportion band into which selected lessons were grouped for any given pupil, i.e. evidence of that pupil's highest English L2 proficiency over the study period.
2. None of these 'max. ratio' results fell within the range 71% A2 to 60% B1 (0.71 A2 to 0.6 B1) due, in part, to the composition of the participant group.

Table 7.3 Global scale for vocabulary control and grammatical accuracy (IILT. 2003: 8)

	A1	A2	B1
Vocabulary control	Can recognise, understand and use a limited range of basic vocabulary which has been used repeatedly in class or has been specifically taught.	Can recognise, understand and use a range of vocabulary associated with concrete everyday needs or learning experiences (e.g. topics or routines that have been introduced and practised in class).	Can recognise, understand and use a range of vocabulary related to familiar classroom themes, school routines and activities. Errors still occur when the pupil attempts to express more complex ideas or handle unfamiliar topics.
Grammatical accuracy	Can use a very limited number of grammatical structures and simple sentence patterns that he/she has learnt by repeated use (e.g. My name is …)	Can use simple grammatical structures that have been learnt and practised in class. Makes frequent basic mistakes with tenses, prepositions and personal pronouns, though when he/she is speaking or writing about a familiar topic the meaning is generally clear.	Can communicate with reasonable accuracy on familiar topics (those being studied or occurring frequently during the school day). Meaning is clear despite errors. Unfamiliar situations or topics present a challenge, however, particularly when the connection to familiar patterns is not obvious.

Units of Work) corresponded to the semantic fields emerging in pupils' oral L2 use. This was apparent whether or not teachers applied the Benchmarks directly in their provision of English language support (the Benchmarks were designed as guidelines; they are not a prescriptive curriculum that teachers must follow). In relation, therefore, to ESL pupils' L2 oral development, it would appear that the Benchmarks descriptors for spoken interaction and spoken production (see Appendix) reflect developing L2 oral proficiency in an accurate and appropriate way. Also, since the descriptors for spoken interaction include an aural dimension which links closely to many of the Benchmarks descriptors for listening, it would seem that the Benchmarks' description of L2 listening skills development may be likewise accurate, although further research would be required in this regard.

Conclusion

Designed to explore the development of L2 oral skills among ESL pupils in Ireland, this study provides empirical evidence that the Benchmarks' description of developing L2 proficiency reflects features of L2 acquisition evident in the actual L2 use of children receiving English language support in Irish primary schools. It is significant that its results are derived from the detailed individual analysis of 18 ESL pupils' L2 acquisition over the study period – investigating each child's specific pathway of L2 development and accounting for differences in age, home language and learning style, as well as for context-related factors such as the influence of interactional patterns. Despite the diversity of its participants, the study's findings as regards the development of L2 oral skills suggest that the Benchmarks' functionally-oriented descriptors provide a 'map' that can be adapted to meet the individual L2 learning needs of ESL pupils in the crucial early stages of their English L2 acquisition. The same study found similar results as regards the development of ESL pupils' L2 reading and writing skills. It thus seems reasonable to conclude that when they are accompanied by teaching approaches that encourage active learning and recognise the individual needs of all learners, context-sensitive adaptations of the CEFR have much to offer educational systems faced with the challenge of integrating children whose home language is not the language of schooling.

References

Council of Europe (2001) *Common European Framework of Reference for Languages: Learning, teaching, assessment.* Cambridge: Cambridge University Press. Available online at http://www.coe.int/t/dg4/linguistic/Source/Framework_EN.pdf

Cummins, J. (1979) Linguistic interdependence and the educational development of bilingual children. *Review of Educational Research* 49 (2), 222–251.

Cummins, J. (2000) *Language, Power and Pedagogy: Bilingual Children in the Crossfire.* Clevedon: Multilingual Matters.

DeKeyser, R. (2005) What makes learning second-language grammar difficult? A review of issues. In R. DeKeyser (ed.) *Language Learning 55, Supplement: Grammatical Development in Language Learning* (pp. 1–25). Oxford: Blackwell.

DES/OMI (Department of Education and Science/Office of Minister for Integration) (2010) *Intercultural Education Strategy 2010–2015.* Dublin: DES/OMI. Available at: http://www.education.ie/servlet/blobservlet/mig_intercultural_education_strategy.pdf

Ellis, R. and Barkhuizen, G. (2005) *Analysing Learner Language.* Oxford: Oxford University Press.

IILT (2003) *English Language Proficiency Benchmarks for non-English-speaking pupils at primary level.* Dublin: Integrate Ireland Language and Training. Available online at http://www.ncca.ie/iilt

IILT (2004) *European Language Portfolio, Primary: Learning the language of the host community.* Dublin: Integrate Ireland Language and Training. Available at: http://www.ncca.ie/iilt

Little, D. (2004) European Language Portfolios for younger learners: Age-appropriate self-assessment grids and descriptors /checklists. Discussion paper prepared for the Language Policy Division, Council of Europe, Strasbourg.

Little, D. (2010) The linguistic and educational integration of children and adolescents from migrant backgrounds. Strasbourg: Council of Europe. Available online at http://www.coe.int/lang→ Migrants → Resources.

Little, D., Lazenby Simpson, B. and Finnegan-Ćatibušić, B. (2007) *Primary School Assessment Kit.* Dublin: Department of Education and Science.

NCCA (1999) *Primary School Curriculum.* Dublin: Government of Ireland. Available online at http://www.curriculumonline.ie/en/Primary_School_Curriculum/

Pienemann, M. (2003) Language processing capacity. In C.J. Doughty and M.H. Long (eds) *The Handbook of Second Language Acquisition* (pp. 679–714). Oxford: Blackwell.

Pienemann, M. (2005) *Cross-linguistic Aspects of Processability Theory.* Amsterdam: Benjamins.

Schegloff, E. (2007) *Sequence Organization in Interaction: A Primer in Conversation Analysis,* Volume 1. Cambridge: Cambridge University Press.

ten Have, P. (2007) *Doing Conversation Analysis.* London: Sage.

Appendix

Global benchmarks of communicative proficiency (IILT, 2003)

	A1 BREAKTHROUGH	A2 WAYSTAGE	B1 THRESHOLD
Listening	Can recognise and understand basic words and phrases concerning him/herself, family and school. Can understand simple questions and instructions when teachers and other pupils speak very slowly and clearly.	Can recognise and understand frequently used words relating to him/herself and family, classroom activities and routines, school instructions and procedures, friends and play. Can understand a routine instruction given outside school (e.g. by a traffic warden). Can understand what is said in a familiar context such as buying something in a shop (e.g. price). Can follow at a general level topics covered in the mainstream class provided key concepts and vocabulary have been studied in advance and there is appropriate visual support. Can follow and understand a story if it is read slowly and clearly with visual support such as facial expression, gesture and pictures.	Can understand the main points of topics that are presented clearly in the mainstream classroom. Can understand the main points of stories that are read aloud in the mainstream classroom Can understand a large part of a short film on a familiar topic provided that it is age-appropriate. Can understand detailed instructions given in all school contexts (classroom, gym, playground, etc.). Can follow classroom talk between two or more native speakers, only occasionally needing to request clarification.

Reading (if appropriate to the age of the pupil) U N D E R S T A N D I N G	Can recognise the letters of the alphabet. Can recognise and understand basic signs and simple notices in the school and on the way to school. Can recognise and understand basic words on labels or posters in the classroom. Can identify basic words and phrases in a new piece of text.	Can read and understand very short and simple texts that contain a high proportion of previously learnt vocabulary on familiar subjects (e.g. class texts, familiar stories). Can use the alphabet to find particular items in lists (e.g. a name in a telephone book).	Can read and understand the main points in texts encountered in the mainstream class, provided the thematic area and key vocabulary are already familiar. Can read and understand descriptions of events, feelings and wishes. Can use comprehension questions to find specific answers in a piece of text. Can use key words, diagrams and illustrations to support reading comprehension. Can follow clearly written instructions (for carrying out a classroom task, assembling or using an object, following directions, etc.).
Spoken Interaction S P E A K I N G	Can greet, say *please* and *thank you*, and ask for directions to another place in the school. Can respond non-verbally to basic directions to a place in the school when the other person supplements speech with signs or gestures.	Can ask for attention in class. Can greet, take leave, request and thank appropriately. Can respond with confidence to familiar questions clearly expressed about family, friends, school work, hobbies, holidays, etc., but is not always able to keep the conversation going.	Can speak with fluency about familiar topics such as school, family, daily routine, likes and dislikes. Can engage with other pupils in discussing a topic of common interest (songs, football, pop stars, etc.) or in preparing a collaborative classroom activity.

(continued)

Appendix (Continued)

	A1 BREAKTHROUGH	A2 WAYSTAGE	B1 THRESHOLD
S P E A K I N G	Can give simple answers to basic questions when given time to reply and the other person is prepared to help. Can make basic requests in the classroom or playground (e.g. for the loan of a pencil) and respond appropriately to the basic requests of others.	Can generally sustain a conversational exchange with a peer in the classroom when carrying out a collaborative learning activity (making or drawing something, preparing a role-play, presenting a puppet show, etc.). Can express personal feelings in a simple way.	Can keep a conversation going, though he/she may have some difficulty making him/herself understood from time to time. Can repeat what has been said and convey the information to another person.
Spoken Production	Can use simple phrases and sentences to describe where he/she lives and people he/she knows, especially family members.	Can use a series of phrases and sentences to describe in simple terms his/her family, daily routines and activities, and plans for the immediate or more distant future (e.g. out-of-school activities, holiday plans).	Can retell a story that has been read in class. Can retell the plot of a film he/she has seen or a book he/she has read and describe his/her reactions. Can describe a special event / celebration in the family (religious festival, birthday, new baby, etc.). Can give an account of an experience or event (travel, an accident, an incident that occurred, etc.). Can briefly give explanations and reasons for opinions and plans.

Writing (if appropriate to the age of the pupil) W R I T I N G		
Can copy or write his/her name.	Can enter newly learnt terms in a personal or topic-based dictionary, possibly including sample sentences.	Can write a diary or news account with accuracy and coherence
Can copy or write words and short phrases that are being learnt in class.	Can write short texts on specific or familiar topics (e.g. what I like to do when I'm at home).	Can write a short letter describing an event or a situation
Can copy or write labels on a picture.	Can write a short message (e.g. a postcard) to a friend.	Can write a brief summary of a book or film
Can copy short sentences from the board.		Can write an account of his/her feelings or reactions to an event or situation
Can spell his/her name and address, and the name of the school.		Can write a short dialogue to be performed by puppets

8 Investigating the Linguistic Skills of Migrant Students in the German Vocational Education System

Patrick Grommes

This chapter discusses the linguistic achievements of students from migrant backgrounds in the German vocational training system. It begins by outlining features of the system and its accessibility to students from migrant backgrounds, then goes on to discuss the aims and objectives of one particular sector of the vocational training system as regards the language development of young migrants. Reference is made to the concept of *Bildungssprache* (academic language) and its relevance for a specific group of students. Based on this discussion we present two case studies, analysing written texts by a Polish and a Turkish student. The analyses reveal that although the students show sufficient general linguistic competence, they lack appropriate skills in *Bildungssprache*. A comparison between these skills, the aims and objectives of the training programme and its actual implementation leads to the conclusion that there may be conflicting goals designed into the system.

Introduction

This chapter reports on research that focuses on the German vocational training system and the integration of migrant students into this system and ultimately into the job market. The issues that underlie the research were part of the motivation for setting up a research programme in the state of Hamburg with funding from the Foundation for Research and Science of the State of Hamburg: the research cluster 'Linguistic Diversity Management in Urban Areas – LiMA'.[1] The LiMA-cluster aims to address questions of multilingual development in the context of urbanisation and migration. One of its main areas of interest is language development in educational settings.

This chapter does not deal with general aspects of the linguistic development of young people moving on from general education to vocational training. Rather it selects a very specific group of students – mainly recent immigrants to Germany around the age of 16 – and a very specific training programme that has been designed to address the educational needs of such students and to support their integration into the job market and ultimately into society.

Our guiding question is: Does the preparatory vocational training programme as offered in the state of Hamburg provide students from migrant backgrounds with the skills they need to compete successfully in the job market? To address this question we will first outline the particularities of the German vocational training system as far as they are relevant to our purposes; we will go on to consider the linguistic issues relevant to the system but also to the students; and then we will present and discuss preliminary linguistic data obtained from students in this training programme in order to assess its outcome and to highlight some problems that emerge from its design.

Educational Factors

The German vocational education system has some features that distinguish it from the systems of most other countries. The feature that is best-known internationally is probably the dual system of vocational training, in which employers and state-run vocational training schools share the task of providing professional training and general education. However, a significant number of applicants do not get access to this system and may end up in a broad variety of programmes. Among these we find the so-called 'transitional system' (*Übergangssystem*). The programmes in this transitional system do not immediately qualify students for a job; rather, they are designed for students who failed to achieve a school-leaving qualification, who are seen to lack basic competences deemed necessary for an apprenticeship, or who have language problems. Thus, 'transitional system' may well be a politically motivated misnomer, since students within this system do not move anywhere in particular, but are kept in a kind of holding pattern.

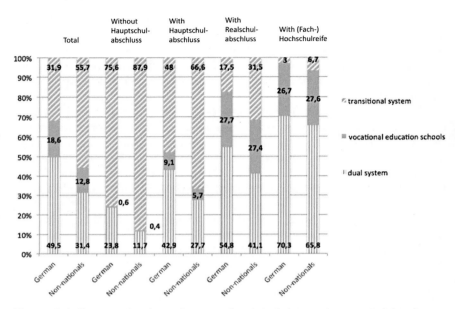

Figure 8.1 New entries into the vocational training system sorted by degree and nationality (adapted from: Autorengruppe Bildungsberichterstattung 2010: 99, Abb. E1-4)

Figure 8.1 shows the biggest barriers to accessing the training market. Students without a school-leaving qualification, and even those with a qualification from a general secondary school (*Hauptschule*), are mostly excluded from the regular market and handed over to the transitional system – whatever their nationality. Figure 8.1 also shows that 55.7% of students with a nationality other than German do not gain access to training under the dual system. Instead they are referred to the transitional system. As there are a considerable number of students with a migration background among German nationals, we can safely conclude that almost two thirds of all potential applicants for apprenticeships who have migrant backgrounds do not get immediate access to the market.

Given that access to the dual system is a challenge even for students with a school-leaving qualification, it comes as no surprise that those who leave preparatory programmes of the transitional system without a qualification, or without completing the programme, face even bigger problems and either turn to further training programmes or take temporary and unskilled jobs, and may end up not being integrated into the labour market and society at all (for a fuller discussion of relevant studies in Germany, see Schumann, 2003). All this raises the question whether the transitional system provides these students with the necessary means to apply successfully for apprenticeships within the dual system.

We will therefore take a closer look at one specific programme offered by the state of Hamburg to what is probably the most disadvantaged group of migrant students: those who arrive in Germany as adolescents with little or no knowledge of German and often patchy educational biographies. The so-called Preparatory Vocational Training Year for Migrants (*Berufsvorbereitendes Jahr für Migranten/BVJM*) is aimed at 16–18-year-old migrant students with unconditional residence permits and language deficits that prevent them from attending regular secondary school classes. The two-year programme aims to provide these students not only with sufficient linguistic proficiency to be able to compete on the job market, but also with broader personal and social competences. In addition it aims to provide them with general technical skills and to orient them towards selecting a suitable trade or profession.

The aims and objectives regarding language development in BVJM classes are set out in the Syllabus for Preparatory Vocational Education Schools (*Bildungsplan Berufsvorbereitungsschule/Bp-BVS*) (BBS [Behörde für Bildung und Sport], 2002). The overarching aim is to develop communicative aspects of soft and hard skills. Regarding the latter, students should be able to access and utilise general and job-specific professional knowledge, to respond to tasks in a goal-oriented, adequate, methodical and autonomous manner, and to critically reflect on their solutions (BBS, 2002: 31).[2] These overall competences are broken down into activities like listening and comprehension, each of which comprises a specific skill set (BBS, 2002: 34). Although many of these skills relate to personal and social competences, some are more closely linked to professional development. For example, comprehension skills include the ability to derive key information from audio-visual media as well as from verbal instructions and task descriptions. Writing skills include style and orthography, but also the ability to write texts on job and training-related issues and to write formal texts such as requests or complaints.

The full skill set listed in the curriculum is even more comprehensive, because the overall aim of the linguistic part of the programme is to enable students to participate fully in society and to compete on the vocational training market, if not on the regular labour market. A secondary aim is to prepare them for the exams that will give them a general secondary school-leaving qualification, which may run counter to the logic of the programme. We will come back to this question in the light of some data, but first we will discuss the linguistic requirements that underpin the skills mentioned above.

Linguistic Factors

Linguistically, typical BVJM students face two challenges. They must learn German for everyday communication in a short space of time at schools that are not necessarily well prepared for this type of tuition; and simultaneously they must acquire German for specific, technical purposes, although not for one specific profession. Rather, the BVJM aims to equip them with competences that are generally required when taking up an apprenticeship or a job. In other words, students have to acquire broader linguistic skills that allow them to act appropriately in a wide range of potential future professions. The required skills thus cannot be limited to learning a specific terminology, neither do they stop at the level of what Cummins (2000) has termed Basic Interpersonal Communication Skills (BICS), although achieving these is also an aim of the BVJM programme. In terms of the widely discussed concept of academic language, students need to acquire competence in educated language use, i.e. they have to learn to deal with formal language in educational contexts, to use language in a way that differs from everyday usage and shows that they can act appropriately in professional contexts.

The concept of *Bildungssprache* (academic language) has become increasingly central to educational and linguistic discussion in German, thanks mainly to the work of Ingrid Gogolin (for example, Gogolin, 2009a, 2009b; Gogolin & Lange, 2011). The term goes back to Habermas (1977), who distinguishes between colloquial language, the language of science, and the language of education. In Habermas's sense, language of education refers to the ability to employ language skills acquired in school in order to access knowledge and participate in educated discourse. This notion has not been abandoned in the discussion initiated by Gogolin, but attention has shifted to the linguistic features of *Bildungssprache*. The essential point is that the use of *Bildungssprache* is not restricted to educational contexts, and it is not simply a feature of classroom discourse or the language used by teachers (Gogolin, 2009a: 270). This distinguishes *Bildungssprache* from what Schleppegrell (2001) calls school-based language or the language of schooling (Schleppegrell, 2004). *Bildungssprache* is also broader than many notions of academic English that focus on lexical, syntactic and discursive features of the language addressed to and used by students in order to follow official curricula (Bailey & Heritage, 2008: 12–14). However, despite its presence in various forms in society at large, *Bildungssprache* is closely associated with educational contexts. For some pupils the foundations for its development – and for the development of literacy – may be laid in early childhood through interaction with their parents. But *Bildungssprache* takes on its full significance when children enter school-based education. Not all classroom discourse is *Bildungssprache*,[3] especially in the earliest stages of schooling, but children are gradually exposed to textbooks and speech that shows features of written discourse rather than informal conversation or narration. A child's – and later an adolescent's – educational success will in part be determined by the degree to which he or she masters *Bildungssprache* productively as well as receptively (Gogolin, 2009b: 268). Although different individuals reach different levels of competence in *Bildungssprache*, its formal and structural features are stable and describable in some detail. Academic language has been extensively discussed in the Anglo-American context; however, a straightforward transfer to other linguistic contexts may not be appropriate. It is therefore necessary to briefly introduce some features of German *Bildungssprache* that have been identified so far.

Gogolin and Lange (2011: 113–114) distinguish between discourse, lexico-semantic, and syntactic features. Discourse features refer to types of speech such as lectures, text types such as reports, or stylistic requirements such as an obligation for objectivity; they also have to do with text structure and length. Lexico-semantic features include phenomena such as a higher frequency of compound nouns, subject-specific terms, compound verbs, and expressions that aim at precision, e.g. regarding the way a task has to be performed – *schmirgeln* ('grind') rather than *glattmachen* ('make smooth'). Use of the less frequent meanings of polysemous words and a shift to more abstract levels of meaning also fall into this category. Instances of this phenomenon occur in Example 1, which is taken from material provided by the Hamburg State Authority for General and Vocational Education to teachers who set exams leading to the general secondary qualification in the preparatory vocational school. The past participle *umbaut* means 'enclosed', but the infinitive of this verb, *umbauen*, can be distinguished from the verb meaning 'convert' only by its phonological stress pattern; and although the past participle of *umbauen* meaning 'convert' is *umgebaut*, we can still assume that this may be an obstacle for the group of students under discussion. Similarly, retrieving the correct meaning of the preposition *nach* ('according to') in the second sentence can be difficult, because it is more frequently used as a temporal ('after') or directional ('to') preposition. Syntactic features include markers of cohesion, complex sentences with embedded or relative clauses, impersonal constructions using the pronoun *man* ('you', 'one'), and complex attributes such as the temporal reference *gleichmäßig über das vergangene Jahr verteilt* ('distributed evenly over the past year'), which has been used in another such test (BSB, 2009: 28).

Example 1

Eine Zimmerei soll ein Gartenhaus aus Holz errichten. Nach den baurechtlichen Bestimmungen darf der umbaute Raum 35 m³ nicht überschreiten. Der Kunde wünscht für das Haus eine Grundfläche von 4 m Länge und 3 m Breite. Bis zum Dachanfang soll es 2,50 m hoch sein. Die Giebelspitze soll vom Boden 3,30 m hoch sein. Berechnen und beurteilen Sie, ob die gewünschten Maße die baurechtlichen Vorschriften einhalten. (BSB 2009: 27)

[A carpentry firm has to build a wooden garden shed. According to building regulations the enclosed space must not be larger than 35 m³. The client wants a floor area measuring 4 m long and 3 m wide. The roof will begin at a height of 2.5 m. The apex of the roof will be 3.3 m from floor level. Calculate the desired measurements and decide whether or not they comply with building regulations.]

So far we have concentrated on formal and structural aspects of *Bildungssprache*, but we have also stated that it entails the ability to participate in educated discourse. The relevant discourse for BVJM students – as for any other student in vocational training – is that of their possible future profession or trade. In these contexts – as in most others – language also has a functional role. It is a tool to direct one's own actions and those of other people: superiors, co-workers, clients and so on. This notion has been brought into the discussion of *Bildungssprache* by Ohm (2010) following Vygotsky (1992). What students need to learn in this respect is what actions can be performed linguistically, and more importantly, what linguistic means are appropriate in a given situation. For instance, in Example 1 they are asked to judge whether or not the planned garden shed complies with regulations. Judging entails considering the facts, i.e. the proposed measurements of the shed, comparing them with building regulations, and coming to a conclusion. In interaction with clients they would also be required to provide a clear explanation of their decision-making process and thus make a case for or against building the shed as planned.

BVJM students are typically aged between 16 and 18, so we might assume that they already possess a general knowledge of some of these linguistic actions. If they had some sort of school-based education in their countries of origin, they may even have received some formal training in this area. Furthermore, from the BVJM syllabus we would assume that training in these linguistic competences is an integral part of the programme; and we would assume that some of these activities play a part in the project-oriented elements of the BVJM programme. Accordingly, we tried to assess the linguistic (*Bildungssprache*) competences of BVJM students using a linguistic task that should be familiar to them and relevant to their future jobs. We chose the text type 'instruction' in order to collect some preliminary data from a small group of students. In the next section we will introduce the stimulus material and present our initial findings.

Empirical Findings

In this section we present two sample texts written by BVJM students. This round of data collection was meant as a small pilot in order to try out various data elicitation procedures. The procedure chosen to elicit the samples derives from the FörMig research programme,[4] which developed and validated tools to assess competence in German (among other languages), focusing on *Bildungssprache* features appropriate to different age groups. The tool *Bumerang* (Dirim & Döll, 2009) was designed to assess students at the point of transition from school to vocational training. They are presented with an advertisement taken from a magazine for young people and inviting applications for an internship at the magazine. The task is to write a formal letter of application and a short text to demonstrate their writing skills. Students are given a series of nine pictures showing the material needed to build a boomerang and the steps one must perform to arrive at a finished product.[5] They are then asked to write a set of instructions that would allow another person to build the boomerang without seeing the pictures. The test material comes with an extensive manual describing the assessment criteria and procedure (Reich *et al.*, 2009). In the examples reproduced below we highlight some of the issues that are linked to the assessment criteria in Reich *et al.* (2009) without going into the detail of the manual.

The student who wrote the text in Figure 8.2 has Polish as her L1. She arrived in Germany two years before the time of the test. She had received nine years of general education in Poland and was in her second year of the BVJM. The second student, whose text is shown in Figure 8.3, is a second-generation Turkish-L1 immigrant who was also in his second BVJM year when the text was written.

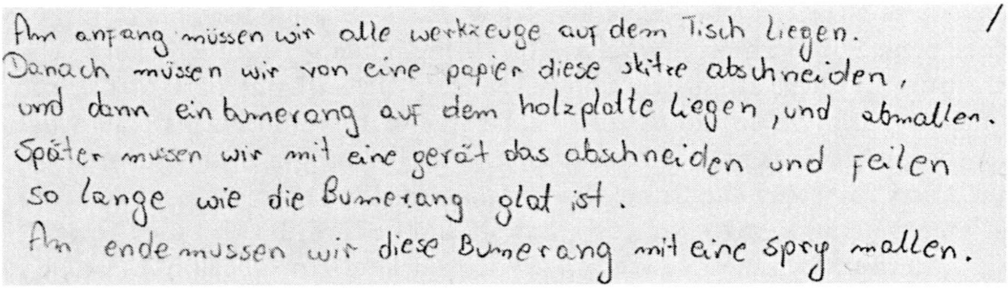

Am anfang müssen wir alle werkzeuge auf dem Tisch liegen.
Danach müssen wir von eine papier diese skitze abschneiden,
und dann ein bumerang auf dem holzplatte liegen, und abmallen.
Später müssen wir mit eine gerät das abschneiden und feilen
so lange wie die Bumerang glat ist.
Am ende müssen wir diese Bumerang mit eine sprüy mallen.

Figure 8.2 Boomerang instruction, Student 0104

[At the beginning we must lie all tools on the table. Then we must cut off of a paper this sketch, and then lie a boomerang on the wooden board, and paint. Later we must cut that off with a machine and file until the boomerang is smooth. At the end we must paint this boomerang with a spray.]

In our discussion of the text reproduced in Figure 8.2 we shall not comment on orthography, the correctness or otherwise of grammatical gender, or errors of inflection (our English gloss attempts to reproduce typical features of the German text). These features are certainly revealing from some points of view, but they are not central to the issue we want to discuss here. At discourse level the text meets the general requirements of the text type 'instruction': individual steps are described in their logical sequence, although the student leaves out steps 4, 7 and 8. Her use of the first person plural pronoun to address the reader is unusual; it occurs in older texts, particularly recipes, but today it is usually seen as patronising.

The omission of steps 4, 7 and 8 corresponds with findings at the lexico-semantic level that seem to indicate an avoidance strategy. The student twice uses the verbs *abschneiden* ('cut off') and *malen* ('paint'). The first instance of *abschneiden* is almost correct, although *ausschneiden* ('cut out') would have been more appropriate; but the second instance is incorrect because the tool used to cut wood requires the verb 'to saw' (*sägen*) not 'to cut'. The meaning of *abschneiden* is close enough to the required one, however, to convey the intended meaning. The student's use of *malen* ('to paint') is similarly generic. She uses it in place of the required *zeichnen* ('to draw') in order to describe the activity of transferring the shape of the stencil to the piece of wood; and then she uses it to denote spray-painting, which in German requires the verb 'to spray'. These features indicate that, with the exception of *feilen* ('to file'), the student lacks technical vocabulary – a conclusion that is confirmed by her use of *eine gerät* ('a machine') instead of *Säge* ('saw').

She shows the fewest difficulties at syntactic level. Her sentence structure is largely correct, and she uses a variety of cohesive devices to sequence the steps in the task. She even uses *später* ('later') to move from step 3 to step 5, which may show that she is aware of having left out a step and is trying to indicate this to the reader.

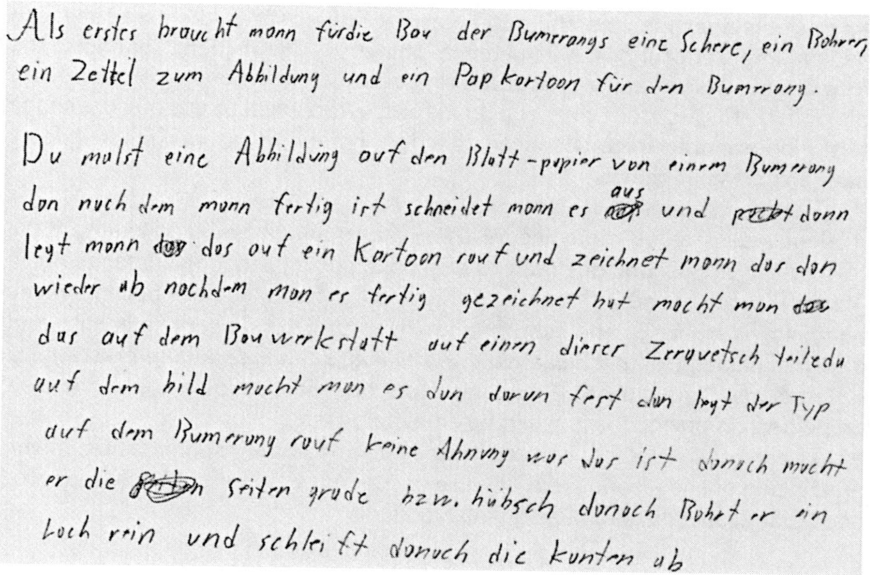
Als erstes braucht mann fürdie Bau der Bumrrangs eine Schere, ein Bohrer, ein Zettel zum Abbildung und ein Pap kartoon für den Bumrrang.

Du malst eine Abbildung auf den Blatt-papier von einem Bumrrang dan nach dem mann fertig ist schneidet mann es aus und dann legt mann das auf ein Kartoon rauf und zeichnet mann das dan wieder ab nachdem man es fertig gezeichnet hat macht man das auf dem Bauwerkstatt auf einen dieser Zerquetsch teiledu auf dem bild macht man es dan darun fest dan legt der Typ auf dem Bumerang rauf keine Ahnung wor das ist danach macht er die Seiten grade bzw. hübsch danach Bohrt er ein Loch rein und schleift danach die kanten ab

Figure 8.3 Boomerang instruction, Student 0101

> [At first one needs for the construction of the boomerang scissors, a drill, a sheet of paper for a figure and a [piece of] cardboard for the boomerang. You paint a figure onto the piece [of] paper of a boomerang then once one is done one cuts it out and then puts that onto a cardboard and one draws that then again [off] it after one is done drawing one makes it on the construction workshop with one of these crushing things there on the picture one makes it then there fast then the guy puts on the boomerang don't have a clue what that is after that he makes the sides even or nice after that he drills a hole into it and grinds after that the edges.]

In the text reproduced in Figure 8.3 we can see that at discourse level the basic structure required for instructional texts is understood and can be reproduced. This student manages to mention all but the last of the steps depicted in the pictures, but he does not list all the tools and materials. However, there seems to be some insecurity when it comes to addressing the reader. The text begins with the correct use of the impersonal pronoun *man*, but then shifts to the informal *du* (2nd person singular, 'you') and later shifts back to *man*. Beginning with step 5 the student switches from addressing the reader to describing the activities of the person shown in the pictures: *dann legt der Typ auf dem Bumerang* ('then the guy puts [something] on the boomerang'). Subsequently he uses the third person singular pronoun *er* to refer to 'the guy'. The student abandons the format and style of an instructional text completely when he comments on his own difficulty in finding the term for the tool used to cut out the shape of the boomerang from the piece of wood: *keine Ahnung was das ist* ('don't have a clue what that is').

The lexico-semantic features of the text are mixed. At verb level this student seems to be more secure than the previous one. For example, he correctly writes schneidet man es aus ('one cuts it out') and later *zeichnen* ('draw') instead of *malen* ('paint'). On the other hand, he does not know the words for workbench and clamp and instead produces a very imprecise and informal description of the activity: *macht man das auf dem* Bauwerkstatt auf einem dieser Zerquetschteile ... daran fest ('one makes it on the construction workshop on one of these crushing things ... fast').

The syntax is largely correct – we even find some subordination in the description of the second step. The use of cohesive devices is slightly monotonous, but again without significant errors.

Discussion

Obviously, findings from an analysis of only two texts cannot be more than preliminary and indicative, but they point in an interesting direction. Here we have two students with significantly different backgrounds: one is a recent immigrant to Germany, whereas the other is a second-generation immigrant who has received all his schooling in the country. But both must have encountered difficulties in finding a place in the dual vocational education system and/or have been assessed as being in need of additional preparatory training, including language training, otherwise they would not have been assigned a place in the BVJM.

Interestingly, their text production is broadly similar, even though the Polish student's text is much shorter than her Turkish peer's. The brevity of her text may be because she has so far had only two years of German language tuition. Despite this difference both students seem to struggle with the same difficulties. They have some general knowledge concerning the requirements of the text type in question, but neither can fulfil them completely; and both have significant difficulties at the lexico-semantic level. For the Polish student this may be explained by her lack of exposure to the German language, but the same cannot be true for the Turkish student. In either case this finding may be thought surprising because both students are attending an educational programme that among other things aims at improving their linguistic skills, particularly in relation to professional requirements. It is all the more striking that both students seem to be relatively competent at the syntactic level: if language tuition in general were the problem, then we would expect difficulties in syntactic competence, too.

This observation raises the question why we get this divergence in linguistic competence between the discursive and lexico-semantic level on the one hand and the syntactic level on the other. Obviously, the first two levels are linked not only to general competence in the target language but to more specialised uses of it. They reflect competence in *Bildungssprache* in its formal and structural features as well as in its function as a tool to direct one's own and other persons' activities. Apparently, the students are not being taught the relevant formal and structural features of *Bildungssprache*. If they are not able to produce a formally correct set of instructions and address their reader correctly, then they lack competence in the productive aspects of *Bildungssprache*. By the same token, they lack its formal and structural features if they do not have command over the terminology relevant to the professional context.

This finding is disturbing when we consider that one of the main aims of the BVJM is to equip students with the competence to communicate proficiently in potential future professional fields. One is therefore prompted to ask whether language education has been assigned to the appropriate slots in the BVJM programme. The syntactic competence of our two students seems to suggest that the German language classes work well. However, these classes seem not to be tailored to the students' future professional needs. Rather, language education for professional purposes seems to have been implicitly delegated to the professional subject classes and the practical projects, such as setting up a repair service and second hand shop for domestic appliances, that are also part of the programme. But in these classes and projects we do not find teachers who are trained in the linguistic aspects of their subjects. They see themselves as subject experts, and often in the vocational training system they are not even professional teachers but trainers in specific trades and professions. This observation is not new, but it comes as a surprise in a programme that has been designed to address the very specific needs of a very specific clientele. And there is one further interesting observation that arises from personal communication with vocational education teachers. One aim of the BVJM programme is to offer students the opportunity to obtain a general secondary school-leaving qualification. However, the exams that lead to this qualification are the same for all students in Hamburg, which means that teachers in the BVJM programme face the problem of reconciling their aim of developing students' communicative proficiency in professional language with the aim of passing exams that have nothing to do with the professional domain. As a result, teachers say that in the first year of the BVJM they aim to give their students general linguistic competence so that newly immigrated students are quickly able to communicate, and at the same time provide some professional skills, because this fits with the aims of the programme and the interests of most students. However, in the second year the focus shifts to the requirements of the exam, so professional requirements are put on the back burner and other linguistic competences get more attention.

Conclusion

The findings and diagnoses presented above are only preliminary and in part anecdotal. But they clearly show that there is scope for further research, and more importantly, a need to reconsider the syllabus and the requirements for educational programmes aimed at supporting and integrating young immigrants.

More research is required on the competence and achievements of migrant students in the vocational training system in order to put the conclusions tentatively drawn in this chapter on a sound footing. Another urgent requirement is a better understanding of what happens from a linguistic point of view in subject and project classes in the vocational training system. Such research would have to investigate linguistic content and communicative requirements, but also teaching styles and teacher training.

Finally there is a political requirement not to design well-intentioned programmes and then leave them to practitioners in the field without monitoring their operation and providing suitable support. At the same time, the formal requirements of a state-controlled examination system need to be reconciled with the everyday needs of immigrants, as designing failure into the system on the basis of conflicting goals does not help integration, it makes it impossible.

Notes

(1) For further information see: http://www.lima.uni-hamburg.de/index.php/en.

(2) '... die Schülerinnen und Schüler in die Lage versetzen, [...] sich berufsübergreifendes und fachliches Wissen anzueignen, Aufgabenstellungen zielorientiert, sachgerecht, methodengeleitet und selbstständig zu lösen und die Lösungen kritisch zu beurteilen [...]' (BBS, 2002: 31).

(3) This is also stressed by Bailey and Heritage (2008: 15–18), who distinguish helpfully between social language (SL) – language used in everyday social contexts, school navigational language (SNL) – the language used to communicate in school and in order to organise school-related matters, and curriculum content language (CCL) – the language used to communicate about content matters, including teaching materials.

(4) The FörMig programme (*Förderung von Kindern und Jugendlichen mit Migrationshintergrund*, 'Support for Immigrant Minority Children and Adolescents') ran from 2004 to 2009 in several German states and continues as *FörMig-Kompetenzzentrum*. Information on FörMig in English can be found at http://www.blk-foermig.uni-hamburg.de/web/en/all/home/index.html; information on the transfer programme is available at http://www.foermig.uni-hamburg.de/web/de/all/home/index.html (at last access, on 27/01/2012, in German only).

(5) The nine pictures show these steps: 1. material and tools; 2. a hand holding scissors and cutting along the lines of a stencil showing the outline of the boomerang; 3. a person using the stencil to draw the outline of the boomerang onto a piece of wood; 4. a piece of wood clamped to a workbench; 5. a person using a jig saw to cut out the boomerang; 6. a person using a rasp to grind the edges of the boomerang; 7. a drill being used to drill holes in the wings of the boomerang; 8. a person polishing the boomerang with sandpaper; 9. a person spray-painting the boomerang.

References

Autorengruppe Bildungsberichterstattung (2010) *Bildung in Deutschland. Ein indikatorengestützter Bericht mit einer Analyse zu Perspektiven des Bildungswesens im demografischen Wandel.* Bielefeld: Bertelsmann.

Bailey, A.L. and Heritage, M. (2008) *Formative Assessment for Literacy Learning: Developing Reading and Academic English Proficiency Together, K–6.* Thousand Oaks, CA: Sage-Corwin Press.

BBS (Behörde für Bildung und Sport) (2002) Bildungsplan Berufsvorbereitungsschule (BVS). Kurs Berufsvorbereitungsjahr für Migrantinnen und Migranten (BVJ-M). Hamburg: Behörde für Bildung und Sport.

BSB (Behörde für Schule und Berufsbildung) (2009) Schriftliche Prüfung in der Berufsvorbereitungsschule im Fach Mathematik zum Erwerb des BVS-Abschlusses, der in seinen Berechtigungen dem ersten allgemeinbildenden Schulabschluss (Hauptschulabschluss) entspricht. Hamburg: Behörde für Bildung und Sport.

Cummins, J. (2000) *Language, Power and Pedagogy: Bilingual Children in the Crossfire.* Clevedon: Multilingual Matters.

Dirim, I. and Döll, M. (2009) 'Bumerang' – Erfassung der Sprachkompetenzen im Übergang von der Schule in den Beruf – vergleichende Beobachtungen zum Türkischen und Deutschen am Beispiel einer Schülerin. In D. Lengyel, H.H. Reich,

H.J. Roth and M. Döll (eds) *Von der Sprachdiagnose zur Sprachförderung* (pp. 139–146). Münster: Waxmann.

Gogolin, I. (2009a) 'Bildungssprache'– The importance of teaching language in every school subject. In T. Tajmel and K. Starl (eds) *Science Education Unlimited: Approaches to Equal Opportunities in Learning Science* (pp. 91–102). Münster: Waxmann.

Gogolin, I. (2009b) Zweisprachigkeit und die Entwicklung bildungssprachlicher Fähigkeiten. In I. Gogolin and U. Neumann (eds) *Streitfall Zweisprachigkeit – The Bilingualism Controversy* (pp. 263–280). Wiesbaden: Verlag für Sozialwissenschaften.

Gogolin, I. and Lange, I. (2011)Bildungssprache und durchgängige Sprachbildung. In S. Fürstenau and M. Gomolla (eds) *Migration und schulischer Wandel: Mehrsprachigkeit* (pp. 107–127). Wiesbaden: Verlag für Sozialwissenschaften.

Habermas, J. (1977) Umgangssprache, Wissenschaftssprache, Bildungssprache. *Jahrbuch 1977* (pp. 36–51). Göttingen: Max-Planck-Gesellschaft zur Förderung der Wissenschaften.

Ohm, U. (2010) Von der Objektsteuerung zur Selbststeuerung: Zweitsprachenförderung als Befähigung zum Handeln. In B. Ahrenholz (ed.) *Fachunterricht und Deutsch als Zweitsprache* (pp. 87–105). Tübingen: Narr.

Reich, H.H., Roth, H-J.and Döll, M. (2009) Auswertungshinweise 'Fast Catch Bumerang' (Deutsch). In D. Lengyel, H.H. Reich, H-J. Roth and M. Döll (eds) *Von der Sprachdiagnose zur Sprachförderung* (pp. 209–241). Münster: Waxmann.

Schleppegrell, M.J. (2001) Linguistic features of the language of schooling. In *Linguistics and Education* 12 (4), 431–459.

Schleppegrell, M.J. (2004) *The Language of Schooling: A Functional Linguistic Perspective*. New York and London: Routledge.

Schumann, S. (2003) Zwischen Chance und Risiko – Jugendliche nach der Berufsvorbereitung. In J. van Buer and O. Zlatkin-Troitschanskaia (eds) *Berufliche Bildung auf dem Prüfstand. Entwicklung zwischen systemischer Steuerung, Transformation durch Modellversuche und unterrichtlicher Innovation* (pp. 69–82). Frankfurt a.M.: Peter Lang.

Vygotsky, L.S. (1992) *Geschichte der höheren psychischen Funktionen*. Münster: Lit.

9 A Corpus-based Analysis of the Lexical Demands that Irish Post-primary Subject Textbooks Make on Immigrant Students

Stergiani Kostopoulou

This chapter reports on a corpus linguistic analysis of subject textbooks used in Irish post-primary education, focusing on the lexical characteristics of six curriculum subjects: English, Geography, History, CSPE (Civic, Social and Political Education), Mathematics and Science. It is the first research of its kind carried out in the Irish context and begins to remedy the lack of empirical information about an important aspect of the linguistic demands that the Irish post-primary curriculum imposes on immigrant students. The chapter begins by outlining the rationale for the research and summarizing the aims of corpus analysis. It then describes the six textbooks-derived corpora and the methodological procedures employed to analyse them and presents the principal empirical findings. These include the most frequent content words together with their significant collocates, and the most frequent 4-word clusters in each corpus. Lexical features are discussed in relation to their semantic value and functional utility in individual corpora. Overall, the empirical analysis uncovers the lexical variation that exists across subjects and provides pedagogically important information on curriculum language as a whole. The conclusion notes some of the implications of the empirical findings for post-primary English language support in Ireland.

The Rationale for a Corpus Linguistic Analysis of Irish Post-primary Subject Textbooks

Although one of the principal aims of the English language support provided for immigrant students in Irish post-primary schools is to help them develop the linguistic resources required for access to the curriculum and academic achievement, research (e.g. Lyons & Little, 2009) reveals that current practice faces a number of challenges. Chief among these, according to teachers' testimony, are (i) the lack of professional knowledge about linking language instruction to the demands of the mainstream subject classroom; (ii) the lack of subject-specific materials;[1] and (iii) the failure of subject teachers to accept their responsibility to facilitate immigrant students' linguistic integration in the subject classroom. A direct consequence of these deficiencies is that English language support is inappropriately or insufficiently linked to the specialized linguistic demands of the post-primary curriculum (Lyons & Little, 2009: 35), failing, as a result, to address immigrant students' needs effectively.

A common denominator linking the above issues appears to be the lack of a clear, empirically based understanding of the linguistic demands that the post-primary curriculum makes of students.[2] Explicit information on curriculum language that accurately captures the requirements of different subjects could (i) inform teacher education, helping teachers to establish direct links between English language support and the subject classroom; (ii) inform the design and development of appropriate materials; and (iii) raise subject teachers' awareness of the linguistic dimension of the content areas they teach and encourage them to appreciate their role.

Starting from the need to make curriculum language explicit and bridge the existing knowledge gap, the present research carried out a corpus linguistic analysis of textbooks used in six subjects of the Junior Cycle (lower secondary) curriculum. Specifically, textbooks for English, Geography, History, CSPE (Civic, Social and Political Education), Mathematics and Science were examined because these subjects are considered fundamental to post-primary education and they are formally assessed through final examinations. The linguistic analysis focused on textbooks because they are 'omnipresent in all kinds of literacy activities', while simultaneously 'interfacing with spoken language in the same mental space of the language user' (Ravid & Tolchinsky, 2002: 230). The language of subject textbooks plays a gate-keeping role in relation to students' access to disciplinary knowledge and academic achievement, and it should be thus made more visible. Although the importance of the oral input students receive in the subject classroom is recognized, this did not form part of the empirical analysis because the variability of teacher discourse (Bailey *et al.*, 2007: 148) could yield inconsistent information and conclusions which could not be easily generalized. If conducted on a large scale, however, a corpus-based examination of teacher talk could yield some useful insights into the challenges that instructional language poses to students and the ways in which it differs from the language of subject textbooks.

The techniques and tools chosen to analyse textbook language were those of corpus linguistics, which facilitate fast, accurate and complex analysis of a variety of linguistic features. Language corpora also provide 'an objective frame of reference' (Bowker & Pearson, 2002: 20) because the information they comprise 'has not been selected in order to confirm existing conscious (or subconscious) biases' (Baker, 2006: 12). Corpus analysis is, further, 'a more replicable process and any analysis can be verified by other researchers' (Adolphs, 2006: 7). A detailed description of the subject-specific corpora that were developed for this research and the methodological procedure that was adopted are described in the following section.

Subject-specific Corpora and Methodology

The data used in the present research comprise six corpora that were designed and developed to represent the language of the curriculum subjects under examination. Each corpus consists of the full contents of four widely used subject textbooks, which cover all three years of Junior Cycle (i.e. lower secondary) education. These were selected in consultation with post-primary teachers and on the basis of frequency of use. The 24 textbooks were scanned and converted into electronic files, which were edited (graphic and visual elements were removed) and stored as text files.[3] The total number of tokens (i.e. running words in a text) in each corpus is given in Table 9.1. The corpora

Table 9.1 Composition of the six corpora built on Junior Cycle subject textbooks (the hash symbol (#) refers to number)

Subject corpus	# of textbooks	# of tokens
English	4	451,784
Geography	4	330,257
History	4	367,708
CSPE	4	213,340
Mathematics	4	336,738
Science	4	328,426

are rather small, especially when compared to the corpora of billions of words that can be built today. It must be remembered, however, that the purpose of the research was to analyse the language of a particular collection of textbooks, not to make generalizations about the English language in general (cf. Bowker & Pearson, 2002: 48).

It is also important to note that the corpora constructed for the present study comprise textbooks written by different authors, in order to neutralize idiosyncratic language use by individual writers.

The methodology used involved a frequency analysis of content words and their significant collocates and 4-word clusters using the WordList of WordSmith tools (Scott, 2004). The rationale behind frequency information is that it can be used as an important criterion in prioritizing what language should be taught; the assumption being that the more often students encounter a word, the more easily and faster they will understand it in their textbooks and learn how to use it productively (see Milton, 2009: 25–43 for a frequency model of vocabulary learning). When applied to the study of word clusters, an additional strength of a frequency-driven approach is that it reveals 'the extent to which a sequence of words is stored and used as a pre-fabricated chunk, with higher frequency sequences more likely to be stored [in the mental lexicon] as unanalyzed chunks than lower frequency sequences' (Biber *et al.*, 2004: 376).

The focus on content words and 4-word clusters was motivated by the instrumental role that vocabulary (single-word items) and lexis (multi-word units; see e.g. Lewis, 1993; Nattinger & DeCarrico, 1992) play in successful second language learning and in learning the language of schooling in particular. Content, or lexical, words (nouns, lexical verbs, adjectives and adverbs) act as the main carriers of meaning, providing access to entire knowledge categories (Corson, 1985). Identifying the most significant collocates of content words, i.e. the words they typically co-occur with 'in their neighbourhood', is also important because words do not exist in a vacuum but 'in the company of other words' (McEnery & Wilson, 1996: 71), which are essential for appropriate word knowledge and use.

Clusters (Scott, 2004), understood as recurrent strings of two or more words that appear more frequently in a particular linguistic register than expected by chance, are pervasive in natural language and especially in subject-specific texts. They typically function as fundamental building blocks of academic discourse (e.g. Biber *et al.*, 1999; Biber, 2006) and shape context-specific meanings (e.g. Hyland, 2008). They have also been found to contribute to the fluency and naturalness of linguistic production by native and non-native speakers of a language (e.g. Pawley & Syder, 1983). On this evidence, both lexical words with their collocates and clusters that repeatedly

occur in curriculum subject textbooks can be viewed as pedagogically important linguistic features that are worthy of investigation.

To single out content words from the frequency wordlists computed by
WordSmith, Nation's (2001: 430–431) function word list was used as a stop-
list filter. Statistically significant collocates of content words were computed
based on the log-likelihood ratio (G^2; Dunning, 1993), a statistical measure
for calculating the significance of word co-occurrence to filter out idiosyncratic collocates, i.e. frequently used word pairs formed by chance. Finally,
4-word clusters were examined (following Jones & Sinclair, 1974) to limit the
scope of the investigation and, more importantly, because these are 'far more
common than 5-word strings' and usually have 'a clearer range of structures
and functions than 3-word bundles' (Hyland, 2008: 8).

For reasons of practical manageability, a relatively high cut-off point was
set for frequency of occurrence (a minimum frequency of 40 times per million words) for the analysis of both content words and clusters. Frequency
counts presented in this discussion are normalized rates of occurrence per
mille (‰) words, and can thus be directly compared across corpora. In addition to minimal frequency requirements, range (i.e. consistency of use across
texts in a corpus) was also used as a criterion for selecting the words and
clusters to be closely examined, the requirement being that a cluster should
occur in at least 75% of the texts making up a corpus (i.e. in at least three out
of four textbooks). This was essential in order to ensure that the idiosyncratic language use of individual textbook authors did not influence the
results. Finally, abbreviations, numbers and symbols (#) were excluded from
the study.

The discussion that follows presents some of the key findings on the
nature of lexical words and clusters in the six corpora and their semantic and
functional associations in subject-specific texts.

The Most Frequent Lexical Words in the Six Corpora and their Collocates

What becomes immediately clear from an examination of the commonest content words in the six corpora is that they are topic-related, that is,
they reflect the distinct thematic concerns and concepts of the different subjects in which they occur. As a result, markedly different lexical sets can be
observed across corpora. The small sample of the top 20 subject-specific
words presented in Table 9.2 illustrates this point.

These words reflect the disciplinary orientation of the six subjects. In the
English corpus, they highlight the literary dimension of the subject, which

Table 9.2 The top 20 most frequent content words in the six textbooks corpora ranked by descending order of frequency (minimum frequency – 40 per million words, minimum range – 75%, normed frequencies per mille words)

N	English		Geography		History		CSPE		Mathematics		Science	
	Word	Freq	Word	Freq	Word	Freq	Word	Freq	Word	Freq	Word	Freq
1	story	2.27	people	3.79	people	4.36	people	6.54	find	6.85	water	9.65
2	like	2.19	map	3.29	war	3.34	action	2.99	cm	5.66	energy	3.93
3	write	1.95	population	3.11	Irish	2.96	community	2.92	number	5.38	used	2.9
4	said	1.84	areas	3.11	government	2.74	rights	2.9	calculate	5.26	light	2.75
5	think	1.73	water	3.05	century	2.16	local	2.78	line	3.65	air	2.66
6	answer	1.67	area	2.82	British	2.01	world	2.33	area	3.6	food	2.57
7	poem	1.66	countries	2.13	new	1.85	work	2.26	value	3.07	test	2.52
8	words	1.49	city	2.11	world	1.67	school	2.12	equation	2.85	heat	2.5
9	people	1.37	river	2.08	became	1.62	government	1.89	point	2.84	experiment	2.38
10	time	1.36	land	1.98	used	1.57	project	1.85	example	2.67	called	2.26
11	make	1.3	following	1.93	made	1.5	European	1.8	given	2.4	plants	2.1
12	read	1.21	figure	1.75	called	1.46	make	1.76	following	2.39	oxygen	2.07
13	good	1.18	south	1.71	year	1.44	Irish	1.69	solution	2.3	tube	2.03
14	give	1.15	world	1.68	land	1.43	class	1.68	angle	2.18	gas	1.91
15	see	1.15	sea	1.67	army	1.34	children	1.67	sides	2.03	place	1.86
16	writing	1.15	large	1.66	great	1.25	council	1.63	length	2.01	method	1.8
17	just	1.1	photograph	1.65	church	1.21	day	1.62	graph	2	carbon	1.79
18	use	1.09	new	1.6	time	1.19	group	1.56	diagram	1.94	plant	1.74
19	new	1.08	high	1.56	following	1.19	groups	1.45	solve	1.89	acid	1.73
20	well	1.05	explain	1.51	work	1.12	think	1.42	sin (sine)	1.89	current	1.71

is primarily concerned with *stor[y/ies]*, and *poem[s]*, *words*, *writing*, etc., inviting students to *write, think, answer, read*, etc. The majority of the commonest words in the Geography corpus reveal the focus of geographical study on people (*people, population*) and their relationships with the environment (*area[s], countr[y/ies], city, land*, etc.). They further refer to visual aids (*map, figure, photograph*). History words are associated with the study of people in institutional contexts (*army, government*) and events (*war*) from the past (*century, year, time*). The very frequent use of past tense verbs (*became, used, called*) reflects the pivotal role played by the past tense in historical meaning-making. CSPE words denote civic, social and political agents (*community, government, council*, etc.), while the most frequent items in Mathematics describe major mathematical concepts (*number, value, equation, sine*) and actions (*find, calculate, solve*). The commonest Science-specific words reveal concepts important to scientific study such as substances and materials (*water, energy, light, oxygen, gas*, etc.). The occurrence of *people* in the top 20 words for English, Geography, History and CSPE but not in the top 20 words for Mathematics and Science is not accidental either, as it is the humanities and social science textbooks that typically discuss people.

Overall, content word analysis shows that the most frequent words in the six subjects are not used at random; on the contrary, word choice is highly restricted by the topics and themes explored and the meanings that are constructed in subject-specific texts. In short, the repeated use of lexical words 'signals and contributes to the uniqueness of the text, that is, what makes this text different from all other texts' (Nation, 2001: 205). These content wordlists could subsequently be used to make language support teachers and students aware of the 'distinct lexical flavour' of the different subject areas. Grouped into semantic categories, they can provide the basis for thematic vocabulary learning that is firmly embedded in the post-primary curriculum.

The examination of the characteristic 'lexical friends' of the commonest content words, reinforces the above point about the interdependence of word choice and thematic content in subject texts. Table 9.3 presents the top 20 collocates of the 10 most frequent words in the six corpora (information on statistical significance and frequency of occurrence has been removed to facilitate a qualitative treatment of collocates).

The grammatical words which are found among the top collocates of content words convey information about the typical grammatical behaviour of node words (colligation; Hoey, 2005). Lexical collocates, on the other hand, show that tendencies of word co-occurrence are also influenced by the informational load of a text. These collocates also show that words are idiosyncratic, in the sense that every single word has a different set of collocates

Table 9.3 The top 20 collocates of the 10 most frequent content words in the six textbooks corpora ranked by descending order of significance based on G² scores (collocates are enclosed in diamond brackets; node = lexical word under analysis)

Subject corpus	Node-collocate pair
English	**story** <the, a, of, in, is, this, to, short, you, tells, or, tell, about, write, set, from, novel, that, read, your>
	like <a, the, you, to, I, what, would, that, it, of, is, this, or, in, was, just, do, dislike, be, she>
	write <a, the, you, to, about, your, paragraph, of, out, for, in, words, letter, story, down, article, an, two, sentences, own>
	said <he, she, I, the, to, mother, you, a, my, and, it, was, that, yes, uncle, me, father, in, as, M>
	think <you, do, I, the, is, about, what, of, that, to, would, it, best, this, why, they, which, a, be, are>
	answer <the, questions, your, following, reasons, follow, give, for, that, then, a, two, this, question, sample, to, of, read, support, poem>
	poem <a, in, the, this, of, is, read, you, or, to, about, questions, from, answer, with, carefully, following, that, line, reading>
	words <the, in, phrases, of, are, that, you, to, using, which, write, a, or, use, key, these, following, with, your, about>
	people <the, to, of, in, are, who, young, a, many, about, how, or, that, they, for, as, be, would, most, on>
	time <the, at, a, of, to, for, in, was, it, first, is, all, that, this, by, he, long, place, I, had>
Geography	**people** <in, of, to, the, live, who, many, for, have, million, young, are, from, work, their, a, migrate, that, areas, living>
	map <the, on, of, sketch, as, extract, ordnance, survey, draw, shown, OS [ordnance survey], area, evidence, page, figure, study, photograph, to, carefully, use>
	population <the, density, of, growth, densities, in, change, distribution, a, high, is, has, diversity, low, pyramid, very, world, to, increase, total>
	areas <in, of, are, rural, the, to, urban, lowland, inner, city, these, such, as, pressure, upland, from, people, low, high, some>
	water <the, of, supplies, is, clean, to, in, supply, a, fresh, from, cycle, for, air, as, into, by, it, condenses, rivers>

area <the, of, in, a, an, map, shown, this, on, is, calculate, sketch, to, photograph, urban, pressure, for, one, that, around>

countries <in, the, developing, of, rich, world, developed, poor, are, to, such, many, poorer, as, have, aid, south, poorest, third, these>

city <the, inner, centre, of, in, a, to, areas, primate, is, suburbs, town, has, are, as, capital, housing, from, or, county>

river <the, a, of, on, its, in, basin, valleys, flows, is, point, valley, flood, course, or, stream, which, bed, bridge, meander>

land <the, of, is, use, in, flat, on, to, uses, agricultural, or, by, quality, from, sloping, land, buildings, values, which, for>

History

people <the, to, of, in, were, many, lived, that, who, more, Irish, history, most, for, ordinary, their, about, a, had, poor>

war <the, world, of, in, civil, cold, during, after, independence, to, ended, end, was, Korean, on, a, years, American, outbreak, when>

Irish <the, to, of, in, volunteers, people, Gaelic, state, agreement, free, by, as, an, were, parliament, British, republic, a, language, government>

government <to, of, British, in, a, Ireland, party, by, that, coalition, act, was, Irish, northern, Fianna, had, fail, set, formed, up>

century <in, international, relations, change, early, social, political, year, of, during, end, first, beginning, decades, a, second, third, BC [Before Christ], AD [Anno Domini], years>

British <government, to, army, of, forces, in, by, troops, Irish, prime, that, parliament, Americans, French, American, the, commonwealth, soldiers, monarch, minister>

new <the, a, of, to, in, were, towns, world, called, built, as, party, lands, ideas, was, orders, constitution, routes, introduced, government>

world <war, the, of, view, European, in, during, after, exploration, discovery, to, new, outbreak, was, ancient, a, on, parts, had, that>

(Continued)

Table 9.3 (*Continued*)

Subject corpus	Node-collocate pair
CSPE	**became** <the, of, in, a, popular, he, more, as, known, leader, very, when, who, minister, so, many, famous, later, soon, they>
	used <to, the, were, was, for, they, as, be, a, by, could, in, steam, methods, tactics, which, of, that, describe, make>
	people <the, young, to, of, in, who, for, are, have, a, by, that, with, many, about, community, homeless, their, older, from>
	action <project, the, an, report, your, on, of, a, you, involvement, this, undertaken, in, part, community, to, for, marks, as, take>
	community <the, in, a, local, of, involvement, to, your, people, action, school, alert, neighbourhood, games, for, European, centre, as, members, groups>
	rights <human, the, of, responsibilities, declaration, to, universal, convention, on, child, abuses, are, for, in, UN [United Nations], dignity, a, that, protection, protect>
	local <the, authorities, authority, a, community, to, government, of, in, your, for, are, councillors, representatives, their, people, councillor, or, with, development>
	world <the, are, we, in, around, small, of, day, a, caring, developing, for, changing, to, third, crossword, war, countries, is, parts>
	work <the, to, of, course, in, module, their, a, for, assessment, on, with, book, who, about, hours, people, they, is, together>
	school <in, your, to, the, a, community, students, for, of, or, go, class, my, on, at, children, number, from, day, an>
	government <the, of, local, to, is, a, in, by, on, policy, coalition, departments, head, for, opposition, Taoiseach, Irish, environment, ministers, has>
	project <action, the, report, on, an, your, a, of, this, doing, part, you, as, was, my, based, in, marks, did, title>

Mathematics   **find** <of, value, to, equation, values, image, a, slope, point, for, coordinates, area, solve, line, graph, if, hence, use, we, number>

cm[centimetre] <of, is, radius, height, length, a, the, its, volume, diameter, by, cylinder, area, has, sphere, width, breadth, calculate, base, in>

number <the, of, is, a, who, to, in, people, times, by, pupils, whole, larger, that, prime, total, on, per, less, second>

calculate <the, of, its, value, area, to, radius, height, amount, mean, interest, total, length, cm, volume, tax, a, in, correct, earned>

line <a, mirror, is, of, on, segment, equation, draw, to, through, point, symmetry, axis, slope, axial, perpendicular, find, parallel, meet, in>

area <the, of, rectangle, is, triangle, calculate, find, volume, its, cm, base, circle, total, perimeter, parallelogram, length, height, width, maximum, in>

value <the, of, find, calculate, minimum, maximum, to, estimate, corresponding, after, equation, is, write, or, down, hence, for, frequency, point, exact>

equation <the, of, solve, an, to, find, in, line, write, this, given, down, form, quadratic, information, is, a, represent, we, value>

point <the, of, on, a, is, intersection, cut, off, line, standard, find, rate, minimum, under, image, central, to, symmetry, coordinates, decimal>

example <for, the, consider, of, is, in, solve, simplify, next, find, type, and, common, if, image, evaluate, sides, has, express, cm>

(Continued)

Table 9.3 (*Continued*)

Subject corpus   Node-collocate pair

Science	**water** <the, distilled, of, in, to, a, is, with, boiling, vapour, beaker, from, dioxide, hard, into, salt, carbon, tap, test, that>
	energy <electrical, heat, to, the, of, is, food, into, chemical, light, in, stored, from, sound, form, potential, sources, by, source, sun>
	used <to, apparatus, is, chemicals, be, the, for, in, are, a, of, can, measure, test, it, an, small, two, separate, make>
	light <the, a, to, of, energy, rays, is, ray, white, from, bulb, that, it, in, travels, refraction, resistor, when, diode, towards>
	air <the, in, to, is, of, oxygen, water, from, dioxide, show, carbon, than, into, vapour, through, with, that, contains, glass, a>
	food <the, of, energy, to, chain, in, chains, is, for, make, web, plants, their, from, types, own, down, photosynthesis, digested, animals>
	test <tube, the, tubes, for, a, to, in, of, water, solution, into, each, used, with, chemicals, starch, presence, paper, stopper, apparatus>
	heat <energy, the, of, to, a, is, in, loss, transfer, water, from, electrical, by, through, conductor, conduction, gently, show, conductors, chemical>
	experiment <to, show, the, this, demonstrate, investigate, that, of, in, a, we, an, will, water, simple, find, examine, mandatory, describe, repeat>
	called <is, the, a, are, this, of, which, tiny, they, in, an, to, particles, cells, process, by, these, because, sometimes, often>

which differ even when the same word is used in the singular or plural. A comparison of the collocates of *area* and *areas* in the geography corpus, for example, shows that only the singular form of the word is used in references to visual aids (*map, sketch, photograph*). Interestingly, the same words can appear in more than one corpus, with different sets of collocates in each corpus. The different collocates of *people* in the corpora for Geography (e.g. *live, migrate, million*), History (e.g. *lived, Irish, history*) and CSPE (e.g. *young, homeless, community*) illustrate this phenomenon, demonstrating how different collocates of the same word provide clues to the information content of a corpus. From this it can be argued that collocational knowledge should be considered an integral part of lexical knowledge, because it marks typical, and thus appropriate, vocabulary use. Collocations become increasingly important in subject-specific language learning in particular because the basic unit of meaning is longer than a single word (Bowker & Pearson, 2002: 26) and words are 'combined in special ways' that differ from Language for General Purposes (Bowker & Pearson, 2002).

Having introduced the commonest content words in the six corpora and some of their favourite lexical 'friends', the discussion proceeds to the analysis of longer lexical patterns, namely 4-word clusters.

The Most Frequent 4-word Clusters in the Six Corpora and their Semantic and Functional Associations

Similar to content word analysis, the frequency analysis of 4-word clusters in the six corpora also reveals semantic connections between lexis and subject-specific content, highlighting once again the variation across corpora. The top 20 clusters in the six corpora, displayed in Table 9.4 below, are discussed separately here in an attempt to isolate the influence of the subject area.

Beginning with the English corpus, most clusters revolve around questions, answers, reasons and subjective viewpoints (*what do you think*). This reflects the emphasis of the English syllabus on helping students to develop their communication skills and their thinking capacity as part of their 'personal growth through English' (NCCA, 2008: 3).

As regards the geography corpus, it appears that 4-word clusters express fragmentary instructions for typical activities, e.g. *draw a sketch map, to support your answer, tick the correct box, study the Ordnance Survey*. Several clusters also refer to information communicated graphically, e.g. *a sketch map of, the*

Table 9.4 The 20 most frequent 4-word clusters in the six corpora in a descending frequency order (minimum frequency - 40 per million words, minimum range - 75%, N = rank order, italics = cluster in all 4 textbooks)

N	English	Geography	History	CSPE	Mathematics	Science
1	give reasons for your	each of the following	in the twentieth century	has the right to	each of the following	shown in the diagram
2	reasons for your answer	draw a sketch map	international relations in the	and answer the questions	find the value of	as shown in the
3	the questions that follow	the west of Ireland	in Ireland in the	the work of the	the values of x	set up the apparatus
4	answer the questions that	a sketch map of	write an account of	why do you think	values of x for	the apparatus as shown
5	and then answer the	the ordnance survey map	the end of the	of the action project	the area of the	is made up of
6	of the following questions	sketch map of the	each of the following	answer the questions that	the value of x	can be used to
7	what do you think	the area shown on	answer the following questions	the questions that follow	the equation of the	what is meant by
8	the end of the	to support your answer	the treaty of Versailles	social and political education	find the image of	the bottom of the
9	two of the following	area shown on the	the age of revolutions	as part of the	at the end of	the centre of gravity

10	do you think the	shown on the map	at the end of	a member of the	find the equation of	a form of energy
11	at the end of	with the aid of	the War of Independence	civic social and political	of x for which	for the presence of
12	fill in the gaps	per cent of the	the agricultural and industrial	of the European Union	divide both sides by	a small amount of
13	one of the following	study the ordnance survey	the League of Nations	Declaration of Human Rights	correct to the nearest	is a form of
14	the rest of the	in the west of	agricultural and industrial revolutions	what do you think	standard rate cut off	experiment to show that
15	each of the following	tick the correct box	of the twentieth century	the rights of the	equation of the line	the mass of the
16	at the beginning of	map of the area	during the Middle Ages	was set up in the	the length of the	carbon dioxide and water
17	in the middle of	the population of the	per cent of the	do you think the	the radius of the	the boiling point of
18	and answer the questions	of the area shown	the Home Rule Party	the European Court of	axial symmetry in the	the density of a
19	give a reason for	is one of the	the Irish Free State	Universal Declaration of Human	the end of the	the top of the
20	this is a very	in the form of	in the Middle Ages	rights of the child	the volume of the	find the mass of

Ordnance Survey map, shown on the map, etc. These demonstrate that the discourse of Geography has a tendency to be expressed multimodally (i.e. the
language of maps, globes, photographs, grids, diagrams, etc.), to encourage
students to 'look through a geographer's eyes' (van Leeuwen & Humphrey,
1996: 30).

In the History corpus two types of cluster stand out: (i) those which
describe past events, issues and figures (e.g. *the War of Independence, the Treaty
of Versailles, the League of Nations, the Home Rule Party*) and (ii) those which
express the notion of time. This is fundamental to the study of history and
can be linguistically constructed in many different ways: 'Any historical
writing is likely to draw on a wide range of linguistic expressions for constru-
ing time' (Coffin, 2006: 10). Among the commonest clusters in this corpus
are those which refer to particular historical eras, e.g. *in the twentieth century,
the Age of Revolutions, during the Middle Ages,* etc., and those which mediate the
chronological ordering of events, e.g. *at the end of,* etc.

Clusters in the CSPE corpus are referents of organizations and titles of
political agreements, e.g. *of the European Union, the European Court of, Declaration
of Human Rights.* There are also clusters that contain the personal pronoun
you and directly address the reader (*what/why do you think*). These mediate
instructions which are similar to those in the English corpus, having to do
with answering questions and justifying personal opinions. This similarity
reflects the common aim of the two subjects to encourage students' active
participation and develop their critical ability. The concept of *rights,* which is
fundamental to the study of CSPE, also features in several clusters.

More technical clusters appear in the Mathematics and Science corpora.
These express fundamental concepts in mathematical and scientific discourse, e.g. *standard rate cut off, the radius of the,* etc. and *carbon dioxide and
water, the density of a,* etc., respectively. They refer to activities undertaken by
students in the two subjects, e.g. *find the value/equation of, divide both sides by,*
etc. and *experiment to show that, find the mass of,* etc. The distinct nature of
4-word clusters manifested in these two corpora stems from the technicality
that is inherent in counting and measurement practices in mathematics and
in experimental work in science.

One common pattern that can be observed in the clusters in all six corpora is the presence of some of the commonest content words within the
commonest clusters, e.g. 'what do you *think*' (English), 'draw a sketch *map*'
(Geography), 'in the twentieth *century*' (History), '*rights* of the child' (CSPE),
'find the *value* of' (Mathematics), 'a form of *energy*' (Science). These words
contribute to the topic-specificity of the corresponding clusters because, as
shown in the previous section, they are evidently topic-based. Even when the
commonest words are not constituents of clusters, concordances reveal that

they appear as the complementation items of clusters (i.e. the words that follow them), e.g. 'the end/rest of the *story*' (English), 'per cent of the *population*' (Geography), 'write an account of [the] *people*' (History), 'the work of the *government*' (CSPE), 'the equation of the *line*' (Mathematics), 'is made up of *water*' (Science). This pattern recalls Sinclair's argument that 'the commonest words are responsible for the commonest patterns or slight variants of these patterns' (Sinclair, 1987: 208), resulting in the pre-patterned nature of language (cf. Sinclair's 'idiom principle'; 1991: 110).

Overall, the analysis of 4-word clusters in the six subject corpora indicates 'important aspects of the phraseology used by writers in specific contexts' (Scott & Tribble, 2006: 132). The variation of these cluster listings across subject corpora adds further evidence to the finding of previous research that each register employs a distinct set of lexical bundles (e.g. Biber *et al.*, 1999). On this basis it can be argued that, in addition to lexical words, 4-word clusters can also be a reliable indicator of subject-based variation (e.g. Hyland, 2008). In pedagogical terms, these clusters should be viewed as important candidates for explicit instruction in language support within the communicative context of curriculum subjects because they are fundamental for students' comprehension and the construction of appropriate discourse (Biber & Barbieri, 2007: 284). Their variation across subject corpora can help language support teachers and students to appreciate the diverse lexical resources that have to be deployed in order to construct subject-specific meaning.

Having discussed the commonest lexical words and 4-word clusters in the six subject corpora, a caveat should be added regarding the generalization of findings. The present findings cannot be generalized to subject-specific language use in these registers as a whole; they are valid only for the language of the corpora in question, as is the case in most corpus studies of English for Specific Purposes. As Sinclair argues, 'no corpus, no matter how large, how carefully designed, can have exactly the same characteristics as the language itself' (Sinclair, 2005: 2). Nevertheless, the present study helps to compensate for the lack of research into the language of Irish post-primary textbooks, providing empirical information that can be exploited in multiple ways in English language support, as argued in the conclusion.

Conclusion

This chapter has provided a corpus-based description of the commonest lexical features of textbooks used in six subjects of the Irish post-primary curriculum (English, Geography, History, CSPE, Mathematics and Science). The purpose of the research was to inform English language support for immigrant students. Although it was possible to present only a limited sample of the findings,[4] several conclusions were drawn about subject-specific language that carry direct pedagogical implications for the language support classroom.

The overall conclusion that emerges from the lexical analysis of all six corpora is that subject-specific texts value distinct sets of interrelated content words, lexical collocates and 4-word clusters, and further, that their lexical preferences are largely determined by thematic (information content) and functional (communicative) requirements. The resulting variation at the level of words, their collocates, and 4-word clusters demonstrates that curriculum language is not a single register but comprises diverse 'dialects' across subjects. This has important implications for pedagogy. When language support is provided in addition to the mainstream curriculum, it should be firmly and explicitly related to curriculum subjects. In general, subject teachers should be better professionalized so that they can focus appropriately on vocabulary; alternatively, in some contexts it may be possible to develop 'dual teaching' approaches, where subject teacher and language teacher work together in the same classroom.

Revealing the commonest lexical items of subject textbooks, the research draws attention to features that should form an integral part of immigrant students' target linguistic repertoire if they are to achieve full access to the curriculum. This empirically derived information can be used to inform decisions about the content, sequence and gradation of the vocabulary component of language teaching. It also has powerful implications for the development of context-specific pedagogical materials and language tests. Underpinned by corpus-based descriptions of subject-specific lexis, teaching approaches, materials and assessment instruments can accurately reflect the type of language that students encounter in curriculum subjects. In this way, direct links can be established between the English language support classroom and the mainstream subject classroom. Teacher education could also make use of the results of this research, raising subject teachers' awareness of the diverse lexical load of curriculum subjects and encouraging them to adopt approaches that take account of the linguistic features of their subject. Arguably, this would benefit all students, including native speaker students with learning difficulties.

By exploring the fruitful interface between corpus linguistics and language pedagogy, the research responds to calls for more applied corpus linguistics studies which are motivated by an interest in second language education and especially in secondary education (e.g. Coxhead, 2010: 466; Flowerdew, 2009: 345). Moving beyond the Irish context, and considering that the linguistic integration of immigrant students is, and will remain, a challenge for all educational systems, the design and methodology of this research have the potential to be adapted for use in other migrant education settings with similar pedagogical needs.

Notes

(1) See, however, the materials developed by the Trinity Immigration Initiative's English Language Support Programme (www.elsp.ie), informed by the present research, and discussed by Lyons in this volume.
(2) To date the only exception is the curriculum framework developed by Integrate Ireland Language and Training. This comprises *English Language Proficiency Benchmarks* (IILT, 2003) which describe the communicative and linguistic demands of post-primary curriculum, and a version of the European Language Portfolio for post-primary immigrant learners (IILT, 2004) designed as a curriculum mediation tool.
(3) I gratefully acknowledge Dr Zach Lyons's help in digitizing the corpora.
(4) See Kostopoulou (2012) for a detailed empirical analysis of the language of Irish post-primary curriculum subject textbooks and examination papers.

References

Adolphs, S. (2006) *Introducing Electronic Text Analysis: A Practical Guide for Language and Literary Studies*. Abingdon: Routledge.
Bailey, A., Butler, F., Stevens, R. and Lord, C. (2007) Further specifying the language demands of school. In A. Bailey (ed.) *The Language Demands of School: Putting Academic English to the Test* (pp. 103–156). New Haven: Yale University Press.
Baker, P. (2006) *Using Corpora in Discourse Analysis*. London: Continuum.
Biber, D. (2006) *University Language: A Corpus-based Study of Spoken and Written Registers*. Amsterdam and Philadelphia: Benjamins.
Biber, D. and Barbieri, F. (2007) Lexical bundles in university spoken and written registers. *English for Specific Purposes* 26 (3), 263–286.
Biber, D., Conrad, S. and Cortes, V. (2004) If you look at. . . : Lexical bundles in university teaching and textbooks. *Applied Linguistics* 25 (3), 371–405.
Biber, D., Johansson, S., Leech, G., Conrad, S. and Finegan, E. (1999) *Longman Grammar of Spoken and Written English*. London: Longman.
Bowker, L. and Pearson, J. (2002) *Working with Specialized Language: A Practical Guide to Using Corpora*. London: Routledge.
Coffin, C. (2006) *Historical Discourse: The Language of Time, Cause and Evaluation*. London: Continuum.
Corson, D. (1985) *The Lexical Bar*. Oxford: Pergamon.
Coxhead, A. (2010) What can corpora tell us about English for Academic Purposes? In M. McCarthy and A. O'Keeffe (eds) *The Routledge Handbook of Corpus Linguistics* (pp. 458–470). London: Routledge.
Dunning, T. (1993) Accurate methods for the statistics of surprise and coincidence. *Computational Linguistics* 19 (1), 61–74.
Flowerdew, L. (2009) Corpora in language teaching. In M. Long and C. Doughty (eds) *The Handbook of Language Teaching* (pp. 328–350). Oxford: Blackwell.
Hoey, M. (2005) *Lexical Priming: A New Theory of Words and Language*. Abingdon and New York: Routledge.

Hyland, K. (2008) As can be seen: Lexical bundles and disciplinary variation. *English for Specific Purposes* 27 (1), 4–21.

Integrate Ireland Language and Training (2003) *English Language Proficiency Benchmarks for non-English-speaking students at post-primary level.* Dublin: IILT.

Integrate Ireland Language and Training (2004) *European Language Portfolio for post-primary learners.* Dublin: IILT.

Jones, S. and Sinclair, J. (1974) English lexical collocations - A study in computational linguistics. *Cahiers de Lexicologie* 24 (1), 15–61.

Kostopoulou, S. (2012) Developing English language support for immigrant students in Irish post-primary schools: A corpus linguistics approach. Unpublished PhD thesis. University of Dublin, Trinity College.

Lewis, M. (1993) *The Lexical Approach.* Hove: Teacher Training Publications.

Lyons, Z. and Little, D. (2009) *English Language Support in Irish Post-primary Schools: Policy, Challenges and Deficits.* Dublin: Trinity College, Trinity Immigration Initiative.

McEnery, T. and Wilson, A. (1996) *Corpus Linguistics.* Edinburgh: Edinburgh University Press.

Milton, J. (2009) *Measuring Second Language Vocabulary Acquisition.* Bristol: Multilingual Matters.

Nation, I.S.P. (2001) *Learning Vocabulary in Another Language.* Cambridge: Cambridge University Press.

Nattinger, J. and DeCarrico, J. (1992) *Lexical Phrases and Language Teaching.* Oxford: Oxford University Press.

NCCA (National Council for Curriculum and Assessment) (2008) *Junior Certificate English – Draft syllabus for consultation.* Dublin: NCCA.

Pawley, A.K. and Syder, F.H. (1983) Two puzzles for linguistic theory: Nativelike selection and nativelike fluency. In J.C. Richards and R.W. Schmidt (eds) *Language and Communication* (pp. 191–226). London and New York: Longman.

Ravid, D. and Tolchinsky, L. (2002) Developing linguistic literacy: A comprehensive model. *Journal of Child Language* 29 (2), 419–448.

Scott, M. (2004) *WordSmith Tools Version 4.* Oxford: Oxford University Press.

Scott, M. and Tribble, C. (2006) *Textual Patterns: Keyword and Corpus Analysis in Language Education.* Amsterdam: Benjamins.

Sinclair, J. (ed.) (1987) *Collins COBUILD English Language Dictionary.* London: Collins.

Sinclair, J. (1991) *Corpus, Concordance, Collocation.* Oxford: Oxford University Press.

Sinclair, J. (2005) Corpus and text – basic principles. In M. Wynne (ed.) *Developing Linguistic Corpora: A Guide to Good Practice* (pp. 1–16). Oxford: Oxbow Books.

van Leeuwen, T. and Humphrey, S. (1996) On learning to look through a geographer's eyes. In R. Hasan and G. Williams (eds) *Literacy in Society* (29–49). London: Longman.

10 Assessing the Impact of English Language Support Programme Materials on Post-primary Language Support and Mainstream Subject Classrooms in Ireland

Zachary Lyons

This chapter is one of several in this book reporting on the work of the English Language Support Programme for post-primary schools (ELSP), part of the Trinity Immigration Initiative (Trinity College Dublin, 2007–2010). It outlines the background to the English language support materials that were developed for use in post-primary classrooms and considers the impact of the materials on teachers' daily practice. The impact study uses a mixed methods approach that combines internet metrics, surveys, interviews and classroom observation. The summary of combined findings suggests that the materials had the greatest impact when used by teachers who were willing and motivated to bring about change and incorporate new tools into the teaching and learning process. The study also suggests that teachers who received training in how to address EAL learners' needs tended to use the materials more frequently.

Introduction

Post-primary school teachers in Ireland use textbooks and other printed materials extensively as vehicles to convey curricular subject content to their students. Subject teachers often report that their students are not maximising their learning potential and are unable to engage with the domain-specific material at a level which ensures comprehension. The innovative approach to curricular language adopted by the Trinity Immigration Initiative's English Language Support Programme (ELSP, 2007–2010) is one way of improving the teaching and learning of the language used in post-primary subject classrooms. From 2007 to 2010 the ELSP developed and exploited an extensive corpus of post-primary subject textbooks, teacher guidelines and examination papers. The open corpus of nearly 5.2 million words supported the analysis of subject-specific language, which in turn informed the development of a large array of materials designed to support the teaching and learning of English as a second language across the first four proficiency levels of the *Common European Framework of Reference for Languages* (CEFR; Council of Europe, 2001).

ELSP Research in Post-primary Schools

Throughout the three years of its existence, the ELSP worked closely with 87 post-primary schools to document the understanding, attitudes and daily practice of language support teachers in dealing with the increasing diversity in classrooms. This research suggested that the challenge at post-primary level was particularly acute for a number of reasons, which are outlined below.

- The older EAL learners are when they arrive in Ireland, the more academic English they must learn in order to catch up with their native speaker peers. EAL students may sound fluent in English within one or two years because they can converse socially with others. However, it takes much longer for them to achieve the same fluency in academic language as their native-speaker peers.
- The academic English used in textbooks and in the classroom is more difficult to understand and cognitively much more demanding for students at this age. They must be able to interpret, infer and synthesise information, pick out main ideas, relate ideas and information to their background experience and recognise the conventions of different genres and their impact on text structure.

- The post-primary curriculum is delivered by subject specialists whose formation has not prepared them to take account of EAL students in their classes.
- Whereas the Department of Education and Skills (DES) funds teaching posts at primary level, it only pays for additional teaching hours at post-primary level. In some schools language support classes are assigned to teachers who do not have a full timetable but have no background in language teaching. This can mean that language support is both marginal and haphazard.
- This lack of adequately trained and supported EAL teachers within the system means that language support tends to be conflated with Special Educational Needs (SEN) and/or resource teaching.

The ELSP's documentation of attitudes and practice in post-primary English language support (Lyons & Little, 2009) indicated a need to move from a perceived emphasis on cultural adjustment and social skills, sometimes with damaging remedial overtones, to a focus on the language and learning skills, including lexico-grammatical skills, required by the curriculum. Sustained exploration of current practice both nationally and internationally revealed that successful language support consisted of a number of elements including: targeting the 'big ideas' of the content; accessing and building upon students' prior knowledge of the content; making sure that new information was comprehensible; using a variety of literacy and vocabulary activities; using cooperative learning activities; and using fair and appropriate assessment strategies.

Developing the ELSP Language Support Materials[1]

Figure 10.1 summarises the steps in the corpus analysis that underpinned the development of the ELSP learning materials. For each subject at both Junior and Senior Cycle (respectively lower and upper secondary), the contents of the most commonly used textbooks were scanned into a computer. The next step involved the use of concordancing software (Wordsmith Tools 4.0), which extracted keywords, collocations and grammar characteristics of the different curriculum subjects. Current teaching materials and methodologies attach much importance to learners' vocabulary acquisition: by learning new words, students can increase their listening, speaking, reading and writing vocabularies and can improve comprehension and production in the target language (Coady *et al.*, 1993).

Research suggests that communicative effectiveness is achieved more successfully by learners with a large vocabulary than by learners with a

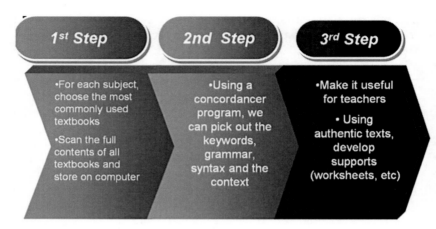

Figure 10.1 Steps involved in corpus analysis

smaller one, and measurements of vocabulary size have been shown to correlate positively with proficiency levels in reading and writing (de Bot *et al.*, 1997; Grabe & Stoller, 1997). Grabe (1991: 392) suggests that 'virtually all second language reading researchers agree that vocabulary development is a critical component of reading comprehension'. Research by Hazenberg and Hulstijn (1996) showed that second language university students tended to lack the academic vocabulary needed to read efficiently; they typically spent between one and two hours reading an assigned text that their native speaker classmates read in about 20 minutes. August *et al.* (2005) found that English language learners in post-primary classrooms who experienced slow vocabulary development were less able to comprehend classroom texts than their native speaker peers; they were also likely to perform poorly on assessments in these areas and were at risk of being diagnosed as learning disabled. Nassaji (2004) found that EAL students who had a larger vocabulary made more effective use of lexical inferencing strategies than their weaker peers.

Research by Barcroft (2004) suggests that the best retention is provided by vocabulary learning techniques that require deeper processing through form and meaning associations (the keyword method). Results also suggest that using the keyword method and direct L1 keyword-translation links in the classroom leads to better L2 vocabulary learning in the early stages of content learning. Research further suggests that explicit learning activities that focus on the word itself are essential for successful EAL vocabulary acquisition (Burke, 2004; Gonzalez, 1999; Johnson & Steele, 1996; Nation, 2003).

Vocabulary teaching research (Burke, 2004; Nation, 2003) suggests that there are several aspects that need to be taken into account when teaching

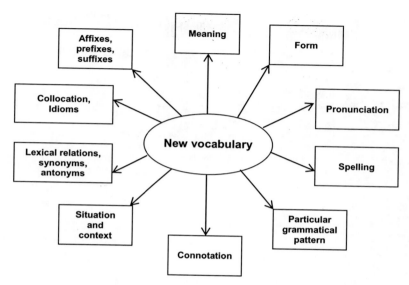

Figure 10.2 Aspects of lexis that need to be taken into account when teaching vocabulary

vocabulary (these are summarized in Figure 10.2). Most of this research implies that the goals of vocabulary teaching must go beyond simply covering a certain number of words on a word list. It is essential to teach techniques that help learners to understand what it means to know a lexical item, providing them with opportunities to use the items learnt but also helping them to develop, use and maintain effective written storage systems for their new vocabulary such as keyword lists, student diaries and so on. (Larsen-Freeman, 2000).

After discussion with our network of teachers and in the light of these research findings, we decided that our materials would focus on vocabulary learning and teaching, emphasising: formal features and grammar; collocation; denotation, connotation and appropriateness; meaning relationships such as synonymy and antonymy; and word, sentence and paragraph formation. Following intensive classroom trials involving 59 subject and language support teachers in 34 schools, 358 units of language support activity were developed for a variety of topic areas in most Junior and Senior Cycle subjects, each unit running to 25–28 pages. The units begin by presenting the key language for the topic in question, which is then exploited in a series of vocabulary-related activities, moving from gap-filling and cloze exercises, through spidergrams and matching activities, to 'writing frames' that help

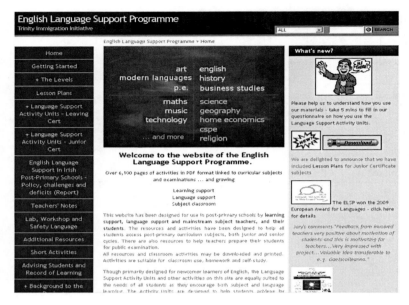

Figure 10.3 The ELSP website

learners to construct essays and exam answers. The progression of the activities approximates to the progression from A1 to B2 in the CEFR.

In addition to the topic-based units, the ELSP team also developed notes for teachers with suggestions for using the materials; additional resources which may be adapted for use across different subject areas and contexts; and a collection of short classroom activities designed to motivate learners and stimulate learning. All these materials were made freely available for download from the ELSP's website (http://www.elsp.ie; see Figure 10.3).[2] Materials and website won the 2009 European Language Label Award.

Impact Study

Teachers have been using these materials in English language support, special education and mainstream subject classrooms since January 2009. From June 2009 to June 2010 an impact study was carried out by the present author using the following instruments: an online survey of teacher feedback; internet usage metrics (Google Analytics); semi-structured focus group interviews with teachers; classroom observations; lesson plans, teachers' notes and teaching diaries; a teacher efficacy questionnaire; and a Levels of Use of the Innovation interview, rating the teachers' level of use and classroom observations.

Online survey (*N* = 143)

The online survey developed by the author consisted of 11 items on a five-point Likert scale, designed to measure strengths and weaknesses of the ELSP materials as perceived by teachers. In addition, two comment-style boxes were provided on the website's homepage from June 2009 to May 2010. Altogether 143 responses were collected. The reliability of the survey was satisfactory (Cronbach's alpha = 0.844). Because the research involved understanding teachers' usage of the ELSP materials the goal was to analyse the quantitative data for general response patterns to the Likert-scale items, and then to illustrate, through the qualitative comments, the teachers' opinions about the materials. The quantitative data were coded on the 5-point scale from *strongly disagree* to *strongly agree*; neutral responses were coded as zero. All data were entered into SPSS 17.0. The qualitative data were analysed through an inductive approach in which themes and patterns emerged from the data.

Internet usage metrics

Usage of the website was recorded for the period September 2009–June 2010 using Google Analytics. There were 14,435 absolute unique visitors to the site from Ireland, 42.22% of them return visitors (from the period before September 2009) and 57.78% of them new; and 68,745 page views, an average of 5.44 pages per visit. Visitors spent an average of 6.98 minutes on the site and there was a 23.71% bounce rate (the percentage of single-page visits and visits that terminated on the landing page). During this period 4.52% of visitors returned to the website between 101 and 200 times, and the site also recorded 10,492 visits from 115 other countries/territories. A total of 29,576 PDF files were downloaded, the most popular being teachers' notes followed (in descending order) by units in English, Mathematics, CSPE (Civic, Social and Political Education), Geography and History (see Table 10.1).

Focus group interviews with teachers (*N* = 15 teachers)

Focus group research draws on the data from a group discussion based upon a chosen topic or topics (Morgan, 1998b). Interviewers usually ask focus group participants to consider and answer questions, and then to make additional comments after listening to the responses of others (Patton, 1990).

Table 10.1 Use of learning objects by curriculum area

Category	Number of PDFs downloaded
Teachers' Notes	3211
English	2551
Mathematics	2390
CSPE	2377
Geography	2303
History	2297

Morgan (1997) notes that focus group research can usefully serve as a supplementary source to embellish another data source such as a survey, or as part of a multi-method study, and is a useful tool for programme evaluations (Patton, 1990). It is especially useful when a researcher needs more generalised group data rather than an 'individual account' (Morgan, 1997, 1998a). For the purpose of this study, I selected teachers with whom I had previously interacted when visiting schools for the purpose of the ELSP survey (Lyons & Little, 2009). Meetings were conducted in the teachers' schools and normally involved 5–8 teachers.

Classroom observation (*N* = 28 teachers)

Classroom observations of 18 language support, 2 learning support and 8 mainstream subject teachers (all were self-selecting after an appeal for participants from the researcher) in 14 schools were conducted between January and April 2010. Teachers were encouraged to follow their instructional plan without special alteration during the observations, which generally lasted between 30 and 50 minutes. Data interpretation involved a thematic analysis of observable behaviours. Teachers were further encouraged to provide materials such as lesson plans and anecdotal notes to show how the materials were being used and to chart their reflections on their use.

Teacher efficacy questionnaire (*N* = 71 teachers)

Teacher efficacy questionnaires were administered at the beginning and end of the 2009–2010 school year, in October 2009 and May 2010 respectively. Teacher efficacy – the extent to which teachers believe they will be able to bring about student learning – is important because teachers with positive beliefs about their instructional capacity are more likely to try out new teaching ideas and materials, particularly techniques that are difficult, involve risks and require control to be shared with students (Moore, 1990;

Shachar & Shmuelevitz, 1997). The questionnaire consisted of 12 items adapted for the purpose from Tschannen-Moran and Wolfolk Hoy (2001): four items for efficacy of engagement, four items for efficacy of teaching strategies and four items for efficacy of student management. The reliability of this adapted instrument, as it referred to teachers' self-efficacy beliefs about curricular literacy areas, was $\alpha = 0.85$ for the pre-test and $\alpha = 0.795$ for the post-test. The results of Cronbach's α reliability coefficients demonstrated an adequate level of reliability and indicated a high level of internal consistency among the items.

Levels of Use of the Innovation (*N* = 16 teachers)

As any educational change or innovation can be intimidating, it was important to have a framework for describing and discussing changes in levels of use of the ELSP materials. As I wanted to explore with each teacher in the study the extent of change in their use of these materials, I decided to use the Levels of Use of the Innovation instrument (LoU),[3] which has been used in educational settings to investigate the stages of change that individuals experience when an innovation is implemented. LoU focuses on the behaviours of individuals as they become more familiar with and more skilled in using an educational innovation. Educational innovations that entail changes in teacher thinking and practice typically emerge from the identification of a need or problem in teaching/learning either through research or by individuals working close to the problem. After an innovation has been created, the next step is to inform others about the innovation through normal communication channels.

Essentially, the LoU identifies the extent to which a teacher has implemented the instructional innovation in the classroom. LoU ratings are achieved through individual-focused interviews and long-term classroom observation (see Appendix 1 for some sample interview questions). The interview begins with a yes/no question and the remainder of the questions are based on the individual's response to this first question. Hall and Hord (2001) identified eight levels of use. Levels zero through two reflect non-user status but include headings such as 'orientation' and 'preparation' that indicate possible future use. Levels three through seven range from mechanical use of the innovation to a re-evaluation of programme quality. As the level of use increases, so does the user's understanding and level of innovation implementation. Table 10.2 reviews these levels. Each level of use is attached to a category that represents central functions that users of the innovation carry out when they are using it. The category descriptions at each level typify the behaviours in which users at that level are engaged.

Table 10.2 Levels of Use descriptors

Levels	Description
0 – Non-use	State in which the individual has little or no knowledge of the innovation, no involvement with it, and is doing nothing toward becoming involved.
1 – Orientation	State in which the individual has acquired or is acquiring information about the innovation and/or has explored its value orientation and what it will require.
2 – Preparation	State in which the user is preparing for first use of the innovation.
3 – Mechanical use	State in which the user focuses most effort on the short-term, day-to-day use of the innovation, with little time for reflection. Changes in use are made more to meet user needs than needs of students and others. The user is primarily engaged in an attempt to master tasks required to use the innovation. These attempts often result in disjointed and superficial use.
4 – Routine use	Use of the innovation is stabilised. Few if any changes are being made in ongoing use. Little preparation or thought is being given to improve innovation use or its consequences.
5 – Refinement	State in which the user varies the use of the innovation to increase the impact on students (or others) within their immediate sphere of influence. Variations in use are based on knowledge of both short and long-term consequences for students.
6 – Integration	State in which the user is combining own efforts to use the innovation with related activities of colleagues to achieve a collective impact on students within their common sphere of influence.
7 – Renewal	State in which the user re-evaluates the quality of use of the innovation, seeks major modifications of, or alternatives to, present innovation to achieve increased impact on students, examines new developments in the field, and explores new goals for self and the organization.

The Levels of Use of the Innovation uses focused interviews to describe the behaviours of individuals as they progress from familiarisation to increased sophistication with an innovation. The LoU was pilot-tested by the researcher in all nine schools in order to define and clarify descriptors for each item and to determine ways to achieve rater reliability. Scoring was determined using the protocols and rubrics (eight levels of use, the seven decision points, and the seven categories) outlined by Hall *et al.* (2006). Cronbach's alpha was 0.909 indicating a high degree of internal consistency. In addition to LoU scores, the interviews also provide an opportunity to collect qualitative data from teachers to illustrate conclusions. The comments made by the teachers were written down during the interview. These data were then used to help triangulate and illustrate research findings. In total, all 16 language support teachers from nine schools provided data for the LoU.

Some Findings

The internet usage metrics revealed a high uptake of the online materials, with 5.44 pages viewed and 6.98 minutes spent on average by each visitor viewing the materials. The low bounce rate (23.71%) indicated that 76.29% of visitors remained on the site to access and download the materials, leading to a high number of PDF files being downloaded (29,576).

Quantitative data from the online questionnaires were fed into SPSS 17.0 to obtain descriptive statistics. A framework was created to categorise teachers' responses to the focus group interview questions into themes in order to facilitate the analysis process. The interview transcripts were subjected to content analysis in order to identify emerging themes and trends. The interpretation of the questionnaire data was supported by the qualitative data obtained during the focus group interviews. The classroom observations were scored according to the Reformed Teaching Observation Protocol (RTOP; Lawson *et al.*, 2002). The RTOP protocol uses five subscales with five items on each subscale with each item described on a five point (0–4) Likert scale. The five subscales are Lesson Design and Implementation, Content – Propositional Pedagogic Knowledge, Content – Procedural Pedagogic Knowledge, Classroom Culture – Communication Interactions, and Classroom Culture – Student/Teacher Relationship.

The responses from the surveys and focus groups centred on two themes: (1) the appropriateness of the materials and (2) their impact. The survey findings suggested that the activities in the units were suitable for use in both language support and subject classrooms by language support, learning support and subject teachers (mean score 4.3 on a 5-point scale ranging from strongly agree '5' to strongly disagree '1'). Of the 143 respondents to the online survey, nearly 97% reported using the materials. 31.9% of this number said they used them at least a couple of times per week, while 68.1% reported daily usage. This confirms that the materials were being used. Among these users, 61.5% said they used the materials for between 20 and 40 minutes during a given class, while 38.5% reported using them for between one and

20 minutes. Some respondents indicated that a lower level of use could be attributed to shorter lessons or to the number of students in a given class.

Of the respondents who reported using the materials, 67% suggested that their teaching styles and practices had changed as a result. This is significant because it strongly suggests that teaching methods were modified as a result of using the materials. Most follow-up comments to this question supported this interpretation; some teachers, for example, reported that the materials offered them the flexibility to explore new and innovative approaches. Some 71% thought that the materials had a perceptible impact on students' attitudes and responses. Some teachers commented that they had noticed higher levels of engagement on the part of their students, which led to improved student focus and greater student–teacher and student–student interactivity.

The data from the focus group reflected the results outlined above: all 15 teachers interviewed agreed that the materials had been beneficial, with the majority reporting savings in time and effort, more convenience, greater choice, new strategies, and the possibility of differentiated instruction (some teachers commented that the materials allowed students with different learning needs to work at their own pace). Typical of teachers' responses was the following comment: 'Sometimes I just despair when I search for materials ... or I find too many resources and have the sense that I am not using the correct ones'. It was also felt that the materials could be used in a whole-school literacy approach as they would benefit some native English-speaking students who find it difficult to engage with the academic language required to access the curriculum. This was reflected in such comments as 'Little by little I am familiarising my [mainstream] teacher colleagues with the resources and activities of the ELSP'.

It is worth noting that of the teachers who were the most enthusiastic users of the materials, the majority (88%) had received some training in how best to use them in conjunction with the mainstream teacher and subject textbook(s). The majority of this training took place during continuing professional development days, school visits or ongoing email support provided by myself.

As well as encouraging students to activate their previous curricular and language knowledge, the teachers felt that the materials allowed them to focus on the language required to communicate curriculum content. This was confirmed during the classroom observations. Twenty-eight teachers permitted me to sit in on either language support classes or mainstream subject classes with a high EAL student population. It was evident that the challenge with EAL learners is to scaffold their comprehension of both the textbook and the teacher's instructions, to make visible the role language plays in the subject and to tap into the learners' relevant background knowledge. The use of the ELSP materials during these classes appeared to help the teacher to identify the main principles, objectives and key vocabulary of the lesson. Thanks to the materials' emphasis on keywords, teachers were able to pre-teach vocabulary, and this approach was reflected in their lesson plans and diaries.

The teachers felt that the materials accessed and built upon students' prior knowledge, perhaps acquired through their first language(s), and encouraged student interaction. The materials also allowed key vocabulary to be emphasised across all content areas (to take one example, the word *bank* in Figure 10.4). The use of the word in different subjects then permitted the teaching of the word's more common, extra-curricular meanings.

The teachers observed that the materials were ideal for cooperative learning activities and found the inclusion of writing frames (Figure 10.5) an extremely useful support for writing essays and exam answers.

Trends in the data from the teacher efficacy questionnaires suggest that teachers had enhanced levels of efficacy. Owing to the small sample size, a test of marginal homogeneity was conducted for specific and item-by-item analysis of self-efficacy, teaching strategies, and efficacy of student management. Testing of all five points of the Likert-type data was rejected

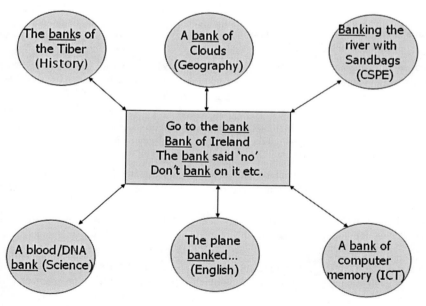

Figure 10.4 Teaching the word 'bank' across the curriculum

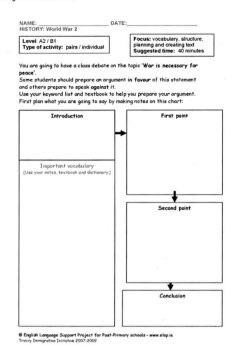

NAME: _____ DATE: _____
HISTORY: World War 2

Level: A2 / B1	Focus: vocabulary, structure,
Type of activity: pairs / individual	planning and creating text
	Suggested time: 40 minutes

You are going to have a class debate on the topic 'War is necessary for peace'.
Some students should prepare an argument in favour of this statement and others prepare to speak against it.
Use your keyword list and textbook to help you prepare your argument.
First plan what you are going to say by making notes on this chart:

Introduction	First point
Important vocabulary (Use your notes, textbook and dictionary.)	Second point
	Conclusion

© English Language Support Project for Post-Primary schools - www.elsp.ie
Trinity Immigration Initiative 2007-2009

Figure 10.5 Sample of writing frame from History unit

because there were not sufficient data to test hypotheses of interest. Cross tabulations were calculated to give frequency counts of the number of times a rating was given for a specific item. Mean scores for the 71 teachers who answered both pre- and post-test items were significantly higher on the post-test than on the pre-test for each of the three subscales. Paired t-tests showed that there were significant differences on the three sub-scales (Table 10.3).

Although many results were not statistically significant, the descriptive data indicate that by using the ELSP materials teachers became more aware of and better able to address learners' needs, such as understanding key grammatical categories (noun, verb, preposition, adverb, etc.); relating meaning to grammatical form in context; understanding the meanings expressed in texts; and expressing appropriate meaning in written work. According to the teachers, the materials provided exposure to a range of authentic texts with a range of functions. They also presented activities that involve planning, exchanging meanings (e.g. in pair work), bridging information gaps, problem solving, reading and listening comprehension, and writing with audience

Table 10.3 Paired t-test outcome of pre- and post-test scores of 71 teachers

		Mean	N	Mean difference	Standard Deviation	Standard error mean	t	p-value
Efficacy of engagement	Posttest	3.89	71	0.84	0.36	0.12	7.49	0.001**
	Pretest	3.05	71					
Efficacy of student management	Posttest	4.26	71	0.9	0.71	0.26	3.11	0.017*
	Pretest	3.36	71					
Efficacy of teaching strategies	Posttest	3.71	71	0.5	0.5	0.17	3.66	0.006**
	Pretest	3.21	71					

**$p < 0.01$; *$p < 0.05$

awareness. The teachers also thought that the materials were learner-centred and apt to encourage reflective teaching and learning in the context of the curriculum; that they would enhance student motivation; that they would make students more aware of the need for goal setting, planning and reflection on their learning; that they fitted in well with the Post-Primary Assessment Kit and with the CEFR scales; that they would foster the development of learning strategies and encourage the use of writing to support thinking and speaking; that they would support social interaction and negotiation in content learning activities; that they could be used to compile a dossier of work kept by the individual student or the teacher (useful in the event of a school inspection); and that they encouraged the use of target language to reflect on learning processes.

The LoU data revealed that the levels of use categories showing the greatest activity were 'routine' and 'mechanical' use. As indicated in Table 10.2, 'routine' suggests that the use of the innovation is stabilised and that activities involving the innovation are being managed smoothly as teachers use the innovation with minimum effort or stress. 'Mechanical use' indicates that the users are focusing efforts on learning about the innovation and developing knowledge and skills in order to use the innovation in a competent manner. One can deduce from these data that many teachers were still in the process of becoming competent users of the ELSP materials.

Concluding Remarks

While the results above indicate the teachers' perception of the efficacy of using the ELSP materials, the qualitative data and classroom observations suggest that the materials had the greatest impact when used by teachers who were willing and motivated to bring about change and incorporate new tools into the teaching and learning process. Teachers also felt that the benefits of using the materials would be neutralised unless teachers were adequately and appropriately trained in how best to use them in conjunction with other curricular tools such as textbooks and subject guides, as well as with the mainstream subject teachers. This research further highlighted that teachers who received training in how to address EAL learners' needs tended to use the materials more frequently; and teachers themselves were of the opinion that this use produced significant improvements in student achievement and in addressing language learning deficits. However, language learning deficits cannot be viewed in isolation. Although the evidence indicates that the ELSP materials can support educational change, they will have little impact without accompanying reform at the classroom, school and DES level.

When teachers were learning to integrate the ELSP materials into their classroom practice, the most important staff-development features seem to include opportunities to explore, reflect and collaborate with their peers while working on authentic teaching tasks and engaging in hands-on, active teaching. In essence, the principles for creating successful language learning environments for children apply to EAL teachers as well.

Finally, the research suggests that the ELSP's focus on teaching and learning the key vocabulary of curriculum subjects, emphasising word, sentence and paragraph formation, made a positive contribution to post-primary language support and mainstream subject teaching for EAL students in Irish classrooms.

Notes

(1) The units were developed by the author, Barbara Lazenby Simpson and Linda Richardson. Thanks are also due to Áine Larkin and Peter McGuire for their early work on the units and for invaluable insights provided by Stergiani Kostopoulou.
(2) This website is now hosted by the National Council for Curriculum and Assessment.
(3) The Levels of Use of an Innovation (LoU) is a dimension of the Concerns-Based Adoption Model (Hall *et al.*, 1973). Concerns-Based Adoption Model Diagnostic tools are used for assessing where the individual members of an organization are in relation to the adoption of an innovation where an innovation is defined as a product or process that produces or is the focus of change in teaching and learning to facilitate

student outcomes (Hall & Hord, 2001). According to Hall *et al.* (1975), the premise of this research methodology is that innovation adoption is a process that is experienced individually rather than collectively.

References

August, D., Carlo, M., Dressler, C. and Snow, C. (2005) The critical role of vocabulary development for English language learners. *Learning Disabilities Research and Practice* 20 (1), 50–57.

Barcroft, J. (2004) Second language vocabulary acquisition: A lexical input processing approach. *Foreign Language Annals* 37 (2), 200–208.

Burke, J. (2004) Learning the language of academic study. *Voices from the Middle* 11 (4), 37–42.

Coady, J., Magoto, J., Hubbard, P., Graney, J. and Mokhtari, K. (1993) High frequency vocabulary and reading proficiency in ESL readers. In T. Huckin, M. Haynes and J. Coady (eds) *Second Language Reading and Vocabulary Learning* (pp. 217–228). Norwood: Ablex.

Council of Europe (2001) *Common European Framework of Reference for Languages: Learning, Teaching Assessment.* Cambridge: Cambridge University Press.

de Bot, K., Paribakht, T.S. and Wesche, M. (1997) Toward a lexical processing model for the study of second language vocabulary acquisition. *Studies in Second Language Acquisition* 19 (3), 309–329.

Gonzalez, O. (1999) Building vocabulary: Dictionary consultation and the ESL student. *Journal of Adolescent and Adult Literacy* 43 (3), 264–270.

Grabe, W. (1991) Current developments in second language reading research. *TESOL Quarterly* 25 (3), 375–406.

Grabe, W. and Stoller, F. (1997) Reading and vocabulary development in a second language: A case study. In J. Coady and T. Huckin (eds) *Second Language Vocabulary Acquisition* (pp. 98–122). Cambridge: Cambridge University Press.

Hall, G., Dirksen, D.J. and George, A. (2006) *Measuring Implementation in Schools: Levels of Use.* Austin, Texas: Southwest Educational Development Laboratory.

Hall, G. and Hord, S. (2001) *Implementing Change: Patterns, Principles, and Potholes.* Boston, MA: Allyn & Bacon.

Hall, G., Loucks, S.F., Rutherford, W.L. and Newlove, B.W. (1975) Levels of use of the innovation: A framework for analyzing innovation adoption. *Journal of Teacher Education* 26 (1), 52–56.

Hall, G., Wallace, R.C. and Dossett, W.F. (1973) *A Developmental Conceptualization of the Adoption Process within Educational Institutions.* Austin: University of Texas, R&D Center for Teacher Education.

Hazenberg, S. and Hulstijn, J.H. (1996) Defining a minimal receptive second-language vocabulary for non-native university students: An empirical investigation. *Applied Linguistics* 17 (2), 145–163.

Johnson, D. and Steele, V. (1996) So many words, so little time: Helping college ESL learners acquire vocabulary-building strategies. *Journal of Adolescent and Adult Literacy* 39 (5), 348–357.

Larsen-Freeman, D. (2000) *Techniques and Principles in Language Teaching* (2nd edn). Oxford: Oxford University Press.

Lawson, A.E., Benford, R., Bloom, I., Carlson, M.P., Falconer, K.F., Hestenes, D.O., Judson, E., Piburn, M.D., Sawada, D., Turley, J. and Wyckoff, S. (2002) Evaluating college science and mathematics instruction: A reform effort that improves teaching skills. *Journal of College Science Teaching* 31 (6), 388–93.

Lyons, Z. and Little, D. (2009) *English Language Support in Irish Post-Primary Schools: Policy, Challenges and Deficits.* Dublin: Trinity College, Trinity Immigration Initiative. Available online at http://www.elsp.ie → Language Support.

Moore, P. (1990) The effect of science in-service programs on the self-efficacy belief of elementary school teachers. *Dissertation Abstracts International* 51 (3), 823-A.

Morgan, D.L. (1997) *Focus Groups as Qualitative Research.* Thousand Oaks, CA: Sage.

Morgan, D.L. (1998a) *The Focus Group Guidebook.* Thousand Oaks, CA: Sage.

Morgan, D.L. (1998b) *Planning Focus Groups.* Thousand Oaks, CA: Sage.

Nassaji, H. (2004) The relationship between depth of vocabulary knowledge and L2 learners' lexical inferencing strategy use and success. *Canadian Modern Language Review* 61 (1), 107–134.

Nation, P. (2003) Effective ways of building vocabulary knowledge. *ESL Magazine* 6 (4), 14–15.

Patton, M.Q. (1990) *Qualitative Evaluation and Research Methods.* Newbury Park, CA: Sage.

Shachar, H. and Shmuelevitz, H. (1997) Implementing cooperative learning, teacher collaboration and teachers' sense of efficacy in heterogeneous junior high schools. *Contemporary Educational Psychology* 23 (1), 53–72.

Tschannen-Moran, M. and Wolfolk Hoy, A. (2001) Teacher efficacy: Capturing an elusive construct. *Teaching and Teacher Education* 17 (7), 783–805.

Appendix

The Levels of Use about an Innovation questionnaire for the ELSP materials

1. Are you using the ELSP materials?

   - If yes, then proceed to 2
   - If no, then proceed to 10

2. What do you see as the strengths and weaknesses of the ELSP materials? Have you made any attempt to do anything about the weaknesses?

3. Are you currently looking for any information about the ELSP materials? What kind? For what purpose?

4. Do you ever talk with others about the ELSP materials? What do you tell them?

5. What do see as being the effects of the ELSP materials? In what way have you determined this? Are you doing any evaluating, either formally or informally, of your use of the ELSP materials? Have you received any feedback from the students?

6. Have you made any changes recently in how you use the ELSP materials? What? Why? How recently? Are you considering making any changes?

7. Are you working with others in your use of the ELSP materials? Have you made any changes in your use of the ELSP materials based on this coordination?

8. Are you considering or planning to make major modifications or to replace the ELSP materials at this time?

9. Have you made a decision to use the ELSP materials in the future? If so, when?

10. At this point in time, what kinds of questions are you asking about the ELSP materials?

11. What are you planning with respect to the ELSP materials? Can you tell me about any preparation or plans you have been making for the use of the ELSP materials?

12. Can you summarise for me where you see yourself right now in relation to the use of the ELSP materials?

Part 3

11 From English Language Support to Plurilingual Awareness

Déirdre Kirwan

The growth in linguistic diversity of the pupil population over almost two decades has provided a challenging, vibrant and stimulating experience for those who teach and learn in Scoil Bhríde Girls' National School (GNS), Blanchardstown, Dublin. Since 1994, when the first non-native speaker of English was enrolled, teachers have dealt with the issue of teaching English as a Second Language (ESL). Priority has been given to enabling ESL learners to have access to their peers and to the curriculum as quickly and efficiently as possible. As a result of their experience teaching in multilingual classrooms, some teachers have begun to develop plurilingual awareness among both newcomer and native-speaker pupils. Using the diverse languages that are present in the classroom, teachers cultivate an environment where children learn to communicate while increasing their awareness of the analytical elements involved in language learning in an informal way. This has created an interest in the exploration of language that has become a spontaneous practice for pupils and may, in addition, aid their understanding at more complex levels of thinking and learning. Such an approach can flourish only in a situation where all languages are valued and where the teacher is equipped professionally to cultivate this kind of educational environment. As principal of the school, the present writer was in the position of being able to observe the impact of the various interacting elements of this developing school milieu and the questions and challenges they posed.

Introduction

This chapter documents the response of school personnel in Scoil Bhríde Girls' School, Blanchardstown, Dublin, from 1994 to the present, to the enrolment of a culturally and linguistically diverse pupil population. Given that language is crucial to cognitive development, to the education process and ultimately to success in school, it was clear that a deeper knowledge of second language learning, in theory and recommended best practice for teaching and learning, would be necessary if all the children of the school were to be enabled to interact socially, gain access to the curriculum and reach their full potential as individuals. The insights gained from such knowledge would also help answer questions and address challenges in a more informed way. Accordingly, I undertook a research project that involved the collection, documentation, exploration and analysis of classroom data over a school year. This yielded a body of knowledge that helped cultivate new and more effective standards of awareness among the school's teachers and school management in relation to policy formation, pedagogical issues and the enhancement of the language learning environment.

With the passage of time and the development of language support structures within the school, the strengths and possibilities that ESL learners, with their varied plurilingual repertoires, can bring to the educational environment have become more apparent. In what follows particular reference will be made to the learning opportunities that are present in a linguistically diverse milieu and how these can be harnessed in order to develop an awareness of language in all children in the school, be they ESL pupils or native speakers of English. I shall argue that the integration of the language experience across the curriculum is of benefit in cultivating not only enhanced language learning in general, but also the development of a plurilingual consciousness. Reference will be made to specific examples of plurilingual interactions that have occurred in particular classes. I shall argue that the presence of ESL learners in the school environment can be a stimulus for their peers, who are essentially monolingual, to become conscious of, appreciate and value language and its communicative function. For this to happen, teachers must be professionally equipped to exploit the opportunities presented in such a multilingual milieu.

Issues in English Language Support

A question that caused concern during the early days of English language support was the disparity among newcomer learners in relation to their developing language proficiency. Some ESL pupils showed little inclination to engage verbally, whereas others demonstrated great eagerness to communicate. Whether or not parents should be encouraged to use their mother tongue when communicating with their children, was another question that was fraught with indecision. Provision for English language support was sanctioned by the Department of Education and Skills (DES) for the first two years of a child's enrolment in school. It was vitally important to ensure that this support was used to best advantage. With these concerns in mind, I decided to explore the language acquisition, learning and development of four groups of ESL learners ranging from Junior Infants (age 4) to Fifth Class (age 11) during the course of one school year, 2005–2006. *English Language Proficiency Benchmarks* (IILT, 2003) based on the proficiency levels defined in the *Common European Framework of Reference for Languages* (Council of Europe, 2001; CEFR) and developed by Integrate Ireland Language and Training for use in Irish primary schools were used as the assessment tool.

Analysis of the research data yielded the following findings:

- a silent phase did not necessarily preclude learning;
- learners who constantly engaged with and through the target language made considerable progress, as did autonomous learners;
- age was a factor, with children in the middle and senior levels making most rapid progress;
- children in the middle and senior groups who had previously developed literacy skills in their L1 made significantly more progress in English language proficiency than their counterparts who had not developed such skills.

These findings served to influence the manner in which English language support was developed and delivered in the school. The school's language policy acknowledged the importance of mother tongues and the importance of English language proficiency for educational success (Kirwan, 2009).

Plurilingual Awareness

As their experience of working in a multilingual environment has increased, some teachers have begun to cultivate language awareness in their pupils in such a way that the learner is enabled to be curious about, explore, analyse and reflect on language. Although we continue to acknowledge and celebrate linguistic and cultural diversity, the notion of language awareness has been expanded to a level where children are encouraged to use their mother tongue – or language of choice in terms of English, Irish or French – for oral expression and written activities. Writing activities are particularly effective where learners use two languages in a parallel text. This approach to language learning is effective in that it values and supports the learner's home language, while at the same time exposing monolingual pupils to the reality of communication in languages other than English (Hélot, 2011). It also develops teachers' learning and enables learners' implicit knowledge and understanding of language to be raised to an explicit level (Baker & Prys-Jones, 1998).

The language competences of newcomer children in these situations can be exploited to best advantage for themselves and their native speaker peers, and there is some evidence to support the notion that children within various groups and classes in the school are operating a plurilingual identity. There are occasions when individual children suggest comparisons between their own language and the language of instruction, English. This can take place in a whole-class setting and in informal discussion among themselves. There are also occasions when they have used the second language of the school, Irish, as a substitute for an English word or phrase and as a basis for comparison with their own L1. This demonstrates that children are making connections between their mother tongue and the languages they are currently learning.

Stimulated and encouraged by teacher suggestion, ESL children are generally the initial and usually most vocal contributors, particularly in the early stages of identifying linguistic comparisons and connections. This is to be expected as they are the people with facility in more than one language, so they have a base from which to make linguistic judgements and assessments.

Third Class

A recent example of this facility for language comparison occurred in a Third Class (age 9) with a newcomer population of 90%.The topic concerned marine life. In response to a child's contribution, the teacher had written the word 'octopus' on the whiteboard. She asked the children how many legs an octopus had and suggested to them that the word itself contained a clue as to the answer. There was silence in the room as children tried to work out what the answer might be. After a few moments, a Romanian child tentatively put up her hand and said she thought an octopus had eight legs. When asked what had brought her to this conclusion she answered that the 'oct' in octopus reminded her of the word 'ocht', which, in Irish, means eight. She was warmly congratulated by the teacher who wrote 'ocht' on the whiteboard. The same child also offered the information that 'opt' was the appropriate word in Romanian. The teacher then asked for the word for 'eight' in any language known to the children in the class. By the time this interaction finished, there were ten different words for 'eight' on the whiteboard. One of the most interesting aspects of this particular event was the response of the native speaker children in the class. They were fascinated as they watched the newcomers animatedly take part in this activity. Although they had no contribution to make themselves, in terms of adding to the list of words accumulating on the whiteboard, they were totally engaged as listeners and observers.

A few days later, in an informal pupil discussion on colour, a child of Irish/Nigerian parentage was overheard to say, in relation to the colour orange, 'In *my* language it's oráiste', ('oráiste' being the word in Irish). Irish is not this child's mother tongue, but her response provides an indication of a positive awareness in terms of language diversity. A further incident in this class showed that the idea of 'finding the clue in the word' had become embedded, for some children at least, when the same teacher introduced the topic of decimals and asked if any of the children were aware of the meaning or function of decimals. A native speaker of English suggested that perhaps decimals had something to do with the number ten and, therefore, with mathematics. The teacher was naturally delighted with this response and asked her how she had come to this conclusion. The response was that the word reminded her of 'deich', which is the Irish word for ten. There is scope for the claim, in this instance, that the child had made a linguistic connection that would be of benefit in terms of her recall, and indeed, her understanding of the concept of decimals.

In Scoil Bhríde GNS, the work of valuing each child's language begins from day one. As children progress through the school, evidence of their developing metalinguistic awareness becomes more apparent. An example of this occurred in Third Class where pupils responded to an allusion made by their teacher to *The Blue Danube* waltz. The children were interested in the music and as a follow-up to their short discussion the teacher asked them to find out the name of the composer and his place of origin. Some days later, two pupils, one of Ukrainian and the other of Filipino origin, brought to school an extensive piece of collaborative research that they had assembled on the topic of Johann Strauss and his music (see Figure 11.1). What was unusual in their presentation was that they had spontaneously included a section where they had recorded the title, *The Blue Danube,* in seven different languages and the country where each is spoken. What is significant is the fact that these children undertook this exercise of their own volition and made all decisions regarding content and presentation. They had taken

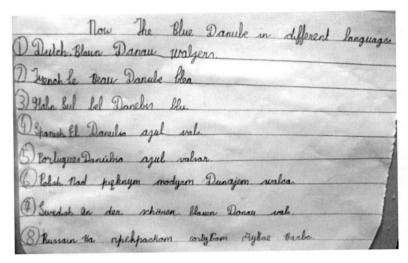

Figure 11.1 'The Blue Danube', Third Class (age 8)

charge of their own learning and had explored and learned more in terms of language, literacy and decision-making than the mere providing of answers to the questions posed by the teacher would do (Holec, 1981).The environment established in the classroom undoubtedly contributed to the independent pursuit of information on a topic that was of interest to the children.

Another example of increasing awareness of language diversity occurred during a lesson on the Second World War. An important question for the children concerned the languages that were spoken by those involved, giving rise to a lively discussion on the variety of languages used. In another instance, an enthusiastic response followed when another teacher asked all the non-native speakers of English in her Third Class to find out how to say 'my name is _____' in their own language. This exercise resulted 15 languages being identified, with many children able to write the phrase as well as produce it orally. One Chinese speaker whose education has happened entirely in Ireland proudly spoke in her language to the class and then announced 'I can't write it but she can' as she pointed to a child, newly arrived from China, who had attended school there for a number of years. This child promptly left her seat, took up a piece of chalk and confidently wrote in Chinese characters the phrase 'My name is _____', which she then read for the class. An interesting feature of this exercise was the palpable desire of the Irish children to be involved. As a result, a number of them came to the blackboard to record the phrase in Irish and then read it for the class. There was a sense that, although their overriding wish may have been simply to be included in the session with their newcomer counterparts, the occasion presented them with the opportunity to actually use their knowledge of Irish in a meaningful way. In these instances curriculum time is being used to best advantage, while language awareness is simultaneously being fostered (Department of Education and Science, 2005).

The children in this class have been encouraged by the language support teacher to listen to and engage with their ESL peers who were involved in a project of writing their own dual language books in the language support class. This activity, undertaken by the pupils in a collaborative way is followed by each individual writing her own story, first in English and subsequently in her mother tongue. All this is done under the guidance of the language support teacher. The stimulus is often an image, perhaps from a poster or photograph. The group looks at the image in silence allowing their thoughts to roam freely. With the help of the teacher, they then discuss their ideas. Attention is drawn to details in the picture that may be expanded and developed. Each child then draws her own story in her copy, a page of which has been divided into six sections. A list of the characters involved accompanies the drawing. This serves the purpose of clarifying the important elements of each story. It also acts as an aide-memoire for the following day when the children write their first draft of the story. Following this, there is further discussion and any amendments or changes are made. Final accounts are then written, with English on the right-hand page and the L1 version of the story on the left (see Figure 11.2 and Figure 11.3).

Some children will be able to write in their L1 unassisted. Others are helped by their parents at home. The books are then decorated, laminated and displayed. This is a moment of great pride for the children who visit adjoining classes and the Principal in order to show off their books and read their stories in both English and their respective mother tongues.

Fourth Class

As children become accustomed to looking for the connections between words in different languages, the practical application begins to fit more easily into lessons. In a Fourth Class (age 10), calculators were being used for a mathematics lesson. The teacher indicated that the right answer contained a nickname for a lion (when the calculator was turned upside down the numbers read as 'LEO'). A Romanian child volunteered that the word for lion in Romanian, 'leu', was almost the same as 'leo'. She explained that it was spelled with a 'u' but sounded the same, 'layoo'. Later, during an English lesson, the teacher asked if anyone knew the meaning of the word 'chauffeur',

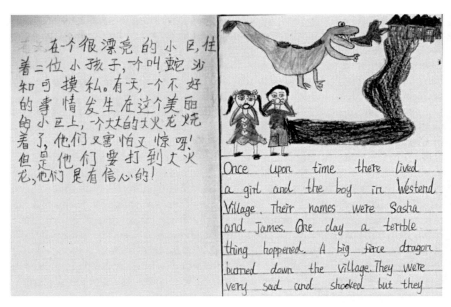

Figure 11.2 Dual language storybook written in Chinese (unassisted) and English (age 8)

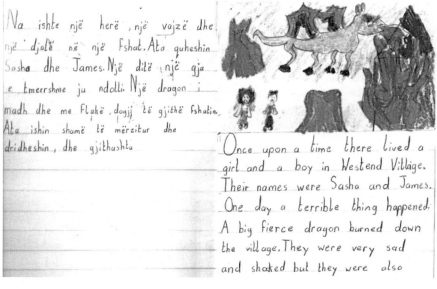

Figure 11.3 Dual language storybook written in Albanian (assisted) and English (age 8)

which occurred in a text the class was reading. She explained that the word had come from French. A Polish child volunteered that she knew what it meant as it was the same in Polish, i.e. 'szofer'. Another child said that she was not sure of the spelling but it sounded like the Ukrainian word 'shofer'. A further contribution came from a child who said the word was spelled in Romanian as 'şofer'. At this point, the teacher drew the attention of the class to the shape and position of the cedilla in Romanian and the 'z' in Polish. The general consensus from the class was that both characters served the purpose of changing the sound of 's'. A period then followed where all children present attempted to pronounce the word correctly in Polish and Romanian. Neither of the children from these countries was entirely happy with the efforts made by their peers, but all enjoyed the exercise.

Children in this group demonstrated their metalinguistic knowledge in their increasing ability to analyse language which they often do spontaneously. When the class was asked to write the sentence 'Hippopotamus means "river horse"' as part of a handwriting exercise, an ESL learner (age 9) commented that in Romanian, 'hippopotamus' was 'hipopotam'. She elaborated by saying that although the word is written with a final 'm' it is actually pronounced 'n'. She also stated that as double letters are not used in Romanian, there is only one 'p' in the initial part of the word. 'Hippopotab' was contributed by another ESL learner as the corresponding word in Urdu. A Polish child took up the discussion and explained that, while the word sounded the same in her language, it was written as 'hipopotamm' with the final 'mm' being pronounced as 'n'. She added that double consonants are used only occasionally in Polish. Another child took the analysis a step further when she provided the Lithuanian word 'begemotas' for the actual animal, adding 'but we say "hipopotamas" for a thing', i.e. a representation of the animal. She then went on to explain that if she had a pencil case in the shape of a hippopotamus she would say 'hipopotamo' (adjective) and that was because it was 'the pencil case *of* the hippopotamus'. The use of the genitive case in the Lithuanian language was being discussed with interest by children in Fourth Class!

In addition to this type of discussion, the children in this Fourth Class enjoyed using different languages for amusement. In Ireland, the roll call to determine who is present in class is traditionally conducted through the medium of Irish, each child answering with the word 'anseo' meaning 'present' or 'here'. Very often, these children will spontaneously decide to confirm their presence in a variety of languages, not necessarily always using their own L1. On the first morning that this happened, the children enjoyed the fun and one native speaker asked the teacher to speak in 'our language' meaning Irish. The teacher obliged and proceeded to correct that morning's mathematics test through Irish. She reported that very few problems were encountered by the children, regardless of their L1.

A further example of the interest shown by this class in language comparisons occurred at Christmas, when they were learning the hymn *Silent Night* in Irish. They used the linguistic expertise available to them in the class to translate the title into as many languages as possible. When they had accounted for five translations, one child asked the teacher if they could 'say it in English' as 'English is a language, isn't it?' When assembling the Christmas crib, the teacher referred to the manger. One of the children asked what a manger was and another child answered that it was a thing used for pig food, adding that her grandmother in Romania used one on her farm. This was supported by a child who said that it was used for animals' food. The teacher then wrote the word 'manger' on the whiteboard and explained that in French, the word 'manger' means 'to eat'. There was a collective 'Ah!' of understanding from the class as they made the connection between the word and its meaning.

A final example of the linguistic connections made by the children in this class occurred when a question in mathematics referred to an 'oblique line'. The teacher gave the meaning as 'diagonal'. An ESL learner (confusing the word) stated that in Romanian the word 'oblig' meant 'you must do something'. The teacher wrote the Romanian word on the whiteboard and asked for similar words in English. A native English speaker offered 'obligatory' and a child who had spent some time in the United States asked if 'obligate' was similar. The difference between the meanings of both 'oblique' and 'oblige' became clear and a Lithuanian child suggested that a good way to remember the difference was that the 'tail' on the letter 'q' in the word oblique was an oblique line itself. At this point, an English native speaker expressed the view that 'it's like as if every word you say in one language, you can say that it's like something else in French, or some other language'. Although it is not possible to provide tuition in all mother tongues that are found in the school, this type of teaching, where languages are viewed and explored in relation to each other rather than in isolation, goes some way to acknowledging, if not actually developing, an integrated language curriculum where children are encouraged to develop their plurilingual repertoires (Little, 2008).

The parallels between the benefits of the language awareness activities outlined and those discussed by researchers are worth noting. The children cited above display a significant ability to reflect on their own learning and discuss their insights in the target language (Little, 1991). Some pupils are also able to engage in analysis of their L1 and how it compares with or differs from English in relation to form and structure. Their writing, reflection and discussion all contribute to their own plurilingual development and help to make their monolingual peers aware of the value of being able to communicate in more than one language.

Drawing awareness of language into curriculum delivery allows for the use and cultivation of individual plurilingual repertoires that can be shared and explored with all members of the class group including ESL learners, native speaker pupils and even the teacher, who becomes a participant rather than a leader in these exercises (Long, 1988).This, of course, demands a willingness and a confidence on the part of the teacher to put herself in the role of the learner when it comes to the exploration of a mother tongue with which she is unfamiliar. This has its own benefits for learning as it helps to create an environment where the contributions of all are valued and everyone present is willing to learn from each other. Children are encouraged to question, compare and contrast the contributions from the different languages being explored. Cultivation of the active involvement of pupils in their own education leads to increased learner responsibility and better learning (Dam, 1995). Being involved in the planning of what and how to learn under the guidance of their teacher has been identified by students themselves as the optimal way of developing proficiency, not only in the target language but in their education generally (Dam & Little, 1999).

Impact of language awareness on additional language learning

In situations where language learning – be it English, Irish, foreign languages or mother tongues – is not only acknowledged but actively valued as an integral part of the comments, explorations and interesting data that form part of a vibrant primary classroom, it is possible to create an environment that values language itself. This may also be important in stimulating children's language learning potential and in supporting the affective factors that can play an important role in allowing language learners to interact confidently with the target language which, in the case of Ireland, may be either English or Irish depending on the ethos and focus of the school (Datta & Pomphrey, 2004; Krashen, 1982). Investigating language, promoting it and encouraging an atmosphere where it is deemed desirable to be able to communicate plurilingually undoubtedly has the capacity to stimulate an awareness of the function of language itself. In Ireland, the Irish language is taught from the beginning of primary education. The presence of newcomer peers who understand and express ideas and information that are important to them in a plurality of languages can be a very useful stimulus for promoting interest in the Irish language as a real and additional means of communication among Irish pupils who are native speakers of English and essentially monolingual. These latter have been stimulated to take part in classroom activities that would be closed to them in terms of their lack of understanding of various mother tongues but which they can access by using Irish. There is no doubt that they want to participate in the plurilingual interactions that take place in the classroom. These native speakers of English see and hear a variety of languages being used to tell stories, to interact and to exchange ideas, thus putting language in its proper setting as a means of communication. In order to be able to do the same thing, they are beginning to spontaneously make their own contributions using Irish. There is every possibility that for the first time they understand that the Irish language has a cognitive and communicative function and is not merely another topic on their timetable. In addition, children are reporting conversations from home, indicating that both they and their parents are discussing issues related to the Irish language. Dual language books are written by newcomers using English and their mother tongues. In Fifth Class, where French is taught for one hour per week, some children are choosing to translate their French class-work into Irish (see Figure 11.4). This approach to language learning can help to cultivate recognition of the fact that Irish has a communicative function in addition to its intrinsic value as part of Europe's linguistic heritage (Little, 2008).

The presence of newcomers and the cultivation of language awareness by teachers present the opportunity to counteract the downward trend in Irish language learning highlighted in a recent report (Harris, 2006).

Pedagogical environment

Two things are necessary if language awareness is to be integrated seamlessly into the delivery of the primary school curriculum. First, a classroom environment is required where awareness of language and how it works is promoted. Acknowledgement of the diversity of languages that exists within the school and wider community, and the enjoyment that can be had from playing with and analysing language, can be cultivated informally as part of daily routine, without in any way adding to an already overloaded curriculum. In order to encourage the kind of thinking that allows for the exploration of language, children must believe themselves to be in an environment where such analyses are not only accepted but also encouraged and valued, where their suggestions and insights are positively affirmed. There must be time, interest and enthusiasm for deviating from the content of the lesson in order to allow for some discussion of language and the various connections across linguistic boundaries. Invariably, teachers who are sensitive to the notion of plurilingualism and the value of additional language learning foster this awareness of language. They set in train a way of thinking that encourages

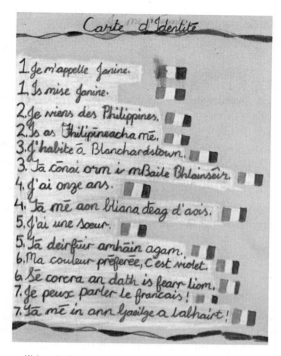

Figure 11.4 'Carte d'identité' in French and Irish (Filipino girl, age 11)

learners to approach a new word or phrase with a battery of information and a degree of flexibility of thought that would not otherwise be available to them. The foregoing examples of children's linguistic contributions show that cultivating a climate of language awareness can aid not only the development of a broad understanding of language itself but can also be an aid to increased understanding at levels of more complex thinking and learning that will support the development of literacy in addition to promoting an openness to different languages and cultures.

A vital element in the fostering of such a climate is that teachers be equipped with an understanding of the importance of languages in the life of the learner, both as a means of interpersonal communication and as the vehicle for cognitive development. An effective way for teachers to make learners' implicit understanding of languages explicit, and to contribute to their understanding of the rules that govern languages, is to include a language awareness component in the content of lessons, in addition to being ready to deviate from a lesson-plan as the opportunity arises. The suggestion that this way of perceiving and dealing with language needs to be cultivated at the pre-service level of teacher education is not innovative. Almost 40 years ago, the Bullock Report proposed that all preparatory courses for teachers should have 'at least 100 hours, and preferably 150 hours' devoted to language in education (Bullock, 1975: 338). Currently serving teachers who are tuned into language teaching, need to exploit occasions for cultivating language awareness. Provision needs to be made for those teachers who wish to learn how to maximise the opportunity to develop the language skills of all pupils, ESL learners and native speakers of English alike. Quality education for learners demands quality formation for those involved in its delivery (Little, 2010). In countries that place a high value on education, seeing it as the vehicle through which their societies are enabled to function successfully, support is provided for ESL pupils, teachers and schools in order to maximise learning outcomes. It is acknowledged that in order to help students to reach their potential, teachers need pre-service training of the highest standards in addition to on-going professional development throughout their careers (OECD, 2004).

Conclusion

Some teachers create opportunities for ESL learners to develop plurilingual competence to the point where it is often the pupils who spontaneously highlight aspects of similarity or interest between the languages with which they are familiar, thus adding to their understanding of the structure and form of language in general. There is evidence that this has had a positive effect, not only on ESL learners but on native speakers of English too.

If learners are to be supported in reaching their plurilingual potential, a key requirement is professional training in language education for teachers so that they will have the expertise and confidence to integrate linguistic experience across the curriculum and contribute to a broader perception of language on the part of their pupils.

References

Baker, C. and Prys-Jones, S. (1998) *Encyclopaedia of Bilingualism and Bilingual Education*. Clevedon: Multilingual Matters.

Bullock, A. (1975) *A Language for Life: Report of the Committee of Inquiry appointed by the Secretary of State for Education and Science*. London: Her Majesty's Stationery Office.

Council of Europe (2001) *Common European Framework of Reference for Languages: Learning, Teaching, Assessment*. Cambridge: Cambridge University Press.

Dam, L. (1995) *Learner Autonomy 3: From Theory to Classroom Practice*. Dublin: Authentik.

Dam, L. and Little, D. (1999) Autonomy in foreign language learning: from classroom practice to generalizable theory. In *Focus on the Classroom: Interpretations* (JALT 98 Proceedings) (pp. 127–136). Tokyo: Japan Association for Language Teaching.

Datta, M. and Pomphrey, C. (2004) *A World of Languages.* CiLT Young Pathfinder 10. London: Centre for Information on Language Teaching and Research.

Department of Education and Science (2005) *Language Policy Profile Ireland.* Dublin: Government Publications.http://www.coe.int/t/dg4/linguistic/Profils1_EN. asp#TopOfPage

Harris, J. (2006) *Irish in Primary Schools: Long-Term National Trends in Achievement.* Dublin: Department of Education and Skills.

Hélot, C. (2011) Children's literature in the multilingual classroom: Developing multilingual literacy acquisition. In C. Hélot and M. Ó Laoire (eds) *Language Policy for the Multilingual Classroom: Pedagogy of the Possible.* Bristol: Multilingual Matters.

Holec, H. (1981) *Autonomy and Foreign Language Learning.* Oxford: Pergamon.

IILT (2003) *English Language Proficiency Benchmarks for Non-English-speaking Pupils at Primary Level.* Dublin: Integrate Ireland Language and Training.

Kirwan, D. (2009) English language support for newcomer learners in Irish primary schools: A review and a case study. PhD thesis, University of Dublin, Trinity College.

Krashen, S. (1982) *Principles and Practice in Second Language Acquisition.* Oxford:Pergamon.

Little, D. (1991) *Learner Autonomy 1: Definitions, Issues and Problems.* Dublin: Authentik.

Little, D. (2008) *Todhchaí na dTeangacha i gCóras Oideachais na hÉireann: Beartas, Curaclam, Oideolaíocht/The Future of Languages in Irish Education: Policy, Curriculum, Pedagogy.* Baile Átha Cliath: Conradh na Gaeilge.

Little, D. (2010) Responding to the challenge of linguistic diversity: some Council of Europe principles and perspectives. Presentation made to 'Diversity: the key to Ireland's future', ELSTA Annual Conference, Dublin, 2 October.

Long, M.H. (1988) Instructed interlanguage development. In L. Beebe (ed.) *Issues in Second Language Acquisition: Multiple Perspectives.* Rowley, MA: Newbury House.

OECD (2004) *What Makes School Systems Perform? Seeing School Systems through the Prism of PISA.* Paris: OECD.

12 Language Diversity in Education: Evolving from Multilingual Education to Functional Multilingual Learning

Sven Sierens and Piet Van Avermaet

This chapter argues that multilingual education is not the only way of responding to language diversity at school; indeed, the large number of home languages present in many schools means that it is impossible to implement traditional modes of bi- and multilingual education. We begin by distinguishing between the multilingualism of educational elites, which involves languages that enjoy a high degree of cultural prestige, and the multilingualism of children from immigrant homes, whose languages are often felt to have no educational value. We then consider the arguments advanced in favour of monolingual and multilingual educational models. Proponents of the monolingual model believe that children from immigrant backgrounds should be immersed in the language of schooling; home languages have no role to play at school because they are seen as obstacles to effective acquisition of the majority language. Proponents of bilingual models, on the other hand, argue that education partly in the pupil's home language provides a more effective basis for learning the language of schooling than immersion, enhances pupils' self-esteem, and helps to preserve immigrant languages. A review of empirical research shows that there is no knock-down argument in favour of one particular model of language education; clearly, no single model can possibly suit all contexts. We propose that there are three strategies for responding to linguistic diversity at school: a constructive language policy; raising language awareness; and facilitating functional multilingual learning. This last is conceptualised as an alternative to the binary opposition between monolingual and multilingual education: a new pedagogical approach that exploits children's plurilingual repertoires as didactic capital for learning.

Introduction

The multilingual context of the school and classroom is a hot topic; it occupies the mind of schools, teachers and society as a whole. A lot of schools are struggling with their multilingual character. Specialists emphasise the importance of multilingualism: it's an added value for all who aim to work and function in Belgium and Europe. Children are encouraged to learn French, English, German, Spanish and Italian and, if possible, to use these new languages at home, with friends and on holidays. On the other hand we see that the multilingualism of immigrant minority children, adolescents and their parents is often considered to be an obstacle to success at school. In Flanders parents are sometimes encouraged to abandon their own language in their conversations with their children and give priority to Dutch. In some cases children are discouraged or forbidden to speak any language other than Dutch while at school. In most cases these measures are not inspired by a negative attitude towards the native language of immigrant minority children. Schools are truly concerned about the learning opportunities available to these children. Nevertheless we do have to wonder what will happen when they hear that learning foreign languages is important for their future but their own 'foreign' language presents an obstacle or handicap for that same future. This chapter explores this aspect of diversity in the educational system, arguing that there is no reason to limit language diversity at school to the organisation of multilingual education (first section). After all, this implies a quite unconventional structural change in the school programme and it is not the most relevant solution for all contexts and schools, given the fact that many schools in Flanders have become hyper-diverse, in the sense that often 10 or more different languages are spoken at school. To deal with linguistic diversity within an educational environment one can use three strategies: a constructive language policy (second section), linguistic sensitisation (third section) and functional multilingual learning (fourth section).

Monolingual versus Multilingual Education

Linguistic diversity or multilingualism is a specific aspect of diversity within the educational programme. Discussion about multilingualism long focused on language teaching: what type of language education fits pupils from underprivileged immigrant backgrounds the best, monolingual or multilingual? Schools choosing a multilingual approach can use more than one language of instruction and administration and teach their regular curriculum subjects in different languages.

In Flanders for ideological reasons, this remains a controversial topic when it comes to children and adolescents from ethnic minorities. However, instead of addressing this discussion from an ideological perspective, we will focus in this section on the available scientific research on the topic as both supporters and opponents seem to interpret the relevant research to suit their own purposes. Generally speaking, both in Flanders and internationally, the debates on this issue are divided into two camps: monolingual (language immersion or submersion) versus bilingual (or multilingual) education. Bilingual education has always been a controversial subject, especially in Flanders, with only a minority of people prepared to defend it. Even immigrant parents and students have different opinions on the subject (e.g. Agirdag, 2010). A clear example is the case of Proposition 227 in California in 1998. In a referendum on bilingual education many of the Hispanic parents voted in favour of the English-only initiative instead of the maintenance of bilingual education. Monolingual education is the mainstream model in the Flemish educational system and is generally supported by society at large. As the Flemish educational system is based on just one official language/language of schooling, most people find it self-evident and normal that students should speak only Dutch when at school (except of course for foreign language courses). The opinion of many teachers is in line with the monolingual norm of a Flemish federal state in which the administrative elite aims at linguistic homogeneity (Dutch) in all domains of public life (education, administration, the law) (Blommaert & Van Avermaet, 2008; Verlot, 2001). Most Flemish people also rely on their common sense and assume that the best way to learn a new language is to immerse yourself in it.

Supporters of monolingual education are convinced that it is best to immerse non-native children in the Dutch language as soon and as often as possible. Within this perspective the home language of these children has no place in the classroom or elsewhere in school and is not included in the curriculum. Supporters of language immersion programmes do not oppose the principle of multilingual education as such (see below). They are however convinced that the use in school of the home languages of children from underprivileged immigrant backgrounds will obstruct the development of proficiency in the language of schooling, a thorough knowledge of which is a precondition for educational success and integration in the labour market and in society generally.

A lot of Flemish schools consciously combine a language immersion model with a monolingual, Dutch-only language policy and ban non-native minority languages entirely. Sometimes these principles find their way into the school regulations (for example: 'no language other than Dutch allowed in the school yard') and students are punished for breaking the rules. Besides the argument of 'integration' there is also the aspect of 'time': whenever children use their home language, they steal away time they could use to practise Dutch and as such slow down the development of the second language (Van den Branden & Verhelst, 2008). From this point of view, some argue that multilingual education, or even the spontaneous use of the home language, leads to 'being zerolingual' and in the end to complete educational failure (Blommaert & Van Avermaet, 2008).

On the other side of the argument, the supporters of bilingual (or multilingual) education are convinced that children benefit from an education in their own language – in addition to or in combination with education in the majority language of schooling, which for them is a second language. They argue that education in the mother tongue provides a more effective basis for learning the language of schooling than total immersion. Second, learning their native language at school would improve the wellbeing of children from migrant backgrounds by supporting positive identity construction, which is known to have a positive influence on school results. Thirdly, teaching non-native languages helps these languages to survive over time. In this perspective providing educational support for minority immigrant languages is an objective of a government policy that acknowledges multilingual education as a positive feature of a multicultural society. The native languages of non-native students are valued for what they are, independent languages, and not simply used as a useful crutch to support the learning of Dutch or improve students' wellbeing and involvement.

The project 'Onderwijs in Eigen Taal en Cultuur' (OETC – Education in Minority Language and Culture) in the 1980s and 1990s experimented with the use of immigrant languages in Flemish schools. In most cases immigrant students were taken out of the classroom and were taught in their own language for a few hours a week (Turkish, Italian, Spanish, Arabic ...). They also followed additional courses in the history and culture of their home country. Initially the purpose was to prepare these children for a return to their home country. When immigrants took up their permanent residence in Belgium the initial objective of the OETC project was replaced by the motives and objectives mentioned in the preceding paragraph. The OETC project was quite successful in the 1980s when about 50 Flemish schools included it in their educational programme. Subsequently the project went downhill. The main reason was a lack of official Flemish financial and organisational support (Delrue *et al.*, 2006). In May 2011, the Flemish Minister of Education took the decision to stop subsidising the bicultural trilingual education model of Foyer, an NGO that ran six elementary schools in Brussels, in spite of its good international reputation and several positive evaluations carried out in the course of its 30-year existence (e.g. Byram & Leman, 1990). In 2008, the city of Ghent started a long-term experimental project in four elementary schools, 'Thuistaal in Onderwijs' (Home Language in Education), in which *inter alia* Turkish children are taught to read and write Turkish when they enter primary school before making the transition to Dutch literacy instruction (Stad Gent, 2007). Today this is the only type of (transitional) bilingual education available to immigrant students in Flanders.

Research on multilingual education: A critical reflection

The United States and Canada has extensive and long-term experience with bilingual and multilingual education for children from immigrant and minority groups, especially Spanish/English programmes for the Spanish-speaking population of the USA. This has generated extensive research on the possibilities and effects of the different language education models. When it comes to the development of theories on the subject, the USA has a lead over its European and Flemish counterparts as well. Supporters of bilingual education can fall back upon the insights of the Canadian educational psychologist Jim Cummins (1979, 2000). In the 1970s he formulated a theory to explain the effectiveness of bilingual education. Based on an interdependency theory of language acquisition, he states that the acquisition of educational skills such as counting, reading and writing, in a language other than the mother tongue, is facilitated by a high level of achievement in the first language. For example, the easiest way to learn to read and write is to learn it in the language you know best, your first language (or better, the formal version of your first language). The Canadian psychologist Wallace Lambert introduced two new concepts, 'additive' and 'subtractive' bilingualism. Additive bilingualism refers to the acquisition of a second language without losing the skills acquired in the first language, mostly because society appreciates and acknowledges both languages as being equal. Subtractive bilingualism refers to a situation in which the acquisition of a second language, often enjoying a higher status, threatens the first language and gradually replaces it. Subtractive bilingualism often occurs when society does not value the first language and feels that it should disappear or be put aside for the benefit of the second language (Lambert, 1974). This is the case for a lot of immigrants to western Europe.

In the USA the contradiction between monolingual and bilingual education grew into a political conflict between the 'English-only' movement and the supporters of 'bilingual education' (Padilla, 1991), which meant that the discussion found itself in an impasse (Köbben, 2003). The available research offered no clear direction, despite the fact that since the early 1970s hundreds of American studies had been published on the subject. However, in recent years new best-evidence syntheses (August & Shanahan, 2006; Genesee *et al.*, 2006) and meta-analyses (Francis *et al.*, 2006; Rolstad *et al.*, 2005) seem to have tipped the balance slightly in favour of strong types of bilingual education programmes. These have modest but consistent positive effects on English language and literacy learning. On the other hand, a recent study by Slavin and colleagues (2011) reports the results of a five-year evaluation study that compared the reading and speaking performance of Spanish-dominant children randomly assigned to transitional bilingual education (TBE) or structured English immersion (SIE) at the beginning of kindergarten. The findings suggest that children learn to read in English equally well in TBE and SIE.

Hence, it is clear that the discussion about which models work best is far from settled. The American scientific research continues to suffer from problems. First, a lot of studies have methodological shortcomings (they are insufficiently comparative, measure only short-term effects, fail to include pre-testing, etc.). After the necessary sifting little research remains from which we can draw well-founded conclusions. High-quality and long-term studies about, for example, transitional bilingual education are scarce, very difficult to set up, and often based on secondary data (e.g. Thomas & Collier, 2002). Ideally, research needs to take account of the following five considerations.

First, studies should commence the day children enter kindergarten and last until they switch to education given exclusively in the second language. This implies that studies should start with sufficient participants to ensure that despite the inevitable drop-out they are able to draw valid and reliable conclusions (Slavin & Cheung, 2005).

Second, there is the problem of comparing chalk and cheese: there are a great many different models of both monolingual and bilingual education (Archibald *et al.*, 2004; García, 2009). Comparing them demands a careful and fair analysis which is sometimes hard to find in the different studies. For example, some studies claim that a certain model of language education works very well, but when you take a closer look, you notice that the alternative models used for comparison are not sufficiently underpinned, i.e. they are not always built on firm foundations. Different studies show evidence of a positive effect of bilingual education, but when it turns out that these studies used as a control group children learning English according to the 'sink-or-swim' method (having to make it on their own without any didactic support), it is no wonder that bilingual education ends up with better scores.

Third, there seems to be a theoretical problem. Some experimental studies show a positive effect of bilingual education on different variables (second language acquisition, psycho-social variables, educational success) but they do not find evidence for Cummins's transfer hypothesis (see above), which thus remains contestable. One aspect is, however, worth remembering: when it comes to achieving a successful transfer from the first to the second language, minimal models, in which only a few hours of the weekly teaching package are devoted to the native language, fall short.

Fourth, scientific research focused for too long on the question of the best model for all circumstances and students: either the monolingual model or the bilingual model, not a combination of the two. This 'either-or' approach has its roots in the desire of policymakers and those active in the educational sector to find an easy way out, a 'catch-all' model. The research, however, suggests that an easy answer or a 'catch-all' model simply does not exist because most researchers start from the wrong basic assumption (Köbben, 2003).

And fifth, research that is premised on programme types rarely comes close to what actually happens in the classroom (Leung, 2005).

It is starting to become clear that all models – monolingual, bilingual and multilingual – have their advantages, and that the choice of a model should depend on the context in which it will be used and the category of students it will address. At least as important to effectively guarantee the quality of an educational model is the quality of the learning environment and the way the pre-conditions are met – both the educational and organisational ones (for example: clearly described objectives, a structured curriculum, guaranteed funding, competent and committed bilingual teachers, sound teaching materials, intensive cooperation within the school team) (August & Shanahan, 2006).

Discussion of monolingual and bilingual education is further complicated by the fact that the educational quality of schools and the educational success of pupils depend on other factors besides language education. There are several variables in play but unfortunately supporters of both educational models sometimes seem to forget this important detail in the heat of their discussions. Language is an important key to success but by no means the only one. However, a lot more research is needed before we can formulate clear and specific answers to new basic assumptions and questions about context and quality. In particular we need research in which researchers and practitioners join forces to develop scientifically supported practical models.

This detour around American research on educational models and theories brings us back to European and Flemish reality. The North American context is quite different from the European and Flemish one. Hence, caution is advisable when considering these North American results and conclusions from a European perspective. Is there a lesson to be learned from the research on language teaching done in Flanders and neighbouring countries? Unfortunately the answer is no. For a start, there are too few projects that focus on multilingual education. Second, western European studies suffer from the same methodological shortcomings as their American counterparts. The conclusion of recent reviews is quite clear: too few studies provide exclusive evidence for the positive impact of bilingual education on western European migrants with a low socio-economic status (Söhn, 2005). An as yet unpublished meta-analysis carried out by Gabrijela Reljić at the University of Luxembourg indicates that bilingual programmes that include the child's first language are superior to monolingual programmes in securing educational success, but this is based on only seven studies selected from over a hundred carried out in Europe to date.

On the other hand, studies providing conclusive evidence of the negative impact of bilingual education are scarce. This implies that in general bilingual education does not impair the development of the second language. This conclusion gives policy makers and those in charge of the educational sector an additional reason to play the card of the monolingual immersion model (which has already happened in The Netherlands). Scientific research does not support the theory that language immersion for non-native students is the best solution in all circumstances, but sometimes political choices are made based on ideology and emotion rather than on scientific research. The problem in Flanders boils down to the implementation of multilingual models. To be able to prove the effectiveness of multilingual models through research, and show that they sometimes work better than the language immersion model, the government should facilitate the implementation of these multilingual models. However, the government refuses to invest further in multilingual education for immigrants, arguing that research studies have failed to show positive effects when using this model. It is important to note that there is barely any research available on the topic and multilingual education (as offered in the OETC project) has never received proper support. In short, multilingual education has never had a chance to prove itself.

Research on multilingual education: The pros

In any case, the current is running against the supporters of multilingual education. To turn the tide they will have to come up with more convincing scientific arguments than they do today. The first argument they use refers to the positive effects of bilingualism. There is quite consistent evidence for cognitive benefits such as increased attention control, working memory, metalinguistic awareness, and abstract and symbolic representational skills even for low-SES groups (Adesope *et al.*, 2010).

A second argument refers to the more general positive results of bilingual education (Baker, 2006; Hamers & Blanc, 2000). At first sight, there is no room for debate here. Bilingual education is organised all over the world and is often successful. Much-quoted examples are the French immersion programmes for English-speaking students in Quebec (Canada) and the Catalan immersion programmes for Spanish-speaking students in Catalonia (Spain). There is little or no dispute about the positive effects of these programmes (Cummins, 2000; Huguet *et al.*, 2000; Lazaruk, 2007). But in almost all cases the programmes involve students who come from high-status groups and are learning a second language in a context of additive bilingualism. For example, English-speaking students who follow a French immersion programme in schools in Quebec are not asked to discard their native language. And in any case, English is far from being a threatened minority language. On the other hand, with a professional career in mind French-speaking students have everything to gain by learning English, the majority language in Canada. International and European private schools in and around Brussels also offer multilingual educational programmes and they encounter little opposition from those who advocate language immersion programmes for underprivileged students. These multilingual programmes target elite students who wish to learn high-prestige languages and who will enjoy greatly increased opportunities to build a successful international career, thanks to their multilingualism.

A third and last argument refers to the strong focus on successful models of multilingual education for immigrant minority groups that are implemented in totally different social, cultural or immigrant contexts. As we suggested earlier, using tried and tested American models can be quite treacherous. Different analyses show that one of the most powerful models of bilingual education is 'two-way bilingual education', a model in which children with different native languages learn each other's language through interaction in the classroom (for example, Spanish-speaking children learn English and English-speaking children learn Spanish). It remains an open question whether this should work in Flemish classes. When organising a few hours per week of native language education for immigrant children already causes a big stir in the media, one may wonder what kind of reaction this 'two-way bilingual education' model would evoke. The Netherlands and Germany have more experience with bilingual education programmes for immigrant minorities than Flanders. A synthesis of the available scientific research in both countries shows mixed results (Driessen, 2005; Gogolin, 2005; Söhn, 2005) and is not very promising for the supporters of bilingual education.

In conclusion, the scientific doubts about the added value of multilingual education in the context of subtractive bilingualism remain. Unfortunately this is the precise context in which a lot of non-native students in western Europe, and Flanders, find themselves (Hamers & Blanc, 2000). It is clear that policy makers and other actors in the educational sector have little difficulty with multilingual education in which students learn languages with a high level of prestige. This point of view derives from the fact that the educational systems of other European countries succeed in delivering competent multilingual students better than they used to. The international reputation of Flanders for multilingualism is at stake and the Flemish educational system threatens to lose its pole position (Delrue *et al.*, 2006). Knowledge of the French language is fading as well, mainly because the federalisation of the Belgian state has psychologically estranged the Flemish and French parts of the country and young people are starting to think in more international terms, preferring to learn English, Spanish and Chinese rather than French. Today multilingual education serves as a means to improve the quality of foreign language education for indigenous children preparing for a future career in a worldwide knowledge economy.

Since 2004 Flemish elementary schools have been allowed to incorporate 'language initiation' into their curriculum. This is an accessible and exploratory form of second language teaching in which children, and toddlers, are initiated in the French language in a playful way (through games, songs, chat sessions with a doll). Although language initiation can be used with any language, French has priority. CLIL (Content and Language Integrated Learning) was introduced in nine Flemish secondary schools and offered students the possibility of following courses such as history and geography in a foreign language (French, English or German). A lot of European countries are experimenting with the CLIL approach, including the Walloon provinces in Belgium (for an overview, see Mettewie & Housen, 2012). The present Flemish Minister of Education favours a more widespread implementation of CLIL but intends to confine it to secondary schools, on the ground that its introduction in elementary schools might endanger the Dutch language skills of too many non-native language speakers.

Dealing with Linguistic Diversity at School, Strategy 1: A Constructive Language Policy

It is quite clear that in the present Flemish educational system it is difficult to advocate an intensive multilingual educational programme in schools with a lot of non-native, underprivileged children, certainly not as a valid alternative to the dominant Dutch language immersion model. The Flemish educational system holds a double (contradictory?) attitude towards multilingual education: it is considered an enrichment for privileged native children but a threat to the Dutch language skills and educational success of non-native, underprivileged children.

This however does not mean that the home languages of these children are of no use at all. In cities such as Antwerp, Ghent, Genk, Mechelen and Brussels the percentage of children with home languages other than Dutch is on the rise; hence, language diversity is a given fact (for Brussels, see Verlot *et al.*, 2003). Their home language is one of the assets these children bring to school with them, and it is part of the multilingual repertoire the school can exploit rather than ignore or ban. After all, there are many ways of dealing with linguistic diversity, from banning home languages (or completely ignoring them) at one extreme to organising multilingual education at the other.

A first and easy option is to introduce a constructive and open language policy that includes all the languages students and their parents speak. This policy is based on separating the language immersion principle from a monolingual school regime. As mentioned before, a lot of schools link their Dutch language immersion programme to a 'Dutch only' school policy. They not only adopt the language immersion principle in class but use it as a criterion for judging all behaviour at school (in the corridors, the playground and the refectory). Children speaking different languages need to seize every opportunity to exercise their Dutch, especially because the opportunities to do so outside school are scarce. Experts on second language acquisition however have their doubts about the argument that 'the greater the exposure, the better'. After all, it seems non-native children master everyday Dutch quite easily (Van den Branden & Verhelst, 2008). Research by Jürgen Jaspers (2005) into the spontaneous speech of Moroccan adolescents in secondary schools in Antwerp shows that they fully mastered different varieties of informal Dutch. The most important obstacle for immigrant-origin students seems to be academic language, which is a lot more abstract and decontextualised than everyday Dutch (Laevers *et al.*, 2004). In secondary technical and vocational schools, non-native students have no problems with the spoken language (Dutch) but struggle to write it correctly. Apparently their 'language problem' has more to do with literacy than with the language in general. To improve the school language and literacy of these non-native students we need years of concentrated teaching effort (Van den Branden & Verhelst, 2008). The language of schooling is best taught and practised in class. Outside the classroom, students use informal varieties of Dutch (the vernacular and dialects). After all, the playground is not the place where children spontaneously use academic language to converse with each other, and the playground does not distinguish between children speaking minority languages and children (and teachers!) speaking Dutch: they all have the same urge to use their own vernacular. In this perspective banning home languages outside the classroom is far from the best way of approaching things.

Schools also use pedagogical arguments to defend their Dutch-only policy. By encouraging the use of Dutch for all communicative purposes, schools hope to discourage the negative use of home languages (name-calling, bullying, social exclusion, forming of cliques, secret language, copying notes). One of the underlying justifications for this approach refers to the fear of losing control over the classroom and the playground. Teachers fear that children who are using their native language will get up to mischief or talk about this and that instead of working on their assignments. When a teacher does not understand what his students are saying, he will find it a lot more difficult to intervene appropriately.

There is, however, a difference between positively encouraging the use of Dutch at school and in class and entirely banning home languages. Experience shows that schools with a student body characterised by a broad variety of home languages do not need to encourage the use of Dutch; students spontaneously use Dutch as their conversational lingua franca. Prohibitive rules about the use of home languages do not seem to improve the use of Dutch either. They do, however, stigmatise the home languages and linguistic varieties of the students and are difficult to put into practice. Controlling the languages used in the playground or the refectory is a near-impossible task; it is simply impossible to ban the use of home languages entirely, even when schools adopt a policy of imposing penalties (which is impossible for teachers to uphold). Schools may opt for a compromise: allowing the use of home languages during recreational time and demanding the use of Dutch in the classroom. When working with toddlers, strict rules about language use are difficult to maintain. Nursery school teachers often need to use the home language of children who to begin with do not understand or speak Dutch. To forbid toddlers to speak their home language is no more realistic than enforcing strict linguistic rules (how would you ever explain it to them?), and it is likely to have a negative impact on their wellbeing.

Responding to Linguistic Diversity at School, Strategy 2: Language Awareness Raising

The concept of language awareness presents schools with another way of responding to linguistic diversity (Devlieger et al., 2011). Interaction between students themselves and between students and teachers remains an important factor in the creation and moulding of attitudes and opinions about language, non-native speakers and multilingualism (Rampton, 1996). The arguments in favour of introducing language awareness in the classroom are primarily social-emotional and social-cultural: to make students receptive to linguistic diversity and to create a positive attitude towards all languages. Using this approach, schools try to stimulate students to open their mind to foreign languages and to motivate them to learn these languages. At the same time language awareness encourages the exchange of explicit knowledge and experience of when and how to use different languages.

Language awareness raising can be used for all foreign languages but it seems logical to focus on the home languages and linguistic varieties already present in the classroom (for example, when singing songs, counting, reciting the days of the week in different languages, language portfolio). A positive attitude towards linguistic diversity may contribute to a better understanding between children in the classroom and elsewhere at school (Genesee & Gándara, 1999; Wright & Tropp, 2005). It also contributes to the wellbeing and the development of the identity of non-native pupils. After all, this approach encourages these children to express their ideas, opinions and feelings in their own language. The attention paid to their native language increases its status, and because these children become experts in their mother tongue, their self-esteem increases and with it, indirectly, their motivation to learn and their school results. At the same time it is important to acknowledge that the 'language awareness' approach is opportunistic in the sense that teachers can only exploit the linguistic resources that pupils bring with them to the classroom, and these are infinitely variable.

The same principles can be applied to parents as well as children. Language awareness raising may be an important way of increasing their involvement (Hélot & Young, 2005): by considering them experts in their native language, just as their children are, schools acknowledge them and are likely to increase their self-confidence in their communication with members of the school team. In the same way parents can be encouraged to use their native language to help their children with their homework, which contradicts the common argument that they absolutely must master Dutch in order to help their children with their schoolwork.

To introduce language awareness into the school and classroom a realistic view of language and its use in an educational context is absolutely necessary. Language is still too often considered to be a linguistic system that should be reduced to an abstract, uniform standard.

In this approach multilingualism refers to 'multiple monolingualism': the level of competence one has in separate, independent languages (Blommaert & Van Avermaet, 2008).

Sociolinguists advocate a more subtle view of multilingualism as a reality in each and every one of us. Even when comparing individuals who speak the 'same' language, we find different linguistic varieties and spontaneous linguistic variation (Blommaert & Van Avermaet, 2008; Van den Branden & Verhelest, 2008). Hence, language is synonymous with multilingualism. Learning languages is a matter of expanding a multilingual repertoire of different genres, styles, registers and linguistic tools (for example: a spoken variant of the standard language, a spoken dialect, a sophisticated professional jargon, everyday jargon, writing, reading). No one can perfectly master all these different aspects of language and use them actively; no one can master a language entirely, not even their mother tongue. Multilingualism is a motley crew of different, unequally divided competences. Every aspect of language is specifically functional: mastering something in one domain doesn't guarantee success in another domain (for example: speaking English fluently doesn't mean you can write it fluently). In conclusion: outside school all students grow up in a multilingual environment; environments differ only according to the level of complexity and multiplicity. When it comes to immigrant children who speak a non-native language, it is clear that the environment they grow up in is characterised by a higher level of complexity and multiplicity.

Exploiting Linguistic Diversity at School, Strategy 3: Functional Multilingual Learning

Between language awareness raising and multilingual education there are still a multitude of opportunities waiting to be discovered that we group together under the banner of 'functional multilingual learning'. This entails that schools use the multilingual repertoires of children and adolescents to ring the changes on knowledge acquisition. Pupils' home languages and language varieties can be seen as didactic capital that is deliberately exploited to foster personal development and increase their chances of educational success. The first language may serve as a stepping stone to the acquisition of the second language and the learning of new content.

The teacher encourages students to help each other in the execution of a task (for example: explaining to a new student with limited knowledge of Dutch what to do) or in the preparation of group work. This approach demands a certain working method: the teaching environment should allow students to interact on a regular basis and should not be entirely teacher-directed. During such intensive interactive moments the linguistic skills of the students help to solve a mathematical problem or to execute a task in physics. We use an example from a physics class to clarify what we mean: levers. The class is divided into groups of three and all groups are given some specific items, some Dutch texts with pictures and illustrations about levers, and a web page of 'Technopolis' with online experiments with levers. Students need to work out how the principle of levers actually works. One of the groups consists of three Turkish students. They are allowed to speak different languages while working on the experiments but need to read the texts in Dutch. If one of them doesn't understand the Dutch text or some parts of it, the other two are allowed to explain in Turkish; and if one of the students doesn't understand an instruction given by the Technopolis website, the others are allowed to clarify the instruction in Dutch. When the teacher joins this particular group he can give the students tips to get back on track if they should need them or give feedback/'feed forward' on how they have performed the task so far. In this way the teacher can assess whether the teaching process, which has taken place in a multilingual context, went well. Nine out of ten teachers will use Dutch as the language of instruction. This approach has several advantages: first the teacher reinforces the insights the students gained about how a lever works and offers adjustments where necessary. When student A explains something to student B in Turkish and the teacher paraphrases this in Dutch, the topics which are acquired in Turkish will reinforce the acquisition of certain concepts and insights about levers in Dutch. This is the core of functional multilingual learning; the insights about levers are gained using different linguistic pathways and academic language skills in Turkish and Dutch are both reinforced. Finally we wish to draw attention to the fact that in everyday life a fine line separates language awareness and the functional use of different languages; especially in kindergarten one approach merges imperceptibly with the other.

Scientific research into the functional applicability of home languages in the classroom is quite recent but shows promising results. Various studies in different countries conclude that when schools acknowledge and use the multilingual repertoires of the students, they present them with better chances of educational success (for example: Jaffe, 2003; Martin-Jones & Saxena, 2001; Moodley, 2007; Moschkovich, 2002; Olivares & Lemberger, 2002; Olmedo, 2003; Peterson & Heywood, 2007; Verhelst & Verheyden, 2003).

An important advantage of this approach lies in the fact that the didactic use of home languages can be introduced into existing courses as a leitmotif. There is no need to alter the curriculum and adapt it to a multilingual approach. What is more, it is not necessary for teachers to know every single home language themselves. The most important aspect of the discussion is the recognition of linguistic diversity at school as an added value rather than a 'problem' or 'deficit'. Linguistic diversity should be used to a maximum to create the best learning opportunities for all children.

To Conclude

It is important to recognise that besides the school repertoire that children need to acquire, they also bring several additional repertoires to school (in Flanders another variety of Dutch, Berber, French, Arabic, Turkish, Polish and so on). If we fail to recognise this diversity as an opportunity for learning and promoting equal opportunities, and consider only one repertoire as the exclusive norm for learning, that repertoire will be assigned a higher value than the others because it is accidentally used more frequently in certain social circles and less in others. If schools advocate the exclusive use of this repertoire, children living in social circles using this repertoire will have a huge head start. And, if schools fail to include the other repertoires as didactic support for the learning process, children using these repertoires will have a lot of catching up to do before they even start their educational career.

In this chapter we have explored the possibilities of exploiting the linguistic diversity in the educational system as an asset for learning, based on the adoption of three strategies: a constructive language policy, linguistic sensitisation and functional multilingual learning.

References

Adesope, O.O., Lavin, T., Thompson, T. and Ungerleider, C. (2010) A sytematic review and meta-analysis of the cognitive correlates of bilingualism. *Review of Educational Research* 80, 207–245.

Agirdag, O. (2010) Exploring bilingualism in a monolingual school system: Insights from Turkish and native students from Belgian schools. *British Journal of Sociology of Education* 3, 307–321.

Archibald, J., Roy, S., Harmel, S., Jesney, K., Dewey, E., Moisik, S. and Lessard, P. (2004) *A Review of the Literature on Second Language Learning. Prepared by the Language Research Centre (LRC) of the University of Calgary*. Alberta: Alberta Learning.

August, D. and Shanahan, T. (eds) (2006) *Developing Literacy in Second-Language Learners: Report of the National Literacy Panel on Language-Minority Children and Youth*. Mahwah, NJ: Lawrence Erlbaum.

Baker, C. (2006) *Foundations of Bilingual Education and Bilingualism* (4th edn). Clevedon: Multilingual Matters.

Blommaert, J. and Van Avermaet, P. (2008) *Taal, onderwijs en de samenleving. De kloof tussen beleid en realiteit*. Berchem: Epo.

Byram, M. and Leman, J. (eds) (1990) *Bicultural and Trilingual Education*. Clevedon: Multilingual Matters.

Cummins, J. (1979) Linguistic interdependence and the educational development of bilingual children. *Review of Educational Research* 49, 222–251.

Cummins, J. (2000) *Language, Power and Pedagogy: Bilingual Children in the Crossfire*. Clevedon: Multilingual Matters.

Delrue, K., Loobuyck, P., Pelleriaux, K., Sierens, S. and Van Houtte, M. (2006) Uit het verdomhoekje van het Vlaamse onderwijs: comprehensief secundair onderwijs, concentratiescholen en meertalig onderwijs. In S. Sierens, M. Van Houtte, P. Loobuyck, K. Delrue and K. Pelleriaux, K. (eds) *Onderwijs onderweg in de immigratiesamenleving* (pp. 191–214). Gent: Academia Press.

Devlieger, M., Frijns, C. and Sierens, S. (2011) *Wetenschappelijk rapport over talensensibilisering in de Vlaamse onderwijscontext: Literatuurstudie praktijkgericht onderwijsonderzoek in opdracht van de Vlaamse OnderwijsRaad*. Brussels: Flemish Education Council.

Driessen, G. (2005) From cure to curse: The rise and fall of bilingual education programs in the Netherlands. In J. Söhn (ed.) *The Effectiveness of Bilingual School Programs for Immigrant Children* (pp. 77–107). Berlin: WZB/AKI.

Francis, D.J., Lesaux, N. and August, D. (2006) Language of instruction. In D. August and T. Shanahan (eds), *Developing Literacy in Second-language Learners: Report of the National Literacy Panel on Language-minority Children and Youth* (pp. 365–413). Mahwah, NJ: Erlbaum.

García, O. (2009) *Bilingual Education in the 21st Century: A Global Perspective*. Oxford: Wiley-Blackwell.

Genesee, F. and Gándara, P. (1999) Bilingual education programs: A cross-national perspective. *Journal of Social Issues* 55, 665–685.

Genesee, F., Lindholm-Leary, K., Saunders, W. and Christian, D. (eds) (2006) *Educating English Language Learners: A Synthesis of Research Evidence*. Cambridge: Cambridge University Press.

Gogolin, I. (2005) Bilingual education – The German experience and debate. In J. Söhn (ed.) *The Effectiveness of Bilingual School Programs for Immigrant Children* (pp. 133–143). Berlin: WZB/AKI.

Hamers, J.F. and Blanc, M.H.A. (2000) *Bilinguality and Bilingualism* (2nd edn). Cambridge: Cambridge University Press.

Hélot, C. and Young, A. (2005) The notion of diversity in language education: Policy and practice at primary level in France. *Language, Culture and Curriculum* 18, 242–257.

Huguet, A., Vila, I. and Llurda, A. (2000) Minority language education in unbalanced bilingual situations: A case for the linguistic interdependence hypothesis. *Journal of Psycholinguistic Research* 29, 313–333.

Jaffe, A. (2003) Talk around text: Literacy practices, cultural identity and authority in a Corsican bilingual classroom. *International Journal of Bilingual Education and Bilingualism* 6, 202–220.

Jaspers, J. (2005) Linguistic sabotage in a context of monolingualism and standardization. *Language and Communication* 25, 279–297.

Köbben, A.J.F. (2003) Het partiële gelijk: pro en contra het 'Onderwijs in de Eigen taal'. In *Het gevecht met de engel* (pp. 122–134). Amsterdam: Mets & Schilt.

Laevers, F., Van den Branden, K. and Verlot, M. (2004) *Beter, breder en met meer kleur. Onderwijs voor kwetsbare leerlingen in Vlaanderen. Een terugblik en suggesties voor de toekomst*. Leuven: Steunpunt Gelijke Onderwijskansen.

Lambert, W.E. (1974) Culture and language as factors in learning and education. In F.E. Aboud and R.E. Meade (eds) *Bilingualism: Psychological, Social and Educational Implications* (pp. 91–127). Bellingham: Western Washington State College.

Lazaruk, W. (2007) Linguistic, academic and cognitive benefits of French immersion. *The Canadian Modern Language Review* 63, 605–628.

Leung, C. (2005) Language and content in bilingual education. *Linguistics and Education* 16, 238–252.

Martin-Jones, M. and Saxena, M. (2001) Turn-taking and the positioning of bilingual participants in classroom discoruse: Insights from primary schools in Britain. In M. Heller and M. Martin-Jones (eds) *Voices of Authority and Linguistic Difference* (pp. 117–138). London: Ablex.

Mettewie, L. and Housen, A. (2012) Challenging language education in Belgium. Dutch, French, English and other foreign languages in the school curriculum: Experiments and policies in Flanders, Wallonia and Brussels. Facultés universitaires de Namur/Vrije universiteit Brussel. Available online at http://www.rethinkingbelgium.eu/rebel-initiative-files/events/sixth-public-event-languages-school-curriculum-and-school-registration-admission-policies/Mettewie-Housen.pdf

Moodley, V. (2007) Codeswitching in the multilingual English first language classroom. *International Journal of Bilingual Education and Bilingualism* 10, 707–722.

Moschkovich, J. (2002) A situated and sociocultural perspective on bilingual mathematics learners. *Mathematical Thinking and Learning* 4, 189–212.

Olivares, R.A. and Lemberger, N. (2002) Identifying and applying the communicative and the constructivist approaches to facilitate transfer of knowledge in the bilingual classroom. *International Journal of Bilingual Education and Bilingualism* 5, 72–83.

Olmedo, I.M. (2003) Language mediation among emergent bilingual children. *Linguistics and Education* 14, 143–162.

Padilla, A.M. (1991) English only vs. bilingual education: Ensuring a language-competent society. *Journal of Education* 173, 38–51.

Peterson, S.S. and Heywood, D. (2007) Contributions of families' linguistic, social, and cultural capital to minority language children's literacy: Parents', teachers', and principals' perspectives. *The Canadian Modern Language Review* 63, 517–538.

Rampton, B. (1996) *Crossing: Language and Ethnicity among Adolescents*. London: Longman.

Rolstad, K., Mahoney, K. and Glass, G.V. (2005) The big picture: A meta-analysis of program effectiveness research on English language learners. *Education Policy* 19, 572–594.

Slavin, R.E. and Cheung, A. (2005) A synthesis of research on language of reading: Instruction for English language learners. *Review of Educational Research* 75, 247–284.

Slavin, R.E., Madden, N., Calderón, M., Chamberlain, A. and Hennessy, M. (2011) Reading and language outcomes of a multiyear randomized evaluation of transitional bilingual education. *Educational Evaluation and Policy Analysis* 33, 47–58.

Söhn, J. (2005) *Zweisprachiger Schulunterricht für Migrantenkinder: Ergebnisse der Evaluationsforschung zu seinen Auswirkungen auf Zweitspracherwerb und Schulerfolg*. Berlin: WZB/AKI.

Stad Gent (2007) *Basistekst 'Thuistaal in onderwijs'*. Gent: Stad Gent, DOOSG, Pedagogische Begeleidingsdienst.

Thomas, W.P. and Collier, V.P. (2002) *A National Study of School Effectiveness for Language Minority Students' Long-term Academic Achievement*. Santa Cruz, CA: Center for Research on Education, Diversity and Excellence, University of California-Santa Cruz.

Van den Branden, K. and Verhelst, M. (2008) Naar een volwaardig talenbeleid. Omgaan met meertaligheid in het Vlaams onderwijs. *TORB (Tijdschrift voor Onderwijsrecht en Onderwijsbeleid)* 2007–2008, 315–332.

Verhelst, M. and Verheyden, L. (2003) *Eindrapport Pilootproject Circus Kiekeboe*. Leuven: K.U. Leuven, Centrum voor Taal & Migratie.

Verlot, M. (2001) *Werken aan integratie. Het minderheden- en het onderwijsbeleid in de Franse en Vlaamse Gemeenschap van België (1988–1998)*. Leuven: Acco.

Verlot, M., Delrue, K., Extra, G. and Yağmur, K. (2003) *Meertaligheid in Brussel. De status van allochtone talen thuis en op school*. Amsterdam: European Cultural Foundation.

Wright, S.C. and Tropp, L.R. (2005) Language and intergroup contact: Investigating the impact of bilingual instruction on children's intergroup attitudes. *Group Processes and Intergroup Relations* 8, 309–328.

13 Exploring the Use of Migrant Languages to Support Learning in Mainstream Classrooms in France

Nathalie Auger

Exploiting learners' L1 proficiency in multilingual classrooms has still to find a place on the educational agenda in France despite interesting experiments in the promotion of language awareness ('éveil aux langues') carried out by Candelier (e.g. 2003). On both sides of the Atlantic, research findings support the view that learners' L1 is always a good foundation for the learning of second/additional languages (e.g. Cummins, 2001; Lüdi & Py, 1986). Nevertheless, until 2002 (MEN 2002b, 2002c, 2002d) the French educational system treated mother tongues other than French as a handicap.

At the beginning of 2000 I set out to discover whether immigrant pupils' mother tongues were used in classrooms. I first studied official policies on teaching immigrant pupils and then observed classroom activities. This ethnographic approach was complemented by interviews with pupils, teachers and parents. My analyses confirmed the general impression that the use of migrant languages is rare; mostly it is thought to be a threat to the teaching and learning of French. My exploration of the different reasons for these beliefs and practices leads into a discussion of how migrant languages can be used in schools and the benefits of such an approach.

General Policies, Specific Pedagogy and Impact on Migrant Languages

I begin this section by summarising the results of my study of policy documents, then go on to describe what I observed in schools and classrooms.

General policy and its impact on migrant pupils and their plurilingual development

A double bind: Welcoming migrants and rejecting their languages

In France discussion of immigration policy has tended to be torn between assimilation and integration. The French motto is 'liberty, equality and fraternity', and France sees itself as a country that is hospitable to immigrants. French schools have always been obliged by law to accept migrant pupils even if their parents came to France illegally. This law and the country's self-image could have led to the use of migrant languages in schools, but this did not happen; other laws and the economic crisis had a completely different effect from what might have been expected. For instance, starting in the late 1970s various bi-lateral agreements were signed between France and immigrants' countries of origin. The aim was to teach newly arrived migrant children their parents' mother tongue. The problem, which still exists, was that there was no connection between the countries of origin and French schools. Language teachers from immigrant countries do not work with French teachers; they give language lessons to pupils outside school. This is regrettable, considering that home languages could support the learning of French and foreign languages.

Languages, the market place and attitudes towards French in France

As Bourdieu (1982) and the sociolinguists Boyer (1997) and Calvet (1994) have argued, the vitality and image of a language are linked to its economic power. Immigrant languages have very little value in the market place. On the other hand, France has always used its national language as an instrument of political and economic power. In order to maintain unity in the country after the 1789 Revolution, one of the objectives was to 'eliminate' (this word was used in texts written by Abbé Grégoire in 1794) other languages (Breton, Occitan, etc.). Until the middle of the 20th century in France, it was 'forbidden either to speak a regional language or to spit', as was written on notices in schools and some public spaces. French schools are still reluctant to give value to migrant or regional languages, but also to any deviation from the norm that is represented by the positive image of the Parisian standard adopted by the media. Social, generational, sexual, geographical and even oral variations from the standard are seen as dangerous for the development of French at school. Of course, this is a way of reproducing elites and preventing people from other classes from gaining power in society (Bourdieu, 1970). Societies usually value bilingualism in languages of high prestige, whereas bilingualism that includes a language of low prestige is often treated as an educational handicap, an obstacle to acquiring the dominant language.

A new direction in the 2000s: Attempts to change the negative image of migrant languages

These traditional attitudes help to explain why migrant languages used to be described as a 'handicap' in the official texts of the French Ministry of Education, and why it was impossible to imagine using them as an asset to develop proficiency in French and bi/plurilingualism.

But in the 2000s the negative image of deprived migrant groups and 'handicapped' native languages began to change in official documents (MEN, 2002b, 2000c, 2000d). Previously the same institutions were responsible for migrant schooling and for providing support in deprived suburbs; now these two functions were assigned to different institutions. In other words, there was an attempt to decouple economic difficulties and language learning, although some politicians continue to link delinquency with lack of proficiency in French (Benisti, 2004; Bentolila, 2007), despite arguments to the contrary from university researchers in linguistics. Assimilation via language is the aim of the hidden French language curriculum; that is why it is so difficult to integrate the use of migrant pupils' languages with mainstream teaching. This particular version of assimilation seeks to unify the nation by allowing only the French language, which contradicts France's multilingual and multicultural reality and denies identity and autonomy to migrant communities.

Ethnographic studies in classrooms: Difficulties in using migrant languages

Co-constructing ethnographic data in schools with teachers, pupils, parents, materials

The study started in 2002 in schools in the south of France and is on-going at the time of writing (Gard and Hérault regions). The research was first carried out in five primary schools (for 6 to 11-year-olds), then it was expanded to include four secondary schools (for 11 to 16-year-olds) and three pre-elementary schools (for 2/3 to 5-year-olds). After that, some other schools in Toulouse and regions around Paris were brought into the study. Some classrooms were dedicated to migrant pupils, some were not, depending on the schools. Despite the heterogeneity of the situation, the aim of the study was to describe attitudes to plurilingualism and plurilingual practices (if any) and then to explain the results. The method combined macro and micro approaches. I recorded and analysed different discourses and practices: teachers, principals, inspectors, pupils, parents. It was then possible to interrogate these data from the perspective of official policies (macro level) on the one hand and the interactions recorded in class (micro level) on the other. This combination of macro and micro levels corresponded to the complexity of the situation.

Discourse analysis and representations of plurilingualism

The methodology I adopted used discourse analysis following the French tradition (Pêcheux in the 1960s) and Anglo-Saxon interactional studies imported into France and popularized by Kerbrat-Orecchioni (1990). Discourses build representations and stereotypes. When they are related to plurilingualism they can reveal the different attitudes that co-exist in schools. The ways in which discourses and representations of plurilingualism intersect have already been explored in Switzerland by Lüdi and Py (1986) and conceptualized by Moore (2006) and Stratilaki (2010).

Turning to the outcomes of the research, a first finding concerns the ambiguous definition of plurilingualism in French schools. This can be linked to a lack of knowledge among teachers regarding the impact on language acquisition of factors like interference, time and variation. If teachers generally do not know how languages function, it is difficult to ask them to engage in language awareness activities with migrant pupils' home languages. Besides, we noticed repeated misunderstanding in communication. Misunderstanding inevitably arises in foreign language classrooms, but it becomes a source of added difficulty if teachers assume that misunderstandings arise with migrant pupils because they are migrants. An ambiguous gesture or mispronunciation, for example, may be interpreted as evidence of a migrant-specific cultural or linguistic problem when it is simply a normal part of language learning.

The researcher asks questions about plurilingualism, teachers answer in terms of bilingualism and monolingualism

During the past ten years, I have repeatedly asked pupils, teachers, school principals and parents what they think about plurilingualism, recorded their responses, and used discourse analysis to study the results. To sum up briefly, plurilingualism is not yet a common word in any of the discourses I recorded. Most of my informants reformulated 'plurilingualism' as 'bilingualism'. Bilingualism is seen as 'perfect' or not – a 'perfect' bilingual being one who speaks both or all their languages like a native speaker. In other words, being bilingual entails possession of two languages that never interfere with each other, whether in pronunciation, syntax, culture, or when they are used for spoken or written communication. This false conception of bilingualism creates difficulties when the researcher proposes the use of migrant languages at school. Languages are still conceived as pipes that are sealed off from one another (Heller, 1996), and the same is believed to be true about identities. In my data bilingualism is presented as entailing two cultural identities that do not impinge on one another. This belief, reinforced by the media message that migrants are a threat to French workers and security, explains why migrant pupils' languages are perceived as a threat to teachers and, more generally, to schools. As one teacher commented, 'when [migrant pupils] use their languages at school, nobody knows if it is to insult us'.

To avoid such reactions, it is necessary to educate teachers and inform parents and pupils so that they become open to other standards and understand plurilingualism as an amalgam of uneven but complementary competences.

A lack of knowledge about language acquisition: Interference and variation

Currently, because of the dominant language policy and ideology, very little information is available on the positive role that migrants' languages can play. Linguistic interference between French and migrants' languages is mostly seen as a problem, not as a sign of developing proficiency in French. Besides, parents, pupils and teachers do not recognize some languages as languages, for a variety of reasons – for example, because they are oral only or have little market value (Amazigh, Romani) or simply because the varieties that migrants speak are more or less distant from standard varieties (for instance of Arabic). This contributes to the belief that the use of migrant pupils' languages is useless and even dangerous to the development of competence in the language of schooling.

The focus on French as knowledge rather than skill

As suggested below, the ability to write French is the ultimate competence that pupils are required to develop. The ability to reflect on texts, with a focus on literary techniques and metalinguistic knowledge, is also considered very important by French teachers. Orthography and grammar are taught until the age of 15 (mostly by giving dictation and requiring pupils to learn rules). We do not dispute the fact that French orthography and grammar can be complicated. Linguists consider French an irregular language. The Académie Française has always been reluctant to normalize irregularity (Siouffi & Steuckardt, 2006), but insisting on linguistic complexity is a way of ensuring that only a small elite will ever master French. Some official texts (e.g. MEN, 2002a) deplore the opaque and selective technical language used by some textbooks and teachers because it does not help pupils to improve their French.

Misunderstanding in exolingual communication and the threat implied by the use of migrant pupils' languages

Misunderstanding between native and non-native speakers is common. The problem can arise from mispronunciation, as a result of which the word in question may come to mean something else or appear to be a curse or simply inappropriate. Misunderstanding can also occur at the syntactic level; for example, the wrong word order may result in a change of meaning, as when the agent becomes the patient (compare 'the cat eats the fish' with 'the fish eats the cat'). Or the problem may be one of tense or a matter of using inappropriate gestures, or the cultural values associated with specific words or phrases may be different. During my ethnographic studies, these misunderstandings arose repeatedly (Auger, 2010). Teachers perceived them as evidence that the media image of various migrant minorities was justified and migrant languages were impoverished. It became a matter of urgency to provide them with information about typical problems of exolingual communication and to propose activities designed to make positive use of migrant pupils' languages.

The Use of Migrant Languages: An Experiment

In official policy texts as well as in the representations of teachers, parents and pupils, the use of migrant languages and, more generally, migrants' cultural background are seen as negative, unusual, exotic.

I will first explain why informing teachers about the concept of interculturality is important if migrant languages are to be used in their classrooms. Then, exploring the use of migrants' languages in practice will lead me to compare and explore whatever languages co-exist in the classroom. Sample activities entitled 'Let's compare our languages' will be proposed as a means of mobilizing migrant pupils' languages as resources to support the development of their proficiency in the language of schooling. A discussion of teachers' and decision makers' reluctance to allow the use of migrant languages will help us to understand how we should work with decision makers both in schools and in the Ministry.

Interculturality: A concept central to understanding the importance of using migrant languages

Interculturality (Abdallah-Pretceille, 1995; Abdallah-Pretceille & Porcher, 1998; Byram, 2011; Zarate *et al.*, 2011) is a synonym for variety, and variety and diversity of apprehension of the world can be perceived as a threat to established systems. The hidden curriculum maintains a French elite (see above section on a lack of knowledge about language acquisition), but the intercultural situation can become an asset when it is used to exchange experiences and see one's own system differently in relation to other contexts. Interculturality leads to shared expertise. In fact, on the one hand, teachers have knowledge pupils must appropriate and, on the other hand, teachers discover that pupils have useful competences which can be exploited to support the learning of French. The status of error changes; we will see later on that the activities I propose help teachers and their pupils to explain things differently.

The activities that will be described below are based on exchange, on reciprocal relationships between teachers and pupils, and make use of past experience. This is not conceived of as a handicap but rather as a resource that can be drawn on to build new knowledge, especially language knowledge (although my aim is not to separate linguistic from other competences, because I prefer to view human beings holistically). The use of migrant languages in an intercultural perspective is a way of exploiting positively the intercultural pedagogical context and of using diversity and even confrontation (between languages, points of view) as a stimulus to discussion. It builds cooperation. The heterogeneity of the group is perceived as a resource and develops empowerment (Caubergs, 2002). The use of their own languages can give migrant pupils the power to increase their knowledge of French, but it also benefits French native speaker pupils, helping them too to develop their competences in French. As Goethe observed, we do not know our own language if we do not also know other languages. The perspectives introduced by referring to different languages give distance to the mainstream language of the classroom and instead of weakening it, strengthen it greatly (as shown by my ethnographic study).

From the positive use of intercultural contexts to the development of language and sociocultural competences

Class discussion that focuses on migrant languages and cultures leads to co-construction of knowledge and skills, which according to social-constructivist theory (Bruner, 1983, 1991; Vygostky, 1934/1997) is the best way to develop competences. It is difficult to interact in a language when one has just started to learn it, but one can listen to the interaction of others as children learning their first language do before they begin to speak; interacting is not necessarily synonymous with speaking. Class discussion helps to encourage a positive attitude to listening to others as well as providing the dynamic that constructs knowledge. It requires participants to use their linguistic and metalinguistic abilities and promotes language learning by stimulating interest in the topic. Teachers need to manage such discussions in a flexible way. Analysing interactions in language classes that used discussion activities, Mondada and Pekarek-Doehler (2005) found that teachers continuously adjusted their instructions, and this helped pupils to develop linguistic as well as sociocultural and institutional competences.

Exploring the use of migrant languages in practice

From vertical to horizontal methodologies

The official French texts on teaching migrant pupils (MEN, 2002b, 2000c, 2000d) say that it is possible to take into account competences that have been developed in other languages, whether at school or elsewhere. However, the texts do not explain how teachers should do this.

My ethnographic studies led me to propose that migrant languages should be used to help pupils develop their French language competences, and, especially at the beginning, that oral activities should be used to avoid discouraging pupils who are not yet able to read and write. That is why oral discussion is one of the most important forms of activity. Allowing the use of migrant languages opens traditional, vertical, transmissive methodology to the intercultural context and makes it possible to develop a 'horizontal' approach in which pupils too can make a contribution.

Using migrant languages to compare the various languages present in the classroom

My research showed that teachers are still largely unaware of interlanguage theory (Corder, 1980). Instances of interference are perceived as mistakes and the image of pupils' languages is mostly negative. Comparing languages can help to develop awareness of the interlanguage process and the inevitable role that error plays in the growth of proficiency. Activities that involve comparison are intercultural because one cannot help making comparisons with one's former experience when faced with a new language and culture. These activities can be used with any child, whatever languages he or she speaks and whatever his or her level of French. For instance, teachers can work on sounds with pupils newly arrived in France, and then move on to vocabulary and syntax. The writing process is not excluded; comparisons can be made between different writing systems, the use of grammar, etc.

That is why I have developed a DVD entitled *Comparons nos langues* ('Let's compare our languages'; Auger, 2005) and a teachers' book with activities to encourage multilingualism in class and activate transfer from one language to another (focusing especially on the language of schooling). The notion of empowerment is very important for the pupils as well as their teachers because, as explained before, the traditional culture of learning and teaching does not really allow empowerment to take place. Thanks to these activities, teachers' and pupils' negative representations of first languages are transformed. Pupils improve readily thanks to their teachers, who were trained to use the DVD. It is clearly a new pedagogical approach for both pupils and teachers in France, recently recognized by the Ministry of Education (MEN, 2009) five years after the European Commission (Auger, 2005).

Our selection of activities (Table 13.1)[1] mobilizes first languages as a resource to facilitate migrant pupils' access to the language of schooling, in conformity with the *Common European Framework of Reference for Languages* (Council of Europe, 2001) and the Council of Europe's platform of resources and references for plurilingual and intercultural education.[2]

Comparing languages in other contexts: Looking for links between languages and people

The word 'comparing' can be misleading because it may imply hierarchy. One should understand that 'comparing' is a pretext to create links between languages, to use migrant languages as resources. Comparison has always played a role in language teaching and learning, for example, when analysing grammar or translating. Recently, it has also played a central role in the European project *Evlang* (Candelier, 2003), which aimed to promote solidarity in linguistically and culturally diverse societies. The *Evlang* activities involve observing different languages with different statuses and at the same time developing metalinguistic reflexion and consciousness of power struggles between languages with a view to avoiding them in the future. This programme has been implemented in Switzerland (Perregaux *et al.*, 2003) and in Canada, especially Quebec (Armand *et al.*, 2007). These activities differ from 'Let's compare our languages' in that they do not use languages pupils already know.

The reluctance of teachers and decision makers

After analysing classroom data and proposing activities which could exploit migrant languages instead of stereotyping them, the study went on to analyse the reactions of teachers, pupils and parents to the use of the 'Let's compare languages' activities.

'A language cannot vary'

Most of the time teachers expressed the view that some languages vary too much to become a resource. They were unaware that any language can have

Table 13.1 Activities (non-exhaustive synthesis board)

Linguistic level	Activities that focus on	Objective	Possible questions (in the mainstream language)
Phonetic level	Sounds	Developing awareness of sound filters	Pupils can listen to and try to repeat various interpretations of animal sounds, machine sounds, expressions of pain, joy and so on in languages known in the class. What sound is made by a horse, a train, somebody who just hurt himself? In French, in other languages you know? Can you identify common features? Why are these sounds different in different languages?
	French vowels (a/e/é/è/in/on/en/u/ou)	Variability of vocalic system	How many vowels are there in French (or another majority language)? And how many are there in your home language? Do the two languages have vowel sounds in common? Are there differences between the oral and the written language? What are they and why do they exist?
	The consonants	Variability of consonantal system	As above + distinction between voiced and unvoiced consonants
Writing system	Relation between sounds and letters	Variation	How can we write 'o' sound in French (*beau, botte, bateau...*), 'en' (*sang, lent...*) etc.? Does this kind of variation exist in your home language?
	Directionality (left to right, right to left, top to bottom, etc.)	Variability	Which way do you open a book in your language? Why?
	Letters	Variability in the number of letters	Compare the letters of the French alphabet with those of the alphabets of other languages you know. Try to name

		used in different languages, role of upper case, lower case, redundancies	the letters of the alphabet in French and in other languages known by members of the class. Are any letters redundant in the sense that they are not pronounced? When do you use capital letters in French? And when do you use them in your native languages? What are the reasons for using capital letters?
	Accents	Optional, depending on the languages involved; expressed using different marks	How many accents are there in French? And in your L1? What is the purpose of using accents? Can we hear the same sound without accents? For example: *raie/ré/revoir/rêve/rêche*
	Punctuation	Variability	How is punctuation used in French? And how is it used in your L1? What does it mean? How do we achieve the effects of punctuation in speech?
Paralanguage	Intonation	Intonation values	Listen to examples (audio/video), pay attention to the way that voices rise and fall. Does intonation have the same value in all the languages you know? Why/why not?
	Relation between intonation and syntax	Possible redundancies and notion of language register	Consider: *Tu pars?* *Est-ce que tu pars?* *Pars-tu?* Put these in order, starting with the most informal and ending with the most formal, explaining which could be used by whom and when. Can you give similar examples from your L1?

(Continued)

Table 13.1 (*Continued*)

Linguistic level	Activities that focus on	Objective	Possible questions (in the mainstream language)
Syntax	Word order	Developing awareness of word order	Consider: *Je lis un livre* Order = subject, verb, object Do the other languages you know observe the same order (for instance, in Spanish, the subject pronoun is optional, in German the verb is in second position in main clauses, etc.)? How are questions formed (in French it depends on the pragmatic intention of the speaker)?
Lexicon		Differences in world view	What kind of objects (in the house, the kitchen for instance) exist in your native country and not in France? How do you translate the names of these objects into French? (Most of the time, there is no translation, the word is directly borrowed from the mother tongue: *tajine*, for example. If one wants to translate, one should use a paraphrase instead of a word.) Which objects exist in France and not in your home country? How could you refer to them in your L1?
	Loan words	Evidence of contact, relationships, common history	What words from your L1 exist in French (or the majority language if it is not French)? For example, the following Arabic words exist in French: *toubib, bazar, kawa, souk*. Do French words exist in your L1? What domains do they refer to (food, housing, etc.)? Why do you think your L1 has borrowed these words?

Words with shared cultural meaning (cf. Galisson, 1991)	Culture-specific lexicon (for example, fish dishes, Christmas, etc.)	Associate cities, regions and traditions to specific words: *bouillabaisse* in Marseille, *camembert* in Normandy, mustard in Dijon, etc. Do the same for other languages present in the class. Associate animals with their supposed qualities: *Malin comme un singe/Smart as a monkey.* Develop awareness that these qualities vary from one language to another. Associate events with cultural objects in French: Christmas: pine-tree, Father Christmas, decorations, etc. Wedding: rice, church, white, etc. Birthday: cake, candles, etc. (Do the same for other languages present in the class and develop awareness that reality is conceived differently by different languages).	
Verb system	Tenses	Different markers: in different languages tens can be marked by verb endings (or not), or by removing the infinitive (or not)	Give examples and compare pupils' L1s with French (or the majority language if it is not French). How do you mark the infinitive? What is its purpose? How do you conjugate verbs in the various languages you know? What is the purpose of conjugating verbs?

(Continued)

Table 13.1 (Continued)

Linguistic level	Activities that focus on	Objective	Possible questions (in the mainstream language)
	Tense and time	Variability in conceptions of time and their relation to tense se	Consider: *Quand j'étais petit j'allais prêcher à la rivière.* *Hier, j'ai pêché à la rivière.* French has two quite different ways of referring to past actions. Is it the same in the other languages you know?.
Mime and gesture	Body and speech	Variability of gesture: the same gesture may mean different things in different languages; languages may use different gestures to convey the same meaning	Do gestures have the same meaning in the different languages present in the class? Are there gestures in your L1 which do not exist in French? When do you kiss in France (man/man, man/woman, woman/woman)? How many times do you kiss each other? When? Where? Why? When do you shake hands? How is it in your L1? Can you explain the similarities and differences?
Verbal interaction	Reflection on dealing with ritual interactions	Variability in dealing with oral routines	From video examples for instance
	Initiating speech	Various ways of taking one's turn to speak	According to the speaker's social position and status. How do you take your turn (for example, starting a conversation)? Do you use *tu* or *vous*? Does this distinction exist in your L1? What purpose does it serve?

	Topics	Note that some topics must be treated carefully. In France these include salary and age (especially for women). What topics must be handled with care in your L1? Why?
	Speech acts and relationships between speakers	Consider a few speech acts ('asking', 'refusing', etc.) and try to classify them according to the formality or informality of the situation: For example, how can you express disapproval of what has just been said? Here are some examples: *Comment?/ sorry? pardon (me)? Non (no)! Ts-Ts, Ce n'est comme ça qu'on dit etc. / you cannot say that.* Give some examples from your L1?
	Variability	
	Variability according to social context	
Non-verbal communication	Relation to time	Find proverbs that express the notion of time in French and the other languages you know? What can you conclude about the perception of time? For example, compare *ne pas remettre à demain ce que l'on peut faire aujourd'hui/don't put off to tomorrow what you can do today* with *avec le temps tout s'en va/how time flies.* (cf. Hall, 1966/1984)
	Societies tend to be more or less monochronic or polychronic	
	Space	In France, what do people do to show that their house is a private space? They put up a fence or a notice: 'beware of dogs', 'private property', 'no trespassing '. What about contexts in which your L1 is used? Not that there are no private signs in the US but the use of guns is allowed. How do people queue? Does the street belong to anybody? What is one allowed to do on the street? And what is one not allowed to do? Why?
	Private space *vs* public space	

(Continued)

Table 13.1 (*Continued*)

Linguistic level	Activities that focus on	Objective	Possible questions (*in the mainstream language*)
Customs and practices	Practices according to situations	Social norms (avoiding behavioural stereotypes: the aim is not to create a guide to good behaviour)	How do you usually act in the following situations in France? • Do you greet or not when you enter a room? • Do you open a present in front of the person who just gave it to you? • Do you say how much you paid for the present you are giving? • If you are a man, do you open the door for a woman? • Do you keep your (cap) hat on indoors? • Can you point your finger at somebody? • Can you be late for an appointment? And what does it mean to be late, how much time is involved? • Can you touch other people (why, how, with what purpose)? • Can you smoke (when and where?) • At what time can you phone somebody? What about L1 situations?
Social and communicative practices	Observe values associated with societal topics	Variability according to socio-historical and geographical contexts	Languages: French/ mainstream language and other languages (associated values, power relationships) Universality and specificities in different countries, regions etc.: relationship to work, family, couple, education, school, healthcare, etc.

different standards according to context. Besides, if languages are only oral, teachers often assume, wrongly, that they are ungrammatical. Even some parents told me that it was wrong to make comparisons with oral Arabic.

'If pupils have knowledge that I don't possess . . .'

Teachers were also reluctant to introduce a 'horizontal' methodology. The traditional vertical, transmissive way of developing language competences in class is still very common in French schools. Accepting that pupils have linguistic skills that they themselves lack is for some teachers a source of considerable discomfort. But we informed teachers that even if they forbid pupils to use their home languages at school, that is inevitably what pupils will do, silently, more or less consciously as they learn the language of schooling. Once again, by providing teachers with information on how languages are learnt, we can help them to change their attitudes and become more confident in the links they create with pupils.

'Some languages are too distant from one another for comparison to be possible'

Migrant languages are sometimes non-Indo-European and teachers often think they are typologically too distant from the language of schooling to use them as a resource. For example, they do not know that Arabic words play an important role in French. They also sometimes overlook the fact that languages that are distant from one another on one level are much closer on another. For instance, German is relatively close to English on the lexical level but relatively distant from English on the syntactic level. The syntactic features of Chinese, on the other hand, share more overlap with English – for example, a SVO word order (Chao, 1968).

'Writing is a transcription of speech'

Some teachers, parents and pupils are shocked because the activities proposed in 'Let's compare our languages' allow them to use the Latin alphabet to write what they hear, even if the migrant's language has a different alphabet or no written form. The belief that writing is an exact transcription of what we hear is a mistake, of course; only the international phonetic alphabet (IPA) is capable of transcribing sounds. The main reason for writing down what is said in class, even approximately, is to establish a visual resource to help develop pupils' competences. It also prevents teachers and pupils from 'sacralizing' writing, something that has been criticized in the official texts referred to above.

'Pupils lack the metalanguage they need to compare languages'

I noticed that some teachers were frightened by the fact that pupils who had not gone to school before arriving in France would not be able to compare languages. But one should not confuse metalinguistic terminology (*verb, adjective, adverb*) with the capacity to reflect on language, which is present in children as soon as they can speak. Metalinguistic terminology is not needed, for example, in order to understand that different languages form the negative in different ways. Metalinguistic terminology can be taught later on.

Opportunities for comparing languages

Another source of reluctance is the school schedule. Teachers repeatedly asked: 'When can we find time to include these activities?' The answer is that they can be included when interference between languages occurs, or when a new grammatical point or speech act is presented. It is not necessary to be a linguist to use these activities; teachers pick up what they need and can create other activities along the same lines according to their needs.

The only way to counteract teachers' reluctance is to provide them with information about languages, how they are learnt, and how they are used to exercise power. I noticed that when I gave teachers or parents such information and at the same time proposed ways of using migrant languages, their reluctance decreased significantly.

Conclusion: Further Steps

In this chapter I have adopted a critical ethnography approach (Heller, 2002). It aims to connect practice to historical moments, taking account of social dynamics. The researcher is socially situated and is responsible for his or her study and research site. Change in this context is seen as transformation or evolution regarding the use of migrant languages in classrooms. The researcher's engagement is also visible in the creation of documents and collaboration with the field. Using the 'Let's compare our languages' activities to explore the use of migrant pupils' language is a first step. A further step would involve allowing migrant pupils to use their home languages in classroom discussion if necessary and extending the activities to all subject classes, rather than limiting them to French classes or classes for migrant pupils. The experience we have accumulated to date could be used in any multilingual class in any other country in Europe and beyond – some interest has lately been shown in North Africa and Canada.

Notes

(1) Video extracts are available free of charge in French at http://www.crdp-montpellier.fr/bsd/afficherBlocSequence.aspx?bloc=481293 and translated into English and German at http://marille.ecml.at/
(2) Available at http://www.coe.int/lang

References

Abbé Grégoire (1794) *Rapport sur la nécessité et les moyens d'anéantir les patois et d'universaliser l'usage de la langue française*. Séance du 16. prairial de l'an deuxième.

Abdallah-Pretceille, M. (1995) *Relations et apprentissage interculturels*. Paris : Armand Colin.

Abdallah-Pretceille M. and Porcher L. (1998) *Ethique de la Diversité et Education*. Presses Universitaires de France.

Armand, F., Dagenais, D., Walsh, N. and Maraillet, E. (2007) L'éveil aux langues et la co-construction de connaissances sur la diversité linguistique. *Revue Canadienne de Linguistique Appliquée* 10 (2), 197–219.

Auger, N. (2005) Comparons nos langues. Démarche d'apprentissage du français auprès d'enfants nouvellement arrivés / Let's compare our languages. Editions CNDP, collection Ressources Formation Multimédia, fabrication: CRDP Languedoc-Roussillon/ CDDP du Gard, DVD (26 min.) et guide pédagogique, 15 pages. European Label for innovative projects in language teaching and learning given by the European Commission in 2004.

Auger, N. (2010) *Elèves nouvellement arrivés en France. Réalités et perspectives en classe*. Paris: Editions des Archives Contemporaines.

Benisti, J.A. (2004) Commission prévention du groupe d'études parlementaire sur la sécurité intérieure. *Rapport sur la prévention de la délinquance*. Assemblée nationale, XXII eme legislature, octobre.

Bentolila, A. (2007) Contre les guettos linguistiques. *Le Monde*, 20 décembre 2007.

Bourdieu, P. (1970) *La reproduction. Éléments pour une théorie du système d'enseignement*, avec J.-C. Passeron. Paris: Minuit.

Bourdieu, P. (1982) *Ce que parler veut dire. L'économie des échanges linguistiques*. Paris: Fayard.

Boyer, H. (ed.) (1997) *Plurilinguisme: «contact» ou «conflit» de langues?* Paris: L'Harmattan.

Bruner, J. (1983) *Le développement de l'enfant: savoir faire, savoir dire*. Paris: Presses Universitaires de France.

Bruner, J. (1991) *Car la culture donne forme à l'esprit*. Paris: Retz.

Byram, M. (2011) From foreign language education to education for intercultural citizenship. *Intercultural Communication Review* 9 (1), 17–36.

Calvet, L.-J. (1994) *Les voix de la ville. Introduction à la sociolinguistique urbaine*. Paris: Payot.

Candelier, M. (ed.) (2003) *L'éveil aux langues à l'école primaire. Evlang: bilan d'une innovation européenne*. Bruxelles: De Boeck.

Caubergs, L. (2002) *Genre et empowerment* – Online document : http://www.atol.be/docs/ publ/MV%20seminaire%20internatl%20Empowerment%20contribution%20 Genre%20et%20Empowerment.pdf

Chao, Y.R. (1968) *A Grammar of Spoken Chinese*. Berkeley: University of California Press.

Corder, S.P. (1980) Que signifient les erreurs des apprenants? *Langages* 57, 39–41.

Cummins, J. (2001) La langue maternelle des enfants bilingues. *Sprogforum* 19, 15–21.

Galisson R. (1991). *De la langue à la culture par les mots*. Paris: CLE International.

Hall, E.T. (1966/1984) *La dimension cachée*. Paris: Seuil.

Heller, M. (1996) L'école et la construction de la norme en milieu bilingue. *AILE*, 71–93.

Heller, M. (2002) *Éléments d'une sociolinguistique critique*. Paris: Didier.

Kerbrat-Orecchioni, C. (1990) *Les interactions verbales*. Vol. 1. Paris: Armand Colin.

Lüdi, G. and Py, B. (1986) *Être bilingue*. Berne: Peter Lang.

Mondada, L. and Pekarek-Doehler, S. (2005) Second language acquisition as situated practice: Task accomplishment in the French second language classroom. *The Modern Language Journal* 88/4, 501–518 (reprinted in *The Canadian Modern Language Review*, 61, 4, 461–490).

Moore, D. (2006) *Plurilinguismes et école*. Paris: Didier.

Perregaux, C., Goumoëns C., Jeannot D. and de Pietro J-P. (2003) *Education et ouverture aux langues à l'école*. Neuchâtel: SG/CIIP.

Siouffi G. and Steuckardt A. (eds) (2006) *Les Linguistes et la Norme. Aspects Normatifs du Discours Linguistique*. Berne: Peter Lang.

Stratilaki, S. (2010) *Discours et représentations du plurilinguisme*. Berne: Peter Lang.

Vygotsky, L.S. (1934/1997) *Pensée et langage*. Translated by F. Sève. Paris: La dispute.

Zarate G., Levy D. and Kramsch C. (2011) *Handbook of Multilingualism and Multiculturalism*. Paris: Archives contemporaines.

Official texts

Council of Europe (2001) *Common European Framework of Reference for Languages: Learning, Teaching, Assessment*. Cambridge: Cambridge University Press.

Inspection générale de l'éducation nationale, Inspection générale de l'administration, de l'Éducation nationale et de la Recherche (2009) La scolarisation des élèves nouvellement arrivés en France, Rapport à monsieur le ministre de l'Éducation nationale, Rapport - n° 2009-082, septembre.

MEN (2002a) L'enseignement du français au collège. Rapport de l'Inspection générale de l'Education nationale 2002-046 (septembre). Paris: Ministère de l'Education Nationale.

MEN (2002b) Modalités d'inscription et de scolarisation des élèves de nationalité étrangère des premier et second degrés. Circulaire n°2002-063 du 20 mars 2002, BOEN n°13 du 28-03-2002. Paris: Ministère de l'Education Nationale.

MEN (2002c) Organisation de la scolarité des élèves nouvellement arrivés en France sans maîtrise suffisante de la langue française ou des apprentissages. Circulaire n°2002-100 du 25 avril 2002. Paris: Ministère de l'Education Nationale.

MEN (2002d) Missions et organisation des centres académiques pour la scolarisation des nouveaux arrivants et des enfants du voyage (CASNAV). Circulaire n°2002-102 du 25 avril 2002. Paris: Ministère de l'Education Nationale.

14 Linguistic Third Spaces in Education: Teachers' Translanguaging across the Bilingual Continuum

Nelson Flores and Ofelia García

Controlling the use of language is a primary way of managing diversity in our current era. Indeed, in current US society, language may be one of the few areas where overt discrimination is still permissible. While it would be considered uncouth to insist that somebody hide their cultural background when interacting with others, it continues to be common for people to insist that only Standard English be used in order to participate in US public life. It is equally common for bilingual American students to receive messages of the inappropriateness of their language practices in US society.

Well-meaning educators, aware of the difficulties experienced especially by *emergent bilingual students;* that is, those students in the US who are still developing English (García & Kleifgen, 2010), insist on teaching Standard American English. Unfortunately, most efforts at doing this come in the form of delegitimizing the students' home language practices. In this chapter, we propose an alternative pedagogical approach that embraces the fluid language practices of bilingual and multilingual students. Building on the concept of third space as articulated by Bhabha (1994), we argue that such an approach makes classrooms into a *linguistic third space* capable of transforming traditional views of language in the US, as well as American ethnolinguistic subjectivities.

This chapter starts with an exploration of the origins of current US language ideologies, connecting them to the development of nation states that was part of the European colonial project. It then examines shifts in critical applied linguistics that have attempted to deconstruct these language ideologies and reconstruct new ones outside of these colonial relations of power. Focusing then on the alternative language practices of two English teachers at a newcomer school for Spanish-speaking immigrants in New York City, the chapter argues that the linguistic third spaces that these teachers construct transcend current hegemonic language ideologies that emerged within the nation state paradigm. We begin by tracing the nature of our current language ideologies in the US.

The Origins of National/Colonial Language Ideologies

The origin of current language ideologies lies with the invention of the printing press. Moved by the emerging capitalist economic system, codified vernacular languages were needed to increase the size of the markets so that the printing press would be profitable (Anderson, 1991). Linguistically heterogeneous speakers had to be moulded into a homogeneous linguistic group.

This creation of homogeneous linguistic groups also had to do with the consolidation of power of the newly emerging European bourgeoisie as part of the development of nation states. Bonfiglio (2010) argues that the codification of a particular grammar and a particular pronunciation produced the bourgeois subject as the speaker of 'the norm', a more correct and perfect language than that of the inferior Other. This creation of a standardized language shifted the focus of language from its communicative aspects toward a focus on correct form as an expression of a static superior national identity. In other words, whether a message was understood was less relevant than whether one articulated the message within the proper form as articulated by nationalist grammarians.

This ideology of the superiority of one language 'norm' was an integral component of the European colonial project. For example, Mühlhäusler (1996) looks at the imposition of a modernist conception of homogeneous and enumerable languages on the Pacific Rim as part of a larger process of colonization. Colonial grammarians sought to codify and name the languages of the Pacific Rim, thus ignoring the fluid language practices that made communication possible in this linguistically heterogeneous setting.

To Mühlhäusler, the categorization of language practices into enumerable and autonomous 'languages' was a form of epistemic violence that did not represent the actual language practices of people.

In summary, the nationalist/colonial language ideology saw language as a tool for the unification of a people under one standard language living in the borders of one territory. This standardization was part of the creation of a bourgeois subject differentiated from the lower classes of Europe and colonial subjects abroad. Language became a tool for managing the lower classes and people of colour all over the world through the imposition of static language forms and an erasure of linguistic heterogeneity.

Critique of Nation State/Colonial Language Ideologies

A critique of nation state/colonial language ideologies has emerged in critical applied linguistics that seeks to excavate subaltern knowledge and challenge the colonizing tendencies in current language ideologies (Canagarajah, 2005; Cummins, 2007; Makoni & Makoni, 2010; Makoni & Pennycook, 2007; Mignolo, 2000; Pennycook, 2010). Critical scholars are creating theoretical frameworks that treat language as a contested space – as tools that are re-appropriated by actual language users. Ultimately, the goal of these critiques is to break out of static conceptions of language that keep power in the hands of the few, thus embracing the fluid nature of actual and local language practices of all speakers.

García's (2009) critique of the current state of bilingual education is demonstrative of this resistance toward nation state/colonial language ideologies. At the core of her argument is a challenge to the homogeneous language constructs at the centre of most language education policy, including those dealing with bilingualism in education. Nation state language ideologies continue to treat bilingualism as the mastery over two separate and distinct languages; that is, from a *monoglossic perspective*. To replace this type of thinking, García argues for adopting a *heteroglossic perspective*, with languages not seen as separable and countable, or associated with nation states. Instead, a heteroglossic perspective acknowledges multilingual speakers' fluid language practices in their full complexity. An education that would respond to this heteroglossic ideology would then leverage multilingual students' complex discursive practices, their dynamic multilingualism, in order to make meaning. García (2009) refers to the dynamic meaning-making discursive processes of bilingual and multilingual populations as (following Cen Williams, 1997) *translanguaging*. In education, translanguaging offers an important alternative to current monoglossic language ideologies, monolingual practices and traditional pedagogies. Translanguaging in education not only creates the possibility that young bilinguals could use their full linguistic repertoire to make meaning, but also that teachers would 'take it up' as a legitimate pedagogical practice in educating those who are linguistically different.

In what follows, a heteroglossic perspective will be taken to describe the fluid language practices of English teachers working with Latino emergent bilinguals in a special high school for newcomer immigrants. Through embracing translanguaging as pedagogy, these teachers are facilitating the development of new subjectivities in their classrooms that defy ethnolinguistic identities defined by a nation state/colonial paradigm.

Creating Linguistic Third Spaces at Pan American International High School

The Pan American International High School (PAIHS) is located in Queens, New York, and serves recently arrived Spanish-speaking immigrant adolescents. The school is part of a network of public government-funded secondary schools that use progressive approaches to educate emergent bilingual students (García & Sylvan, 2011). The school's pedagogical approaches include utilizing all of the students' language practices as tools in the learning of academic English. The use of bilingualism in education doesn't then emerge from structures of language allocation or curriculum, but rather 'from the students up'. Although English is the language of instruction according to plans submitted to government officials, the schools' collaborative group learning structures facilitate students' use of their home language practices when meaning-making in the classroom. How teachers, supposedly teaching 'in English' respond to these fluid language practices and 'take them up' to educate is the subject of this chapter.

During 2010–2011, we conducted observations of all teachers of 9th and 10th graders, and more intensively of Math and English teachers, to attempt to answer our overarching research question: *How does Spanish support English language development in a school where all students speak Spanish, but not all teachers do?* (García & Flores, 2011). In this chapter we focus on the language practices of two of the teachers of 'English' who are at different points on the bilingual continuum. Whereas one is a fluent bilingual who speaks English and Spanish, the other is 'picking up' Spanish language practices from her students. Specifically, we look here at how these two teachers, with different bilingual proficiency, use translanguaging as a pedagogy to educate these students for whom translanguaging is also a common language practice at home and in the community.

The snapshots that are offered here are based on audio-recordings of lessons conducted by these two teachers, as well as field notes written by us as we observed the teachers in their interactions with students. All actual quotations are from transcriptions of the audio-recordings. While we are very aware of the fact that linguistic third spaces are not only created by teachers, the nature of our data only allows us to analyse the creation of linguistic third spaces from the teachers' perspectives.

The first teacher, who will be referred to as Ms C, is a Chilean-American born in the US who grew up using English and Spanish. We will focus on the ways that she systematically incorporated translanguaging strategies to facilitate the development of linguistic and cultural third spaces in her classroom. In particular, we will analyse one observation we conducted of a weekly event that she called 'Hip-Hop Monday'.

The second teacher, who will be referred to as Ms S, is an Indian-American whose language practices include Gujarati, Hindi, Urdu, English and (now) Spanish. She reported taking Spanish in high school, but not using it on a regular basis until working at PAIHS. While Ms S planned translanguaging in ways that facilitated the creation of linguistic third spaces, her planning was less systematic and more spontaneous. We will focus here primarily on her interactions with students during her 'English' lessons in the course of our observations. Putting these two teacher snapshots together allows us to illustrate the ways that teachers at different points on the continuum of bilingualism create linguistic third spaces through translanguaging. In addition, we look at the effects of translanguaging as a pedagogical practice.

Ms C's Classroom

As mentioned above, Ms C has a special session of her 'English' class every Monday that she calls 'Hip-Hop Monday'. This section describes the overall structure of Hip-Hop Monday and demonstrates how it is structured in such a way as to create linguistic third spaces. In addition, one session of Hip-Hop Monday will be described to illustrate how linguistic third spaces look in practice as translanguaging is consciously incorporated into a lesson plan. We will demonstrate how Hip-Hop Monday undermines nation state/colonial language ideologies and facilitates the development of fluid ethnolinguistic identities that are culturally and linguistically transformative for both Ms C and her students.

Every Hip-Hop Monday centres around two songs on a particular topic, usually a topic dealing with social justice around US Latino/Latin American issues – one in Spanish, and one in English. It is this juxtaposition of two songs on a related topic but in different languages that lies at the core of the

linguistic third spaces created every Hip-Hop Monday. Students are introduced to the topic through listening to the Spanish song, which connects to
their Latin American national identities. They analyse the song with a critical
socio-political, as well as language/literary lens, using language practices that
incorporate Spanish features as well as English features in order to provide a
deep critical and creative analysis. They then translate a section of the song
into English in writing using their full linguistic repertoire, sometimes incorporating Spanish features, sometimes English features, always both. They do
so using dictionaries, asking each other questions and always collaboratively
in heterogeneous groups that consist of students at different levels of English
language development. As we will see, putting Spanish and English alongside
each other, many times with features that are 'trans' – blends of both – starts
to construct an ethnolinguistic identity that is not solely Latin American and
Spanish monolingual, and not solely Anglo US and English monolingual, but
a US Latino bilingual identity. Students are then exposed to the same topic
again through listening to an English song and orally analysing the song using
the translanguaging of their evolving discourse. They then translate in writing
a section of the song into Spanish, translanguaging actively and constructing
their discourse not solely from an English-language perspective, but through
the use of complex bilingualism that does not separate English from Spanish.
As will be seen in the description of one Hip-Hop Monday below, this constant going back and forth between seemingly static languages and ethnolinguistic identities allows for the emergence of fluid border identities that
transcend national borders and challenge homogeneous language constructs.

In one session, Ms C is teaching the students about *'los desaparecidos'* ['the
disappeared'] in Chile during the dictatorship of Augusto Pinochet. Ms C
begins the lesson by presenting a PowerPoint with images to build background knowledge on the US-backed coup in Chile that brought Pinochet to
power. While the PowerPoint is written in English, key terms are written in
Spanish. In addition, both Ms C and the students interact with the
PowerPoint in linguistically fluid ways. One exchange between Ms C and a
group of students demonstrates what this sounds like.

Ms C: Well I don't know where they were from, but they got money
          from the United States. But they came and they bombed it.
          The President Allende was inside.
Student: *¿Murió?*
Ms C: And he died *y murió.*

Ms C begins the exchange in English. A student indicates her understanding
of what Ms C says by posing a question in Spanish. Ms C responds to her

question in English, but then reiterates it in Spanish. This repetition in Spanish not only acknowledges the original language of the question, but also emphasizes the point for the entire class. There could be no misunderstanding. President Allende died and the language in which it was expressed did not change the tragic nature of it.

Ms C continues with this exchange and enlarges the linguistic third space through sharing her own personal connection with the death of President Allende, as a Chilean-American.

Ms C:	And my uncle who I told you about, right¿ Didn't I tell you¿
Students:	Yeah.
Ms C:	He was inside also because he worked in the government.
Student:	¿Y se murió también¿
Ms C:	No, he didn't die that day. He was taken then to the concentration camp. So Allende died. *La gente no sabe si se suicidió o lo mataron. Es como un misterio histórico en Chile.* But then who took over¿ The picture of him is right there.
Student:	Pinochet.

Ms C develops a linguistic and cultural third space by permitting and participating in fluid language practices in her interactions with students, as well as by sharing her experiences as a Chilean American. First, a student expresses his interest in knowing more about her uncle in Spanish. Ms C acknowledges his interest, though she answers in English. However, she then uses Spanish to emphasize the key point that she wants students to take away from the presentation – namely that Allende died and it is unclear whether he committed suicide or was murdered.

This linguistic third space culminates in Ms C emphasizing in Spanish the connection between the military coup in Chile and the experiences of other Latin American countries:

Ms C:	*Hay gente desaparecida todavía en la Republica Dominicana, Haití,* Peru (says it with an American pronunciation).
Student:	(mockingly exaggerating an American accent) Peru.
Ms C:	Peru. *Perú.*
Students:	(continuing to mock) Peru, Peru.
Ms C:	(laughs) *Perú.* Alright. So this is not only Chile. There are many places that this has happened.
Student:	*México.*
Ms C:	*México.* Yeah.

Ms C is able to transcend the borders of individual Latin American countries and to support students in the construction of a Pan-Latino third space through the shared experiences of Latin American *desaparecidos*. At the same time, the going back and forth between Ms C's Anglicized 'Peru', and the Spanish *'Perú'* after students mock her pronunciation, extends the Pan-Latin-Americanism to include a Latino US identity. The identities that the students are constructing (and that Ms C is helping develop) as US Latinos cannot simply be expressed in Spanish, or in English, but need a translanguaging discourse to transcend the realization that their new country is partially responsible for the disappearance of many of their own people in their other countries. To develop these complex understandings they cannot be simply North American, or simply Latin American; they cannot be simply English speakers, or simply Spanish speakers. Instead, they must accept their role and responsibility as new US Latinos. Their translanguaged discourse opens up the possibility of a more just US future that would include Latinos as equals. This is a classroom moment when national and linguistic boundaries are transcended, as students and teacher express shared histories and solidarity with one another's struggles, beyond nationality or language.

The second part of the lesson is centred on listening to a song in Spanish about the disappearances in Chile. Ms C now has the students listen to and watch a music video by the Chilean hip-hop group *Subverso*. After listening to this Spanish-language song, students answer a series of questions written in English. At times the nature of the questions inevitably requires students to answer in Spanish. The following interaction concerning one of the questions demonstrates this point:

Ms C: What do you hear multiple times?
Student: *Dónde están.*
Ms C: *Dónde están.* Good.
Student: *Matar.*
Ms C: *Matar.*
Student: *Verdad.*
Ms C: *Verdad.* Nice. So you just write it right there.

In short, while the questions are in English, because the song is written in Spanish it is, in fact, impossible not to answer some of the questions in Spanish. Therefore, the task by necessity requires the fluid use of language and translanguaging. More importantly, the Spanish use on the part of the students cannot possibly be interpreted as 'a crutch', since an English answer would have been incorrect. For example, to have said that 'where are they' was repeated multiple times would not have been accurate, since what was actually repeated multiple times was '*dónde están*'. The students' fluid linguistic abilities become an asset, a necessary tool in navigating the classroom discussion, as opposed to something that should be avoided at all costs.

After hooking students through the incorporation of the Spanish hip-hop that many of them listen to daily, Ms C then turns the students' attention to an English pop song entitled 'They Danced Alone' by Sting. By pairing this song with a Spanish hip-hop song, Ms C positions Spanish/English and Latin America/US alongside each other, helping students construct a transcultural and transnational Pan-Latino US identity that affirms their multiplicities and the dynamic interrelationships of their developing language repertoire and ethnolinguistic identities.

The music video is about Chilean women dancing the national dance, which is traditionally done with a male partner, by themselves, as a form of protest against the disappearance of their men during the Chilean dictatorship. In introducing the song, Ms C connects back to students' national identities:

Ms C: [Sting] saw in 1987 what was happening in Chile and he wrote this song about it, right? *El escribió esto porque supo lo que estaba pasando.* And he wrote the song called *La Cueca Sola* because *La Cueca* is, what? *Qué es La Cueca en Chile?*

Student: *El baile nacional.*

Ms C: Good. So here is a picture of the national dance. Here's a picture. Do you see it? *El baile nacional.* Like in the Dominican Republic what would the national *baile* be?

Student: *Merengue.*

Ms C: *Merengue.*

Student: *Bachata.*

Ms C: *Bachata.* In Chile, *La Cueca, La Cueca.*

Ms C begins this exchange by stating in English, and emphasizing in Spanish, the reason Sting wrote the song – namely that he wanted to raise awareness about the Chilean situation. She then has a Chilean student in the class explain in Spanish that La Cueca is the national dance of Chile. Once affirming this student's national identity, she then once again shifts the classroom discourse back to a more fluid pan-Latino identity through an acknowledgement of the national dance of another country – the Dominican Republic. But then through translanguaging, English is added to the mix of language practices, going beyond Latin American identities to construct a complex and multiple US Latino identity. As opposed to gradually replacing Spanish by English, Ms C develops the students' comfort with translanguaging and the discursive fluidity characteristic of bilingual communities.

A linguistic third space is developed in the interaction between a language (Spanish) and style (hip-hop) with which students are more familiar, and a language (English) and style (pop) which are less known. Thus, students not only cross national and linguistic borders (Rampton, 2006) but go beyond them. As a result, they make meaning of the consequences of the Chilean dictatorship in a way that speaks directly to their developing subjectivities as US Latinos. Issues of social justice are at the centre of this translanguaging, as injustices are neither hidden nor blamed on others, but engage students' sense of responsibility for a more just world. In this educational context, English becomes a tool to add to global understandings and incorporate multiple subjectivities, instead of being simply an instrument for marginalization and the construction of Otherness. A translanguaging pedagogy becomes a way of transcending national/colonial language ideologies. Yet the question remains as to how a teacher who has less experience with Latin American culture and the Spanish language can facilitate the development of these spaces. It is to this that we now turn.

Ms S's classroom

As mentioned above, Ms S grew up in a multilingual environment and now self-identifies as speaking five languages, although she has also spoken other languages at different points in her life. Ms S's multilingualism has allowed her to develop a strong understanding for the communicative aspects of language and has made her less concerned with form than with using language effectively. Therefore, despite what a more traditional approach to language would consider 'ungrammatical' or 'broken' Spanish, we will demonstrate that Ms S is a successful user of Spanish in that she is able to use it to leverage comprehension and learning among students. She is thus able to create linguistic third spaces that allow both her and the students to take on fluid ethnolinguistic identities, as well as fluid language practices.

Some of the translanguaging that Ms S uses in the classroom is planned. This oftentimes comes in the form of translating key terms of the day into Spanish to scaffold instruction and build on students' prior knowledge. This translanguaging also makes students notice cognates, an important clue to unlocking the meaning of a new language. For example, in a lesson early in the year on comparing and contrasting, Ms S wrote the following on the board:

Aim: Why do we compare (*'comparar'*) and contrast (*'diferenciar'*) things, ideas, or people?

Do Now: To compare is to find similarities (*'similares'*) in two things.
            To contrast is to find differences (*'diferencias'*) in two things.

By positioning Spanish alongside English keywords, students are able to juxtapose their prior understandings with terminology in a new language.

Most of the linguistic third spaces that Ms S developed during our observations are spontaneous, as she navigates communication with her students in a language that she has not used extensively prior to arriving at the school. Rather than accepting a monoglossic ideology that would position her as a 'Spanish Language Learner', she uses features of Spanish as she translanguages, to engage her students in learning and meaning-making, as well as to encourage the addition of English features to their linguistic repertoire.

An incident that occurred during a public student presentation illustrates this point. After being pressured by other teachers to present in English, a student completely shut down and refused to speak. Ms S started to communicate with the student through a translator, but ended up having a direct conversation with the student, utilizing translanguaging strategies. Her message was completely understood, as she expressed the importance of taking risks languaging. In so doing, she became a model of the very experimentation that she was encouraging in the student. It is one thing for a teacher to encourage students to take risks, and quite another for a teacher to model what taking these risks might look like.

In translanguaging, Ms S also frequently positioned herself as the novice in relation to her students who are speakers of Spanish and who can incorporate more English features into their Spanish discourse than she can incorporate Spanish features into her English. In one exchange, Ms S uses Spanish to communicate an important idea to the students, but also asks for assistance from the students in helping her convey her message:

Ms S: *Escribir una comparación* with Julio and myself. Can someone say it in Spanish?
Student: *Que tiene que comparar ellos.*
Student: *Algo que ellos tienen en común.*
Ms S: We both have hair. Both of us are human. We both have homework.
Student: You are the same high school
Ms S: We both go to the same school every day.

Here Ms S begins the exchange in Spanish, but immediately positions students as the experts by asking if somebody could say in Spanish what she wanted them to do. This attempt on her part at using Spanish, while acknowledging her needs, creates a linguistic third space where students feel empowered in what they know and are then more comfortable taking on English features into their linguistic repertoires. After she provides some models for what a response in English might be, a student also comes up with an answer in English. Ms S then paraphrases what the student says without offering any corrections.

This routine continues throughout the exchange, with Ms S primarily using English, but also using Spanish, to get key points across. She continues:

Ms S: *¿Qué es diferente en nosotros? Tamaño,* size.
Student: Your skin, different color.

Ms S makes an effort to make herself understood using Spanish, and the students make an effort to make themselves understood using English. Indeed, Ms S and her students are constantly making an effort to communicate with one another using fluid language practices, though all with the purpose of adding more English to the linguistic repertoire of students, and adding more Spanish to the linguistic repertoire of Ms S.

Yet, interestingly, despite the fluid ethnolinguistic identities and dynamic language practices utilized by both Ms S and her students during this particular class period (and in general), there was still a resistance on the part of students to accept her as a legitimate user of Spanish, or themselves as legitimate users of English, as indicated in the continued discussion of the differences between Ms S and her students:

Student: You speak English and we speak Spanish.
Ms S: But you guys speak English too....
Students: No!!!
Ms S: But I speak Spanish too.
Students: No!!!!!!!!!

In short, despite the existence of linguistic third spaces in the classroom, for the students it was still difficult to position Ms S as a Spanish speaker or themselves as English speakers. This indicates the continued effect of monoglossic language ideologies even in such a heteroglossic classroom – namely, that if one does not fit an idealized conception of a 'native speaker', one cannot be positioned as a legitimate user of a language.

Despite the apparent contradiction between perceived language identities and actual language use expressed by the students here, there were many instances where Ms S was, in fact, a successful user of Spanish, and when the students through their interactions with her were successful users of English. One does not need to be 'fully bilingual' in order to translanguage in ways that facilitate the creation of linguistic third spaces. It is true that Ms S translanguaging creates different linguistic third spaces than Ms C. Ms

C is able to use her extensive familiarity with Spanish and English, along with her wealth of understandings of Latin American and US culture, history and politics to interact with students in ways that construct a pan-Latino identity and encourages emergent bilinguals to dynamically take up features from English into their original Spanish-only linguistic repertoire. Ms S uses her supposed lack of knowledge of Spanish to model for students how to privilege the communicative aspects of language over form. In this way, she too is able to break out of nation state/colonial language ideologies and demonstrate ways to create fluid ethnolinguistic identities that transcend national and linguistic borders.

Conclusion

Schools most often reflect national and colonial relations of power. The language ideologies that schools use and foster has been used throughout history as an important instrument for nation states to manage diversity, control and marginalize populations that are different, and consolidate power. Recently, however, there has been an epistemological shift, as language minorities have demanded their language rights in education, and as some societies have yielded to their demands for the inclusion of their languages in education. Despite the growth of bilingual education programs throughout the world since the second half of the 20th century, bilingual education programs remain instruments of control, as bilingualism is perceived to be the simple addition of two autonomous languages. Thus, even in bilingual education practices, the complex discursive practices that characterize all bilingual communities have been shunned.

This chapter highlights the case of two teachers of 'English' in a secondary school for Latino newcomers who are learning English. The two case studies show how the use of translanguaging in education constructs a third space that makes possible the development of students' dynamic language and cultural practices, and thus a meaningful education. Contrary to popular belief, the insistence on using only the dominant standard language in monolingual education or in carefully compartmentalizing the two languages in bilingual education cannot break the language hierarchies that exist. If we wanted to ensure the full participation of all citizens, including those who are linguistically different, we would have to let go of the static definition of acceptable language use that has been part of the European colonial project. The two cases here considered clearly show that translanguaging has the capacity to transcend language and cultural hierarchies, facilitating a functional interrelationship of discourses and identities that is necessary for minority students' healthy development linguistically and educationally. The two cases further show that translanguaging as a pedagogy does not necessitate a fully bilingual teacher; what it does require is the teachers' willingness to engage in learning with their students, becoming an equal participant in the educational enterprise that should seek, above all else, to equalize power relations. Translanguaging as a pedagogy offers much promise to enable linguistic and cultural constructions that transcend the nation state relationships of power.

References

Anderson, B. (1991) *Imagined Communities: Reflections on the Origin and Spread of Nationalism* (revised edition). London: Verso.

Bhabha, H. (1994) *The Location of Culture*. New York: Routledge.

Bonfiglio, T. (2010) *Mother Tongues and Nations: The Invention of the Native Speaker*. New York: de Gruyter.

Canagarajah, S. (ed.) (2005) *Reclaiming the Local in Language Policy and Practice*. Mahwah: Lawrence Erlbaum.

Cummins, J. (2007) Rethinking monolingual instructional strategies in multilingual classrooms. *Canadian Journal of Applied Linguistics* 10 (2), 221–240.

García, O. (2009) *Bilingual Education in the 21st Century: A Global Perspective*. Malden: Wiley/Blackwell.

García, O. and Kleifgen, J.A. (2010) *Educating Emergent Bilinguals: Policies, Programs and Practices for English Language Learners*. New York: Teachers College Press.

García, O. and Flores, N. (2011) A study of the Pan American International High Schools: Developing bilingualism in a common language model. Submitted to PAIHS, October 10, 2010 (mimeo).

García, O. and Sylvan, C. (2011) Pedagogies and practices in multilingual classrooms: Singularities in pluralities. *Modern Language Journal* 95 (3), 385–400.

Makoni, B. and Makoni, S. (2010) Multilingual discourses on wheels and public English in Africa: A case for 'vague linguistique'. In J. Maybin and J. Swann (eds) *The Routledge Companion to English Language Studies* (pp. 258–270). London: Routledge.

Makoni, S. and Pennycook, A. (2007) *Disinventing and Reconstituting Languages*. Clevedon: Multilingual Matters.

Mignolo, W. (2000) *Local Histories/Global Designs: Coloniality, Subaltern Knowledges, and Border Thinking*. Princeton: Princeton University Press.

Mühlhäusler, P. (1996) *Linguistic Ecology: Language Change and Linguistic Imperialism in the Pacific Region*. London: Routledge.

Pennycook, A. (2010) *Language as a Local Practice*. London: Routledge.

Rampton, B. (2006) *Language in Late Modernity. Interaction in an Urban School*. Cambridge: Cambridge University Press.

Williams, C. (1997) *Bilingual Teaching in Further Education: Taking Stock*. Bangor: Canolfan Bedwyr, University of Wales.

15 From 'Monolingual' Multilingual Classrooms to 'Multilingual' Multilingual Classrooms: Managing Cultural and Linguistic Diversity in the Nepali Educational System

Shelley K. Taylor

In a position paper entitled *Education in a Multilingual World*, UNESCO (2003: 12) describes societal multilingualism as a way of life, not a problem to be solved, since complex multilingual societies are the norm in many parts of the world. It further suggests that any 'problems' that multilingualism poses should not be attributed to culturally or linguistically diverse (CLD) children, but to educational systems that have not adapted to complex realities and do not provide quality education that takes learners' needs into consideration. Thus, UNESCO (2003) places the onus on educational systems to adapt to and manage diversity.

This view of where the onus lies in managing diversity in education is not necessarily shared by dominant group members, as the following example illustrates. A move to introduce instruction through the medium of Arabic in the primary grades in a predominantly Arabic-speaking neighbourhood in a Canadian city was met by public outrage, and comments such as: 'They always say English is the hardest language to learn, so I don't see how learning Arabic 60% of the time is going to help with English', and: 'They need more English. To me, I'm tired of having to bend to all these immigrants coming to Canada' (Wolfson, 2007). These comments do not support UNESCO's view that educational systems, not CLD children, must adapt to fit the needs of diversity; rather, they frame minority languages (their use, maintenance, promotion and revitalization) as socially divisive, the 'business' of minority group members, and problematic overall. Minority language researchers such as Baker (2011), Cummins (2009), Edwards (2009), Panda *et al.* (2011) and Skutnabb-Kangas and Heugh (2012) concur with the UNESCO view, with Edwards (2009: 123) observing that, although 'conditions in industrialized and developing countries are very different, teachers in both settings have a shared interest in supporting linguistically diverse students'. Viewed thus, countries such as Canada, Ireland and Nepal that may initially seem worlds apart share common needs; they need to manage cultural and linguistic diversity (CLD) in education, and they need to manage public sentiment that ranges along a continuum from supporting to opposing UNESCO's view of who or what must adapt to diversity.

This chapter introduces a model of multilingual language education (MLE) designed to manage diversity in education – mother tongue (L1) based instruction at the primary level (L1-based MLE) – and outlines CLD and dominant group members' reactions to the program in the Nepali context. A unique aspect of the Nepali initiative is that there are some 140 reported languages in the country (Giri, 2011; Yadava, 2007), making L1-based instruction for all a major undertaking and many-layered process. Edwards (2009) observes that public sentiment or 'ruling passions' vary from country to country and class to class, and play a role in shaping national educational priorities. This chapter will consider whose interests the L1-based MLE program serves, how it has been implemented, and what other countries grappling with how to manage CLD in education can learn from the Nepali response.

Challenges in Introducing L1-based MLE

Alidou *et al.* (2006) support UNESCO's (2003: 6) view of where the onus lies in managing CLD in education, going so far as to say that 'while language is not everything in education, without language, everything is nothing in education'. The latter quote sums up the results of the report they compiled for UNESCO and the Association for the Development of Education in Africa. The report summarizes their assessment of mother tongue and bilingual education programs in sub-Saharan Africa: the best way to provide quality education and achieve sustainable development is to provide L1-based bilingual instruction until the end of primary schooling.

Their report is supported by NGOs and specialists in English language teaching (e.g. Coleman, 2011). Webley (2006), an official with *Save the Children*, views poverty and discrimination as the root causes of inequitable access to education. She views the latter combined with family background (i.e. levels of education, social class, etc.) as key indicators of educational achievement. Webley (2006) notes that hungry, suffering people focus on survival before education, a view shared by McConnell-Ginet and Whitman (see Harbert *et al.*, 2009), who acknowledge the important role that poverty plays in deciding the outcomes of language planning efforts. Webley also notes, however, the important role that L1-based, bi-/multilingual education plays in children's educational success; however, as the Canadian example illustrated, these views are not shared by all. Despite decades of research support for L1-based instruction in Western contexts and a growing body of research conducted on the same in developing countries, many dominant group members view CLD in education and bi-/multilingual language education as problematic.

When 'More' is *Less*, not *More*, and the Management of Linguistic Diversity in Education

To some, the notion of minority language children receiving instruction through a minority L1 is illogical as folk belief holds that children pick up language from their surroundings ('like little sponges'). It therefore seems illogical that children can be surrounded by talk without having access to it – or education. Perceptions of logic aside, research does not support the belief that *more* instruction in a second, dominant societal language (L2) results in *more* L2 learning for minority language children. Instruction in a language children understand (e.g. their L1) can lead to more content learning in the short term, and more L2 learning in the long run (Heugh *et al.*, 2007; Ramirez *et al.*, 1991). (See Cummins (1991) for discussion of the 'interdependence hypothesis'.)

A longitudinal study conducted by Parrish *et al.* (2006) revealed that there is no single roadmap to success for CLD learners, despite the popular belief that *more* is *more* (i.e. that *more* L2 instruction results in *more* L2 learning).

Characteristics of schools and school boards identified in the latter study as contributing to CLD children's academic success included:

- a common vision of priorities and expectations for CLD learners;
- teachers' and other staff members' capacity to address CLD learners' needs;
- a school-wide focus on developing L2 proficiency in CLD learners;
- systematic assessment generating data to guide policy and instruction.

These characteristics support Cummins' (2009) claim that language is not the only factor in CLD learners' educational achievement. Little (2010: 16) concurs that when respect and support for the L1 are linked to respect and incorporation of CLD children's local knowledge in the curriculum, their identities are affirmed (not stigmatized) and it is more possible for teachers and administrators to address CLD children's needs.

Yet belief in the *more* is *more* hypothesis runs deep and continues to limit CLD children's access to bi-/multilingual education programs as individuals have the power to influence how governments manage CLD in education; they have the power to affect the lives of those whom Tollefson (2002: 4) describes as having 'little influence over the policy making process'. The belief that *more* is *more* also leads some CLD individuals to set up their own roadblocks and obstruct their own access to L1-based instruction.

The Lure of 'Goddess English'

The value of L1-based instruction is a recurrent theme in Coleman's (2011) collection of papers on English language teaching (ELT) in developing countries in Africa and Asia; however, even governments and ELT researchers who are aware of research such as the above and UNESCO's (2007) *EFA Global Monitoring Report 2007* can be confronted with 'ruling passions' in the form of public demand for English. CLD parents and communities sometimes hold ambivalent views towards L1-based instruction, preferring non-local languages as the medium of instruction – including state languages such as Nepali, and international languages such as English.

Coleman (2011) and Pandey (2011) discuss the recent introduction of 'goddess English' to India's old 'untouchable' class (Dalits). A Dalit writer, Chandra Bhan Prasad, introduced English as a 'goddess' to other Dalits in a village in Uttar Pradesh to introduce them to the power of English. She introduced the goddess as standing atop a computer to show Dalits that they can 'use English to rise up the ladder and become free forever' (Pandey, 2011).

Prasad equates English with gaining upward mobility and the power needed for formerly 'untouchable' Dalits to replace those currently at the top of the social scale.

Dalits make up 40% of the population in the region surrounding the village (Pandey, 2011). Even though India and Nepal abolished the caste system long ago (see Government of Nepal, 2001: 3), Dalit children are still discriminated against at school because the school system is dominated by higher castes. Inequities such as forcing Dalit children to sit and eat separately at school take a toll on school retention rates and, perforce, on literacy rates as well. At 55%, their literacy rate is 10% lower than India's national average (Pandey, 2011), and the situation is similar in Nepal where:

- 19.6% of all children do not enrol in school;
- 45.4% of those enrolled drop out before Grade 5;
- 14.5% drop out in Grade 1;
- the drop-out and illiteracy rate for indigenous, ethnic minority and stigmatized minority (Dalit) children is disproportionately higher than the national average (Government of Nepal, 2007).

These data explain why the percentage of CLD children from stigmatized indigenous/minority backgrounds that are able to read and write is lower than the national average of 54% (Government of Nepal, 2007: 13). Decision-makers in countries such as Nepal must not only manage issues of linguistic diversity in education, but also of cultural diversity as the two combined lead to academic achievement rates for CLD children that are significantly below the national average. The L1-based MLE program reported on in this chapter was introduced to tackle CLD children's higher than average drop-out and illiteracy rates head-on, and to begin to make amends for decades (if not centuries) of mishandling diversity in education.

Introducing L1-based MLE into Nepal to Manage CLD in Education

Although Nepal is not an immigration country, its L1-based MLE program does provide a good example of a country grappling with how to meet the educational needs of CLD children. Though a multilingual country, the monarchy only granted primacy to Nepali under the guise of 'national unity' throughout its 240-year reign (Awasthi, 2004). CLD children received Nepali-medium instruction whether their L1 was a tribal[1] or minority language, even though over 50% of the school-aged population spoke a language other than Nepali as their L1 (Giri, 2011; Yadava, 2007). For most of its reign, the monarchy's approach to managing CLD in education was to ignore the 140 languages other than Nepali – an approach to 'managing diversity' that led to a decade of violence prior to the Maoists taking power in 2007. In Giri's (2011: 198) words, CLD groups asked for 'separate territorial divisions in Nepal in order to ensure their ethnic, linguistic and cultural survival'. During the civil war, language issues became a political battleground.

After the Maoists took power, they introduced an Interim Constitution (Nepal Law Book Society, 2007) guaranteeing tribal/minority children's right to L1-based instruction (Yonjan-Tamang *et al.*, 2009). This move coincided with the Finnish government providing technical assistance to the Nepali Ministry of Education and Sports, and the development and implementation of an L1-based MLE project. The goals of the initiative were in sync with both UNESCO (2003, 2007) and the Government of Nepal's (2001, 2003, 2007) 'Education for all' (EFA) objective of reducing the poverty rate in Nepal by increasing the national literacy rate, and the new Maoist government's goal of ending ethnic strife motivated by perceptions of linguistic and cultural inequities (Giri, 2011; Government of Nepal, 2007). The attempt to develop a prototypical, L1-based MLE model program, train educators to deliver the program and materials developers to support it, and implement a pilot program prior to cascading the model to all 140 tribal/minority groups was both innovative and daunting.

Managing CLD in the Pilot Project

The joint Nepali/Finnish L1-based MLE project was piloted in nine languages in seven primary schools spread over six districts, and was intended to eventually extend to all tribal/minority language groups across the country (Nurmela *et al.*, 2011; Taylor, 2010, 2011). It responded to both national and international EFA goals for literacy development (and poverty reduction), and the 7th EFA goal of using local languages and mother tongues as the media of culturally relevant, indigenized instruction to meet the sociolinguistic, cultural and political goals and needs of tribal/minority groups (United Nations, 2007).

The MLE program featured:

- initial literacy and numeracy instruction through tribal/minority children's L1;
- the introduction of Nepali as a second language (L2) and English as a foreign language (EFL) throughout the primary grades;

- a transition to Nepali-medium instruction beginning in the junior grades;
- ongoing instruction in the L1 as subject after transitioning to Nepali-medium instruction.

The formal project goals were: (a) to develop the capacity of tribal/minority communities to create local, L1-based MLE programs in the primary years, (b) to introduce culturally relevant pedagogy and (c) to develop materials that would facilitate linguistically/culturally responsive teaching (i.e. not just translations of mainstream Nepali content) (Hough *et al.*, 2009). Under the auspices of the project, teacher training manuals were initially developed in nine languages, with six more (for a total of 15) completed in summer 2009. Finland's involvement in the project ended at the end of 2009, but the Nepali government committed to cascading the program and teacher training so that all CLD learners could benefit from L1-based instruction in the framework of an MLE program (for a detailed description of the components of the framework, see Taylor, 2010).

In the years immediately prior to the Maoist government taking power and the introduction of the Nepali/Finnish MLE project, the Nepali monarchy had produced L1-based materials, but they were just translations of existing curricular materials into tribal/minority languages; they did not reflect local worldviews and the tribal/minority communities rejected them (Giri, 2011). In contrast to this, the Finnish technical team consciously adopted a bottom-up, community-based approach to materials development for the MLE project (Hough *et al.*, 2009). It was designed to hinge curriculum development on traditional indigenous knowledge (TIK), including beliefs, values and teaching practices. The intention was for local communities to take control of the content and methods of teaching and learning, and to have a voice in educational policy-making at the national level in keeping with the United Nations Declaration on the Rights of Indigenous Peoples (United Nations, 2007). Paragraphs 13 and 14 of the Declaration give indigenous peoples the right to control the content of their teaching, and to deliver it in an appropriate way (through culturally/linguistically responsive pedagogy).

TIK transmitted through the elders' (or IK holders') oral language played an important role in content teaching and in the initial materials development phase of the project as the elders possessed a vast knowledge of their culture, history and traditions: 'they had specialized knowledges pertaining to the land, the spiritual belief systems and the customary lore of the community' (Nurmela, 2009b: 21). These knowledges, presented in the form of storytelling, were documented and became the basis of locally developed pedagogical materials. While one team member, Nurmela (2009b), was conducting a site visit, she took field notes of topics that IK holders discussed with children in the primary grades in an MLE school. The topics ranged from traditions, festivals and group histories to creation tales. Children illustrated the stories, and the IK holders wrote the children's comments under their drawings, thus developing materials for later use as authentic, locally developed materials. The stories were also audio-recorded.

In subsequent workshops that she provided for teachers involved in the project in its various locations and for materials developers assigned to the project by the Ministry of Education, who were fluent in the tribal/minority languages represented in the project, Taylor noted reluctance to trust their own local knowledge as they felt only IK holders had the authority to speak for their communities. Taylor (2011) therefore introduced workshop activities through which they came to see that their local knowledge was valid too. Techniques were also presented for seeking out children and community members' knowledge about locally relevant topics, writing about this knowledge, and producing more L1 materials as many more materials were needed to offer full primary programs in the various L1s.

The community described by Nurmela (2009b) and members of other communities whom Taylor met over the course of the workshops she offered were heartened by the culturally/linguistically responsive pedagogy that children were receiving in the pilot schools, and they reported soaring retention rates. Whereas the national average for Nepali-speaking students staying in school from Grade 1 to Grade 5 (ages 6 to 11) increased from 58% to 79% between 1999 and 2004, it was not uncommon for 50% of tribal/minority children in Nepali-medium schools to drop out of school in Grade 1 (Nurmela et al., 2011). Early reports from the MLE project schools indicated that CLD learners were staying in school for the primary years, which would increase their literacy rates; however, achievement of the EFA goal of quality primary education was less clear-cut.

Quality Control in 'Multilingual' Multilingual Classrooms

Different pilot schools adopted different linguistic and grade groupings in any particular classroom. Of the seven schools initially involved in the project, five were classified (in a rather oxymoronic fashion) as 'monolingual' multilingual programs as all children shared the same mother tongue. Their programs could still be classified as 'multilingual' as from Grade 1 onwards, the children received instruction in their L1, their L2 (Nepali) and in EFL. Two schools were classified as 'multilingual' multilingual programs as children came from different L1 backgrounds (Nurmela, 2009b). As a result, several models of grouping children were adopted in the MLE schools from the viewpoint of single or mixed grade classrooms, one or more language groups in single grade classrooms, and one or more language groups in mixed grade classrooms. Other variations included whether several teachers came into a classroom throughout the day to teach their own specialty courses ('subject teaching') or one classroom teacher stayed in the classroom for the whole day and taught all the subjects ('grade teaching'), either in a single-grade or mixed-grade classroom.

The classroom with the highest degree of linguistic diversity, a Grade 1 classroom with over one hundred children, was located where Nurmela's (2009b) observations of involving IK holders in oral classroom activities took place. The children came from four different home language backgrounds (Uranw, Tharu, Maithili and Nepali). As described by Taylor (2011), the situation for the subject teachers who came into the classroom was far from ideal, but the children's retention rate was extremely high – indication of the community's appreciation of receiving L1-based, culturally responsive pedagogy and recognition of their rights (United Nations, 2007). However, whether the program met the EFA criteria of 'quality' education that took the learners' needs into consideration in that classroom was questionable, as is described in the next section.

There are four language families in Nepal: Indo-European (Indo-Aryan), Tibeto-Burman, Austro-Asiatic, and Dravidian – which only 0.13% of the population speaks (Yadava, 2007). One of the four languages in this Grade 1 classroom, Uranw, was a Dravidian language. Whereas with time (e.g. in the older grades) and teacher 'translanguaging',[2] children who spoke the three Indo-Aryan languages could pick up on cognates and partially understand when one of the other Indo-Aryan languages was being used as the language of instruction, they would not come to understand the Dravidian language without direct instruction in the language or extensive interaction with Uranw-speakers in the local community. The opposite also held true for the children whose home language was Uranw.

Instruction in the classroom was primarily delivered in a consecutive language manner. That is, a subject teacher (e.g. of social studies) would enter the classroom and deliver a lesson in Language A, then deliver the same lesson in Language B, then in Language C and, finally, in Language D. Then the next subject teacher (e.g. of mathematics) would do the same, and so it continued throughout the teaching day (Nurmela, personal communication). A multilingual Nepali researcher present in that classroom observed that while the teachers (who were multilingual in all four of the children's languages) occasionally translanguaged between the three Indo-Aryan languages, they did not do so between those languages and the Dravidian language (Kedel, personal communication). Although the children were technically receiving L1-based instruction in each of their L1s, the teachers did not focus their attention on the children for three-quarters of the time because of the consecutive language teaching approach.

Film footage taken of the classroom by Nurmela (2009a) at extended intervals, which Taylor viewed, showed the children behaving in a highly vocal (loud!), unruly manner when the teacher was providing instruction in one of the three languages that was not their L1 (e.g. they jumped on desks, and ran in and out of the classroom). The behaviour was not typical of the school – not even of the older cohorts in bilingual ('multilingual' multilingual) classrooms; it was confined to the Grade 1 classroom (Nurmela, personal communication). From the community's perspective (from parents to IK holders and other community members, right down to the children), even if the Grade 1 classroom situation was not ideal, they were aware that they had a right to L1-based instruction and appreciated the adaptations to managing CLD that had been made in the school; they also appreciated the fact that their children were no longer receiving corporal punishment for not speaking a language they did not know (Nepali) upon school-entry in Grade 1 (Taylor, 2011).

Although the children's learning conditions were better than before, they were in no way receiving what most parents would view as acceptable learning conditions for school-starters (lower class sizes in the primary grades, instruction in a language they understand or provision of scaffolds for language learning). Neither was Parrish et al.'s (2006) criterion of teachers with the capacity to address CLD learners' needs met. Finally, the children did not have access to the sorts of L1-based MLE program supports needed to meet the UNESCO (2003, 2007) and Government of Nepal's (2001, 2003, 2007) EFA objective of increasing the national literacy rate to reduce poverty.

During one of the workshops, Taylor met with the director of the school that housed the massive Grade 1 classroom and one of its Grade 1 teachers. They discussed possible solutions (hiring another teacher, dividing the language groups, adding on additional classrooms in the school, community volunteers). While those solutions would have been plausible in wealthier countries or in schools for more elite Nepalis, the country's financial realities precluded all of them in the context of this Grade 1 classroom. Indeed, Nepal is the 12th poorest nation in the world and, as such, depends on donor countries for 50% of its educational budget (Collins, 2006; World Bank, 2001). Taylor met with a government level education official to discuss the workshop results, and seized the opportunity to explain the school's need for more funding. The official's view was that 'multilingual' multilingual classrooms were the norm and the answer to managing multilingualism in education in and of themselves. This begs the question of whether he would enroll his own child in a similar instructional setting, a topic that is discussed with regard to ruling passions below.

All of the communities that participated in the project were highly cognizant of their rights and quite politicized, as were the workshop participants. The inception of the L1-based MLE program was not only due to the Maoists' view that enshrining minority language rights in the constitution would help Nepal emerge from language issues as a political battleground (Giri, 2011); it was also attributable to a grassroots movement spearheaded by organizations such as the Nepali Teachers' Federation and the Nepal Federation of Nationalities (Yadava, 2007). Therefore, there was widespread support for the program, regardless of its warts and growing pains; however, more resources (e.g. smaller class sizes and fewer L1s than in the Grade 1 classroom described) were needed for the EFA goal of quality primary education to be met. Where further understanding was needed was in the area of psycholinguistic principles of multilingualism and literacy development. While grouping numerous language groups in a classroom full of 100 pupils in Grade 1 may technically meet the needs of L1-based instruction in a country with Nepal's linguistic complexity, it stretches the limits of what any program can offer in terms of meeting EFA goals for quality primary education.

Ruling Passions

Contrary to what one might assume, neither the 'monolingual' multilingual nor the 'multilingual' multilingual issue, nor even 'goddess English', is the stumbling block in the current MLE cascading process. Giri (2011) notes reluctance on the part of the Maoist government to support the tribal/minority groups' CL and economic goals. He suggests that the Maoists come from higher castes, were schooled in the Nepali language, want to maintain its hegemonic control of power, and 'allow' the MLE program to exist while undermining its chances for success by not providing the infrastructure it needs to succeed (teacher education, materials development, reasonable class sizes, etc.); the infrastructure that is widely deemed most conducive to supporting culturally/linguistically diverse school-starters (Ontario Ministry of Education, 2012).

Giri (2011: 205) further suggests that the Maoist government only supported the MLE initiative to appease the Finnish donor while engaging in 'invisible language politics' (i.e. strategies and tactics aimed at furthering a monolingual Nepali ideology). This suggestion puts the unwillingness to provide the funding needed for the Grade 1 program to thrive of the educational official described above in a new perspective.

Bhattarai (2012) supports some of Giri's (2011) claims, but not his pessimism. Although Bhattarai (2012) agrees that unsupportive state language policies are impeding efforts to cascade the MLE program, he notes that there is still strong political support for L1-based MLE among CLD tribal/minority groups. With its strong grassroots base, public demand for the program is not waning. Dhakal (2010) corroborates this view, noting that the Nepali School Sector Reform Programme planned to launch MLE classes in 7500 schools by 2015 and 17,000 schools had already started teaching students in their L1s as early as 2010.

Discussion and Conclusion

Many layers must be considered in the introduction of the L1-based MLE program into Nepal. These include whose interests the program serves, how it is taken up and implemented, and what other countries grappling with CLD in education can learn from the Nepali response. Tollefson's (2002: 4) observation that how policy-makers manage diversity in education affects 'the lives of individuals and groups that have little influence over the policy making process' pertains to the Nepali situation as, historically, tribal/minority groups' ruling passions (their desires for L1-based instruction) were not heard. The MLE program was intended to give them voice in the classroom and later, through greater success rates in education, in the halls of power. The extent to which tribal/minority politicians will succeed in writing 'L1-based instruction as right' into the final draft of the constitution, or whether a monolingual (Nepali) ideology or 'goddess English' will prevail is not yet clear; theirs is a story in the making.

What is known is that Nepal must achieve enrolment of all children in Grade 1 and retain them throughout primary school to raise its national literacy and poverty rates (Government of Nepal, 2007). To do so, it must manage CLD in education – if not through L1-based MLE, then through other programs that are equally or better adapted to meet Nepali children's cultural/linguistic and socio-economic needs, and provide them with quality education; it must 'identify those left out of school and prepare policies specifically for them' (Government of Nepal, 2007: 27). The L1-based MLE program was designed to reach that goal.

Nepal provided a shining example of a country not only managing, but introducing forward-thinking legislation for CLD in education by guaranteeing the right to L1-based instruction to CLD children from over 140 language groups. Additionally, the grassroots support that the project received was exceptional in light of Harbert *et al.* (2009) and Webley's (2006) observation that groups struggling to meet their basic needs focus more on survival than on education. Though the Grade 1 classroom described in this chapter indicates that the MLE implementation process was not working completely seamlessly, the tribal/minority populations it served expressed satisfaction with the program and requested a faster cascading process (Dhakal, 2010).

Time will tell if factions within the government are merely paying lip-service to MLE to appease tribal/minority groups while harbouring a monolingual (Nepali-only) ideology, or if they will provide the infrastructure needed for L1-based MLE programs to be successfully cascaded and meet CLD children's right to quality education. The Nepali education system is in a process of 'becoming'. It has the potential to develop into an educational system that not only adapts to, manages and accommodates diversity, but also sets the bar for what 'developed' countries such as Ireland and Canada can become.

Notes

(1) As the term 'tribal' (not 'indigenous') is used in Nepal, it is used throughout this chapter.
(2) The term 'translanguaging' refers to strategies used by educators in bilingual teaching situations that develop both languages and foster content learning. Baker (2011: 288) describes the teaching approach as 'less concerned with language separation in the classroom than strategic language integration'. Translanguaging in a multilingual classroom is more complicated than in a bilingual classroom.

References

Alidou, H., Boly, A., Brock-Utne, B., Diallo, Y.S., Heugh, K. and Wolff, H.E. (2006) *Optimizing Learning and Education in Africa – the Language Factor: A Stock-taking Research on Mother Tongue and Bilingual Education in Sub-Saharan Africa.* http://unesdoc.unesco.org/images/0014/ 001460/146090e.pdf, (accessed 13 January 2009).

Awasthi, L.D. (2004) Exploring monolingual school practices in multilingual Nepal. PhD thesis, Danmarks Pædagogiske Universitet [Danish University of Education].

Baker, C. (2011) *Foundations of Bilingual Education and Bilingualism* (5th edn). Bristol: Multilingual Matters.

Bhattarai, T. (2012) Language education in Nepal: Perspectives on policy provisions relating to medium of instruction in the linguistic minority contexts. Paper presented at 10th Annual Hawaii International Conference on Education, 5–8 January. Honolulu, Hawaii.

Coleman, H. (2011) Developing countries and the English language: Rhetoric, risks, roles and recommendations. In H. Coleman (ed.) *Dreams and Realities: Developing Countries and the English Language* (pp. 9–21). London: British Council. http://www.teachingenglish.org.uk/sites/teacheng/files/Z413%20English%20Development%20Book.pdf (accessed 3 January 2012).

Collins, S. (2006) World report: Assessing the health implications of Nepal's ceasefire. *The Lancet, 368*, 907–908. http://download.thelancet.com/pdfs/journals/lancet/PIIS0140673606693537.pdf, (accessed 22 August 2012).

Cummins, J. (1991) Interdependence of first- and second-language proficiency in bilingual children. In E. Bialystok (ed.) *Language Processing in Bilingual Children* (pp. 70–89). Cambridge: Cambridge University Press.

Cummins, J. (2009) Transformative multiliteracies pedagogy: School-based strategies for closing the achievement gap. *Multiple Voices* 11 (2), 1–19.

Dhakal, M. (2010) Multi language education luring students, *The rising Nepal*, 4 July. http://www.gorkhapatra.org.np/detail.gopa.php?article_id=36996&cat_id=4 (accessed 13 July 2010).

Edwards, V. (2009) *Learning to be Literate: Multilingual Perspectives*. Toronto: Multilingual Matters.

Giri, R.A. (2011) Languages and language politics: How invisible language politics produces visible results in Nepal. *Language Problems and Language Planning* 35 (3), 197–221.

Government of Nepal (2001) *'Education for all': National plan of action (2001–2015)*. Kathmandu: Ministry of Education.

Government of Nepal (2003) *Education for all: Nepal national plan of action*. Kathmandu: Nepal National Commission for UNESCO in collaboration with UNESCO. http://www.google.com/url?sa=t&rct=j&q=&esrc=s&source=web&cd=1&cts=1331307052214&ved=0CCQQFjAA&url=http%3A%2F%2Fwww.nncu.org.np%2Fpublications%2Feducation_for_allnational_plan_of_action.doc&ei=HyJaT_nUI8WTiQfam6mnDQ&usg=AFQjCNENgQmBuyaz-xkIxPhuAd3VSyJyQg (accessed 9 January 2009).

Government of Nepal (2007) *Interim Constitution of Nepal 2007*. Kathmandu: Government of Nepal.

Harbert, W., with McConnell-Ginet, S., Miller, A. and Whitman, J. (eds) (2009) *Language and Poverty*. Bristol: Multilingual Matters.

Heugh, K., Benson, C., Bogale, B. and Gebre Yohannes, M.A. (2007) *Final Report: Study on Medium of Instruction in Primary Schools in Ethiopia*. Research report commissioned by the Ministry of Education, Addis Ababa, September to December 2006. (http://www.hsrc.ac.za/research/output/outputDocuments/4379_Heugh_Studyonmediumofinstruction.pdf) (accessed 22 August 2012).

Hough, D., Magar, R.B.T. and Yonjan-Tamang, A. (2009) Privileging indigenous knowledges: Empowering MLE in Nepal. In A. Mohanty, M. Panda, R. Phillipson and T. Skutnabb-Kangas (eds) *Multilingual Education for Social Justice: Globalising the Local* (pp. 146–161). New Delhi: Orient BlackSwan.

Little, D. (2010) The linguistic and educational integration of children and adolescents from migrant backgrounds: Concept paper. Council of Europe Policy Forum: *The Right of Learners to Quality and Equity in Education – The Role of Linguistic and Intercultural Competences*. Geneva, Switzerland, 2–4 November. http://www.coe.int/t/dg4/linguistic/ListDocs_Geneva2010.asp#TopOfPage (accessed 7 April 2012).

Nepal Law Book Society. (2007) *Interim Constitution of Nepal* (2007). Kathmandu: Nepal Law Book Society.

Nurmela, I. (2009a) The multilingual Gr. 1 MLE classroom (video documentary, available as part of Nurmela's fieldwork). MLE project: Kathmandu, Nepal.

Nurmela, I. (2009b) The story of elders in mother tongue education in Nepal built upon notes from my field journal. *Indian Folklore* 32 (April), 21–23.

Nurmela, I., Awasthi, L.D. and Skutnabb-Kangas, T. (2011) Enhancing quality education for all in Nepal through indigenised MLE: The challenge to teach in over 100 languages. In T. Skutnabb-Kangas and K. Heugh (eds) *Multilingual Education and Sustainable Diversity Work: From Periphery to Center* (pp. 151–177). New York: Routledge.

Ontario Ministry of Education (2012) *Supporting English Language Learners in Kindergarten: A Practical Guide for Ontario Educators.* Toronto, Canada: Queen's Printer for Ontario.

Panda, M., Mohanty, A.K., Nag, S. and Biswabandan, B. (2011) Does MLE work in Andhra Pradesh & Odisha? – A longitudinal study. *SWARA* 1 (6–7), 2–22. National Multilingual Education Resource Consortium newsletter. http://www.nmrc-jnu.org/nmrc_img/Newsletter_6%20&%207_Proof%206_19%20Nov%202011%20%281%29.pdf (accessed 13 January 2012).

Pandey, G. (2011) An 'English goddess' for India's down-trodden: A new goddess has recently been born in India. She's the Dalit Goddess of English. *BBC News South Asia.* http://www.bbc.co.uk/news/world-south-asia-12355740 (accessed 15 February 2011).

Parrish, T.B., Merickel, A., Pérez, M., Linquanti, R., Socias, M., Spain, A., Speroni, C., Esra, P., Brock, L. and Delancey, D. (2006) *Effects of the Implementation of Proposition 227 on the Education of English Learners, K-12: Findings from a Five-year Evaluation.* Washington, DC: American Institutes for Research.

Ramirez, J.D., Pasta, D.J., Yuen, S.D., Billings, D.K. and Ramey, D.R. (1991) *Longitudinal Study of Structured Immersion Strategy, Early-exit, and Late-exit Bilingual Education Programs for Language Minority Children (Vols. 1–2).* San Mateo, CA: Aguirre International.

Skutnabb-Kangas, T. and Heugh, K. (eds) (2012) *Multilingual Education and Sustainable Diversity Work: From Periphery to Center.* New York: Routledge.

Taylor, S.K. (2010) Beyond bilingual education: Multilingual language education in Nepal. *Colombian Journal of Bilingual Education/GiST Education and Learning Research Journal* 4 (1), 138–154.

Taylor, S.K. (2011) MLE from Ethiopia to Nepal – refining a success story. In T. Skutnabb-Kangas and K. Heugh (eds) *Multilingual Education and Sustainable Diversity Work: From Periphery to Center* (pp. 178–196). New York: Routledge.

Tollefson, J.W. (2002) *Language Policies in Education: Critical Issues.* Mahwah, NJ: Lawrence Erlbaum.

UNESCO (2003) *Education in a Multilingual World.* http://unesdoc.unesco.org/images/0012/001297/129728e.pdf (accessed 8 January 2009).

UNESCO (2007) *EFA Global Monitoring Report 2007: Strong Foundations* (2nd edition). Paris: UNESCO.

United Nations (2007) United Nations Declaration on the Rights of Indigenous Peoples. http://www.un.org/esa/socdev/unpfii/en/drip.html (accessed 8 January 2009).

Webley, K. (2006) Mother tongue first: Children's right to learn in their own languages. *ID 21 Insights.* http://www.id21.org/insights/insights-ed05/index.html (accessed 13 January 2012).

Wolfson, M. (2007) Arabic pilot project will be curtailed. *The Windsor Star.* http://www.canada.com/windsorstar/news/story.html?id=976a1e64-3cb0-4c89-8fec-fb7f20e0a4f7&k=45221 (accessed 3 December 2011).

World Bank (2001) *World Development Report: Building Institutions for Markets.* New York: Oxford University Press.

Yadava, Y.P. (2007) Linguistic diversity in Nepal: Perspectives on language policy. Paper presented at the Seminar on Constitutionalism and Diversity, 22–24 August,

Kathmandu. http://74.125.77.132/search?q=cache:6KgHrJ1aIRMJ:www.seameo. org/_ld2008/doucments/Presentation_document/Yadava_Linguistic_Diversity_ Nepal.pdf+Uranw+Ethnologue&cd=1&hl=en&ct=clnk&gl=dk&lr=lang_da|lang_ en|lang_fi&client=firefox-a (accessed 6 March 2010).

Yonjan-Tamang, A., Hough, D. and Nurmela, I. (2009) 'All Nepalese children have the right to education in their mother tongue'– but how? The Nepal MLE program. In A. Mohanty, M. Panda, R. Phillipson and T. Skutnabb-Kangas (eds) *Multilingual Education for Social Justice: Globalising the Local* (pp. 241–249). New Delhi: Orient BlackSwan.

16 The Ecology of Mobile Phone Use in Wesbank, South Africa

Fie Velghe and Jan Blommaert

Although education is intuitively understood as located in the institutional realm of schools and adjacent formal learning environments, it is good to remind ourselves of the fact that such formal learning environments are surrounded by complex *informal* learning environments, and that learning and teaching, if you wish, are features of an enormous range of everyday social practices performed individually as well as in small peer groups and (increasingly) in large virtual networks. In addition, the boundaries between formal and informal learning environments are leaky, and skills and knowledge acquired in each of them percolate into the other (remember Ben Rampton's (2006) accounts of how popular music entered urban UK classrooms, and how school knowledge of German entered the playful interaction of adolescent learners). New technologies – Internet and mobile communication devices – have complicated and intensified the development of such informal learning environments and have shaped a space for new, informally developed, patterns of literacy and numeracy. While such patterns bear similarities with formally acquired patterns of literacy and numeracy, they nevertheless are new and extraordinarily complex (see e.g. Kress (2003) and Lankshear & Knobel (2011); Davidson & Goldberg (2010) address the wider implications).

In environments where access to formal learning environments is or has been constrained, such new technologies often grow into prominence as tools and gateways to the acquisition of skills and forms of knowledge otherwise not available. This is the case with the only new technology that has been more or less democratically spread over the world, and this chapter will engage with the ways in which mobile phones have acquired such prominence in a particular space: a township near Cape Town, South Africa. We will show how mobile phones have become a 'placed resource' there – a resource that has acquired specific functions by virtue of its 'ecological' insertion into broader local economies of knowledge and resources (Blommaert, 2003: 619). New resources such as mobile phones do not operate in a vacuum and do not improve or deteriorate the local conditions of life *per se*. They do so in relation to what is already there in the way of resources, and their effects depend strongly on their 'degree of fit' into local repertoires and modes of communication (Hymes, 1966: 119). This chapter is, thus, an attempt towards situating the use of mobile phones as learning devices in the broader local communicative, social and cultural framework – an elementary ethnographic endeavour.[1]

Introduction

Mobile phones have become a necessity in the daily life of people all over the globe, including the developing world. According to the International Telecommunication Union (ITU, 2010a) the developing world's share of mobile subscriptions increased from 53% at the end of 2005 to 73% at the end of 2010. Until the arrival of mobile phones, people in the global south only had minimal access to telecommunication technologies, since the uptake of landline networks is very limited owing to insufficient service delivery, high installation costs and financial constraints (see also Hodge, 2005 and Esselaar & Stork, 2005). Thanks to basic but cheap mobile phones, the introduction of prepaid non-subscription plans (Minges, 1999) and the 'caller party pays' system, even people at the bottom of the income pyramid have mobile phones. For the first time they can take part in the telecommunication society and fundamentally change their communication.

Mobile phone penetration in South Africa is the highest in Africa, standing at well over 100 mobile cellular subscriptions per 100 inhabitants (ITU, 2010b). This high penetration rate of mobile phones was confirmed during fieldwork in Wesbank, a post-apartheid township in the suburbs of Cape Town, South Africa. Here, 83% of the people questioned were in possession of a mobile phone.

A lot of research has been done on the social and cultural impact of mobile phones on daily life in developing countries, on how mobile phones can be used for developmental purposes, how they foster economic growth and the wellbeing of the poor and how phones can close the so-called 'digital gap', the disparity in Internet access and use between the developed and the developing world (for an overview, see Donner, 2008). This chapter looks at how daily life in an impoverished area like Wesbank affects the appropriation of the mobile phone and how mobile phone use is adapted to lives in this community.

The way in which the phone has been integrated into society cannot be separated from the specific culture, economy and history of a society (Nkwi, 2009). Mobile phone use is embedded in existing social and economic practices and realities, so by surveying the main characteristics of life in Wesbank we may understand the broader dynamics of the use of mobile phones in such areas. An important aspect of that specific background is the low level of formal education enjoyed by large numbers of township dwellers. Consequently, informal learning instruments such as the mobile phone can be used to upgrade the skills and competences of local people, and this educational dimension is an integral part of the work we do in Wesbank. Mobile phones can be informal learning instruments in at least two ways. As communication tools they help users to access information that may involve processes with an educative effect on the one hand and information for real-life purposes that may serve an educative function on the other.

We give a brief description of the history of Wesbank, followed by an explanation of our research method and a description of the data, before engaging with the main characteristics of Wesbank and discussing their consequences for the use and appropriation of mobile phones and the circulation of the literacy resources that accompany mobile phones. We will show how mobile phones create new possibilities and opportunities, whereas poverty and other realities are major constraints on the full use of their potential.

The field

Wesbank was built in 1999 as part of the Reconstruction and Development Programme (RDP), a South African policy framework designed by the first democratic government in South Africa in 1994 to tackle the economic, spatial and racial legacies of apartheid and to improve government services and basic living conditions for the poor.[2] The housing part of the RDP aimed to provide one million subsidized houses before the year 2000, and was a response to a crisis in housing owing to internal migrations from rural areas into the cities after apartheid. Wesbank was the first post-apartheid housing project in the Cape Town area that was not segregated along racial lines but was intended to give homes to deprived people, irrespective of colour and descent. This first so-called 'rainbow community' had to host 25,000 residents in 5149 fully subsidized houses, reallocating people who had never owned a house before or who had been living in informal settlements for most of their lives (see Figure 16.1). The actual number of residents in Wesbank is currently estimated to be much higher, as extended families live together on one plot, and people have been building shacks in the backyards of their houses. Owing to the socio-economic criteria applied to the selection of the inhabitants, the population in Wesbank is very diverse (Blommaert *et al.,* 2005). Black, coloured, (some) white people and a growing number of African immigrants are living in the same community; the majority of the population are coloured and Afrikaans-speaking. The houses have an average size of 25 square metres, are built with brick walls and corrugated iron roofs and are not insulated. Every house has a living room, a very small bathroom with a toilet and a washing table, and one bedroom.

Basic service delivery is minimal. Although two were planned, there is only one high school in Wesbank – insufficient for the number of teenagers in the area. There are three primary schools, although according to the official South African norm there should be five. Recall that the Wesbank population in general is characterized by low levels of formal education; inadequate educational infrastructure of course tends to reproduce such features across generations. Given the inadequacy of school infrastructure, the objective need for additional informal learning environments, tools and practices is clear, and mobile phones can play a role in that.

Figure 16.1 Street view of Wesbank (Photo: Fie Velghe)

For three years, Wesbank has had its own day clinic, but the clinic is open only for babies, children and TB and HIV/AIDS patients. The nearest hospital is in Delft, a neighbouring community. For two years now, Wesbank has had its own taxi (minibus) rank and a Multi-Purpose Centre. Apart from 'shebeens' (illegal pubs, often used as a meeting space by township inhabitants) and informal, small-scale shops, there is only one – relatively expensive – supermarket in the community. Unemployment and sub-employment are massive; gangster activity and crime rates are very high, but there is no police station in the area.

Methods and data

The data reported here were collected during four months of ethnographic fieldwork in Wesbank early in 2011, with a special focus on cell phone use among middle-aged women.[3] The study included 11 face-to-face interviews with (mostly coloured) women and one group interview with women attending the crafts club of the Wesbank Senior Citizen's Organisation at the Multi-Purpose Centre. The interviews were held in the houses of the women and lasted for about one hour each. Most of the interviews were conducted in English or a mixture of English and Afrikaans. Interviewees were selected and introduced by two well-known community workers, who were present at our first meeting with them.

Other data included questionnaires administered in the high school and in one of the primary schools and completed partly by the pupils and partly by their mothers.[4] In total, eighty questionnaires were returned (almost 50%). Observations and informal conversations were recorded in a fieldwork diary and a lot of time was spent in the community. One of the informants kept a mobile phone diary, in which she wrote down all the text messages and phone calls she made and received during a couple of weeks.

The Conditions for Mobile Phone Usage in Wesbank

Let us now review some of the conditions for the use of mobile phones in Wesbank. As we explained above, the use of such devices is strongly entrenched in local socio-economic conditions, and we will review three major ones: poverty, crime and unemployment.

Poverty

The lives of most Wesbank residents are characterised by poverty and unemployment. As Wesbank was intended to relocate 'maximum subsidy' (i.e. minimum income) families (Achmat & Losch, 2002), poverty character-ised the eligible population from the first days of Wesbank's existence.

Recent unemployment rates for the area are not available; the latest report dates from 2001 and mentions 60% unemployment among the active population in the area. This figure even increases for women (70.4%) and black people (76%) (Nina & Lomofsky, 2001). According to Sharon Penderis (personal communication, 2005) 'the deprivation of Wesbank can be attrib-uted to low wages, low educational qualifications, an unskilled or semi-skilled workforce, rising unemployment, part-time seasonal work or insecure informal sector employment, lack of job opportunities in the wider region, long home-to-work journeys, and the financial inability of residents to seek for employment'. Current unemployment estimates are even higher, although more people found their way to informal sector employment and social secu-rity systems such as child support, disability support, care for the elderly, etc. According to Newton (2008) 77% of those living on the site have to survive on a monthly income of R400 (€39 in September 2011) or less.

This general impoverishment is no obstacle to having a mobile phone. As mentioned above, 83% of the people interviewed or questioned had a phone at the time of the fieldwork. Only 3.4% had never possessed a phone before. The remaining 13.6% once had a cell phone, but it got lost, stolen or broken. 69.7% of the people interviewed bought their cell phone themselves. 21.3% got it from a family member and 9% got the phone at their current job. Asked about the negative consequences of having a cell phone, only 10% mentioned the extra financial burden a cell phone creates. The high uptake of mobile phones was confirmed in the interviews, in which people stressed the fact that it is very exceptional to find someone without a cell phone, as phones are so cheap nowadays.

Financial constraints do, however, deeply affect the use of cell phones. Let us now look at five main influences of the economic reality in Wesbank on cell phone use.

Phone sharing

Poverty influences the way in which inhabitants of Wesbank share mobile phones. As most of the people have a phone, people do not share phones because the devices are scarce – a phenomenon often discussed in research on mobile phone use in developing countries (e.g. de Souza e Silva et al., 2011). According to Samuel et al. (2005), in many African countries a mobile phone is a household asset, not a personal or individual one.

Cases of shared use in Wesbank because of device scarcity are very rare, with some exceptions of – especially older – people who don't have a handset of their own. People share their phones because they don't always have money to buy airtime: sharing out of financial instead of device scarcity. Asked if she was sharing her phone with someone else, a mother answered: 'when there is airtime on it's not mine'. Mothers also mentioned that their phones become a shared phone from the moment the children come home from school.

'Please call me'

Another remarkable way of using the mobile phone within the daily reality of financial constraints is the frequency of free 'please call me' (PCM) messages. PCM is a free service offered by the provider; it allows a free text message to any other number with a request to call back. Those free messages – often limited to a daily amount[5] – read 'Please call me' and feature the number requesting the call-back, followed by an advertisement. Nowadays, one can add a short personal message to these PCMs and personalise the telephone number with one's own name or nickname. Eleven percent of the respondents mentioned sending such free messages as one of the three things they do most on their cell phone.

The use of a PCM message is comparable to the practice of 'beeping', 'flashing' or 'missed calling', a practice already discussed in several studies on mobile phone use in the developing world (Donner, 2007; Sey, 2007; Slater & Kwami, 2005; Ureta, 2008). Users call an addressee and hang up before this person answers. Donner (2008) sees the practice of leaving those intentional missed calls as an example of 'how the process of appropriation by users in the developing world leads to the creation of "new" mobile use' and as 'an example of an ongoing interaction between social practices and technological factors' (Donner, 2007: 3) in which users modify technology for their own purposes according to their own social and economic conditions, often in a desire to cut costs. This is what Zainudeen et al. (2006: 7) call 'telecom use on a shoestring'. South African providers initiated the PCM messages as a way of limiting the strain of missed calls on network traffic. Their strategy seems to have worked: in none of the interviews or questionnaires was the practice of 'beeping' or 'flashing' mentioned, unlike the use of free PCMs. Observe, in passing, the complexity hidden in this phenomenon: even though very little in the way of propositional content is transmitted, and even though the literacy skills involved are hardly spectacular, these 'phatic' messages are important tools for sociality and conviviality: phone-generated and transmitted 'gestures' that keep channels of communication and social relationships alive.

In common with a 'beep fatigue' (Donner, 2007) the high use of PCMs also generates irritation among Wesbank residents. The irritations and complaints run parallel to the 'rules of beeping' (Donner, 2007), such as the 'richer guy pays' rule, the fact that one can only send a PCM for urgent or important reasons and when one really does not have any airtime left. If one wants to ask for a favour or wants to make a good impression, it is not advisable to use a PCM. Moreover, too many PCMs annoy the receiver.

Topping-up

Only one out of ten informants was using a post-paid contract system of R100 (€10) airtime per month. Running a flourishing taxi business with her husband, this informant was financially better off than most of the other respondents. She was mostly using her phone for business purposes and her monthly bills were covered by profits from the family business. All the other interviewees charged their phone with a pre-paid card system, in order to avoid the risk of not being able to pay the monthly bills. The small amounts of airtime purchased were quite remarkable. Top-ups of R5 or R10 (respectively €0.5 and €1) were most common, enough for one or two short calls.

Most of the interviewees only charged airtime when a call needed to be made and when there was money available to do so, followed by some days or weeks without airtime in which the PCMs or free calling minutes to same-provider numbers were used. MTN, for example, one of the most popular providers among the residents of Wesbank, offers free calling minutes to other MTN members at the weekend and during off-peak hours. The mobile phone is thus used almost like a pay phone, as people only use the money they can afford to spend, and calls end abruptly when the credit is spent.

Appropriation of the phone

Use of features of the mobile phone that are not free of charge is limited. Almost no one in Wesbank installed or used the voicemail service, as no one wanted to run the risk of calling someone in vain and having to pay for it.

Free mobile phone applications however are maximally used. As most of the people in Wesbank do not possess many technological devices, the mobile phone is used for a broad range of purposes. During the interviews and in the questionnaires, people mentioned that they used their mobile phone as a lamp, a radio, a calculator, a still camera, a laptop, a watch, an alarm, a video camera, and a gaming device. We can see how a seemingly simple and monofunctional device acquires a complex range of functions in contexts such as those of Wesbank. Local knowledge, rooted in the challenging social conditions characterizing the place, prompt quick and accurate learning and development practices in which objects such as phones are explored for vastly more purposes than the one envisaged by their engineers and product developers.

Learning how to use the internet was high on the agenda of most of the people questioned. However, the extra costs that this would generate were (next to device and Internet illiteracy) the main reason why most people had never used the Internet before. Access to Facebook, Google, internet banking, Windows and email on the mobile phone were the things that were desired most. Note that these desires and ambitions were not predicated on a detailed knowledge of the literacy resources, skills and competences involved in them.

Access to emergency services

Calling the emergency services from a mobile phone is not free of charge. One can only call to the Capetonian toll-free 107 emergency number – to be transferred to the relevant emergency service such as ambulance, the police, fire or traffic services – using a Telkom phone or a payphone (Telkom is South African's largest communications company). Calling from a cell phone to the 107 number is impossible, so one has to call to the dispatching centre on a regular number, charged at domestic rates.[6]

Although Telkom payphones are scattered along Main Road in Wesbank – many of them permanently out of order however – for reasons of safety and efficiency residents prefer to call the emergency services from inside their homes by mobile phone. Residents did find a way to circumvent the telephone charges by calling the call centre of their cell phone provider. The call centre then redirects the call toll-free to the emergency services. Such redirection can sometimes take (too) long, but most people felt that they didn't have any alternative, as calling at domestic rates is too expensive.

Crime

Crime rates in Wesbank are very high, although it is very difficult to obtain recent crime statistics of the area. The latest statistics from the Kuilsriver Police[7] at our disposal date from July 2004 and mention 18 (residential) burglaries, 11 common and four violent robberies, five rapes and one attempted and one effective murder for that month (Depypere & Velghe, 2006). High unemployment rates, the constant inflow of new residents and, consequently, high population density, the large number of illegal shebeens, easy access to alcohol, drugs and firearms, the absence of a police station in the community, and the flourishing, deeply rooted presence of two big and several small gangs are regarded as the main causes of the high crime rates in the community.

Calling emergency services

As a consequence of this, 26% of the respondents acquired a cell phone for safety reasons. All interviewees could recall at least one incident for which they had used their mobile phone to call an emergency service; only one third of the residents who filled in the questionnaire had never used their mobile phone to call one of the emergency services.

Especially the older women felt safer with their own handset. If something happens with themselves or in the neighbourhood, they can just call the emergency services from inside their homes. The feeling of (personal) safety and the fact that one is always only one phone call away from emergency services such as the ambulance or the police recurs in many mobile phone studies all over the world. Many studies show that the concern for safety is the primary motive for women to acquire a mobile phone, and also an important one for men (Katz & Aakhus, 2002). It is not at all surprising that in an unsafe area like Wesbank mobile phones create a sense of safety and connectedness that is new to many residents.

Children and cell-phones: MXIT

More than 72% of the youngsters who answered the questionnaires in Wesbank had a mobile phone of their own. Those youngsters were all between 14 and 19 years old. When their parents were asked, more than half of them gave 'safety' as the main reason why they decided to give their children a phone of their own.

Especially owing to negative press coverage over the years, urban legends and true stories, MXIT, a very popular mobile phone-based instant messaging program, had a bad reputation among many respondents. Media, government, educational institutions and parents stigmatize the MXIT messaging service, connecting it with drug addiction, cyber harassment, immorality, abuse, adultery, and unbridled sexual behaviour, and regard it as a free-zone for unsafe behaviour, rudeness and pornography (see also Chigona & Chigona, 2008; Chigona et al., 2009a). In addition, MXIT is a site for exploring and circulating 'heterographic' writing codes (of the kind 'CU@4'; see Blommaert & Velghe, 2012) – also something which is widely perceived as 'bad' and 'deficient' writing.

However, in contrast to Chigona and Chigona (2008) and Chigona & Chigona (2009b) not all the parents interviewed were entirely negative about MXIT. Several parents also mentioned positive aspects of MXIT, applauding the fact that it is thanks to MXIT that their children spend more time inside the safe environment of the home, instead of hanging out in the streets. From inside their houses, under the watchful eye of their parents, children are now able to chat with their friends and to keep in touch with their social networks in and outside the community.

The youngsters themselves reported the above-mentioned positive consequences of MXIT as well. 'I spend more time inside the house', 'I stopped walking around' and 'It changed my life completely because now I can stay away from the *danger outside the house'* are some of the answers they gave when asked about the changes a mobile phone has brought in their lives.

Theft and robberies

In Wesbank, thefts and robberies – often quite violent – of mobile phones also have become a new lucrative crime among the gangs in the community. One third of the persons questioned who didn't have a mobile phone at the moment of the survey had lost their previous handset through theft.

The risk that one runs of being robbed, however, does not prevent people from carrying their phone whenever they leave the house. Having a mobile phone and being connected at any time and in any place seemed to be more important than the danger generated by carrying a phone. Unwritten 'do's and don'ts' on where and when (not) to use and show your phone do exist and influence the use of the phone in the community. Switching off the sounds of your phone in public places is one such rule. This is to prevent potential thieves from knowing you have your phone on you, in the event that someone calls or sends a text message while you are in a public place. Calling or texting while walking or standing on the street is hardly done. Most South African women we met, and especially the women living in the poorer areas confronted with high crime rates, carry their handset between their bosom and their bra, as pockets and handbags are too obvious hiding places for potential thieves.

Unemployment

Job seeking

As mentioned above, unemployment rates for the community of Wesbank are very high. New communication technologies such as the mobile phone have the potential to simplify access to the labour market. Although it was clear that women did not optimally use their phone in searching for employment, most women were aware of the potential created by mobile phones and, especially, mobile internet. Most of them applauded the fact that daily travels to job centres are no longer necessary. Job seekers now only have to travel once to distribute their curriculum vitae, on which their mobile phone number is mentioned, and then wait for a phone call at home. The fact that employers can reach them on their handsets makes it possible to save considerable travel costs to and from centres of employment.

Although the Internet has created an alternative way to apply for jobs – looking for online job advertisements, sending one's curriculum vitae by e-mail, social networking sites and instant messaging programmes such as MXIT offering free advertising spaces (see Figure 16.2), etc. – the use of mobile Internet to find employment is still very limited among residents of socially

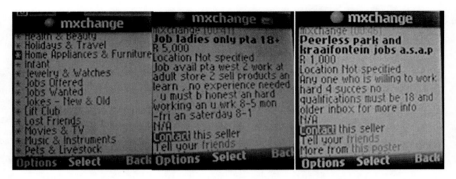

Figure 16.2 MXchange application on MXIT, job section (picture: Fie Velghe)

excluded and poor communities, although the interest in online job seeking is quite high (see also Chigona *et al.*, 2009a; Donner *et al.*, 2011). Evidently, the lack of accessibility of Internet facilities has an effect on the development of literacy skills and competences required for the use of the Internet – as we saw above, not many residents in Wesbank have a precise idea of the various and complex skills and competences involved in internet usage.

According to Donner *et al.* (2011), in South Africa's highly stratified economy, particularly professional and service-sector jobs in the formal economy are likely to be advertised online by one of dozens of listing services. As a consequence, many formal-sector employers in urban South Africa assume potential employees to have access to the Internet, expecting job seekers to post their CV on the web for example. As most middle-aged women in Wesbank are Internet and computer-illiterate, they miss out on those more secure job opportunities. In line with other literature (Chigona *et al.,* 2009a; Miller, 2007) there were also many Wesbank residents who firmly believed in the traditional methods of finding a job (face-to-face contact, job advertisements in print, printed and personally distributed curricula vitae, etc.).

Informal economy and job creation

Owing to the lack of access to formal sector employment, informal businesses are booming. Grocery stores, craft shops, fruit stands, tyre shops, electrical repair shops, hair dressers and shebeens are scattered around Wesbank, in residential premises, in containers or in makeshift stalls.

In line with many other studies in the developing world (see for example Donner, 2005), interviewees confirmed that having a mobile phone helped their small businesses, organizations or other informal activities. Although mobile phones are no panacea for small entrepreneurs in Wesbank, in the

Figure 16.3 Advertisements for (informal) businesses with cell phone number (pictures: Fie Velghe)

sense that they are not rapidly expanding business and customer networks outside the community, they do strengthen ties with existing clients and within the community itself (see also Sey, 2011, for similar findings in Ghana). Clients are able to reach the business on their phones, appointments and orders can be made over the phone, networks can be broadened, and a cell phone number can be displayed on business publicity and advertisements (see Figure 16.3).

Discussion and Conclusion

According to Sey (2011), studies on the impact of the use of ICTs in poverty-reduction programmes and other programmes that would benefit the poorest and most excluded sections of the population have focused on the potential generated by the spread of ICTs, without actually discussing how this potential can be translated into reality. This is, according to Sey (2011), in line with other studies that have emerged after the invention and uptake of every new ICT in the past. Print media, radio, television, video, fixed telephones, and the Internet have all raised new hopes for transforming the fortunes of the poor in developing countries. A vast amount of literature, for example, has focused on the opportunities that cheap and easily accessible mobile phones would bring to close the so-called 'global digital gap' that was created by unequal access to the internet between the developed and the developing world. Initially, however, one had hoped that the internet would be the panacea to finally bring information to the poorer and under-developed parts of the world.

The importance of those studies cannot be denied, and several studies and development programs that use mobile phones as a development tool have definitely proved to be effective (see for example Aker *et al.*, 2010; Ekine, 2010; Reuben, 2007). Still, it is important to keep in mind that ICTs are always embedded in social and economic realities and practices which define people's use of them. Although mobile phones can help to (re)shape and elaborate the economic, political, cultural, linguistic and social capital of the people and of society, one first has to look at how society (re)shapes and influences (the use of) the technology. As society and technologies are dialectically related, one should be cautious in extrapolating findings and studies from one continent, country or society to another. The conditions of uptake and use are always uniquely local, and they depend on the 'degree of fit' within the broader range of communicative resources, knowledge and skills.

For Wesbank residents, communication, connectivity and safety seemed to be the three main reasons for purchasing a phone. Family and friends were the two main groups in their networks. Exceptionally, some interviewees used their phones for business purposes. The adoption of a mobile phone strengthened networks with clients and made business communication easier, but didn't necessarily lead to a growth in turnover. Mobile phones do, however, seem to broaden and strengthen social networks, especially with relatives and friends outside Wesbank. Mobile phones also created new networks and enabled people to re-imagine themselves, often through the use of MXIT. In open chat rooms, one is able to virtually meet people from outside the community and from all over South Africa. This enables people to break out of their immediate environment at low cost without having to leave it physically. And finally, the use of mobile phones, especially in chat modes such as MXIT, offers an otherwise absent learning opportunity to Wesbank residents: they acquire modest but highly effective literacy skills enabling them to maintain their networks and relationships, and expand them on occasion, even in the face of severely challenged literacy backgrounds (see Blommaert & Velghe, 2012, for the case of a severely dyslectic woman and her texting practices). Modest and highly 'specialized' forms of literacy, such as the capacity to send PCM messages or use 'heterographic' textspeak codes, make a difference in the lives of many Wesbank residents.

That the adoption and use of mobile phones is profoundly influenced by the daily realities and constraints that determine specific societies, communities and livelihoods becomes very clear when one takes a closer look at the residents' use of mobile phones. Looking at the mobile phone use of middle-aged women and their children living in poverty, it became clear that the increased capabilities and potential that a mobile phone would be able to bring depended 'on how other aspects of their livelihoods are organized' (Sey, 2011: 387). According to the same author, 'high levels of mobile phone adoption do not guarantee development outcomes, especially if other elements in the livelihoods environment (e.g. vulnerability context, livelihood assets, transforming institutions and structures, livelihood strategies) are not appropriately aligned' (Sey, 2011: 387). In Wesbank, poverty proved to impose a major constraint on the full use of the potential of mobile phones, and severely influenced the way and the frequency with which residents used their handsets. First of all, 'anytime anywhere' communication and 'perpetual contact' (Katz & Aakhus, 2002) with relatives and friends was simply not possible due to financial or safety issues. Second, the extent to which mobile phones can be used for developmental purposes (job seeking, business growth, sharing of information, the closing of the 'digital gap', etc.) was restricted because of the unaffordable costs that this creates. People living in poverty are forced to continuous cost–benefit analyses on every cent they spend. Spending money on communication technology only seemed to be acceptable when one could benefit from it in the short-term at the lowest cost possible. The literacy skills they could acquire, therefore, were determined by access to the tools and facilities available to them: modest medium-tech objects such as mobile phones.

The insertion of mobile phones in the communicative economies of a community such as Wesbank's, is thus something that yields both opportunities and constraints. The opportunities are well-known: the creation of an informal learning environment in which new skills and competences can be acquired and developed, notably new forms of literacy and understandings of the patterns of communication enabled by the use of phones, and in which consequently new social relations, networks and identities can be shaped. These opportunities and effects are quite formidable; elsewhere, we described how a severely dyslectic township woman was able to use minimal forms of mobile texting in order to create and maintain an intricate social network of friends and relatives (Blommaert & Velghe, 2012). We have also seen how a form of chatting on mobile phones allowed a middle-aged woman from Wesbank to engage in love relationships with middle-class men and so create networks and forms of mobility beyond the township (Velghe, 2011). In both cases, elaborate collective informal teaching, learning and scaffolding practices were involved, and mobile phones provided opportunities and results never obtained in formal education. The potential is real and important.

The constraints, on the other hand, are quite formidable as well. They are imposed by the historical conditions that determined and still determine the development of this community – poverty and marginalization, low levels of education and schooling, risks involved in the mere possession of devices such as mobile phones. The 'infrastructure', so to speak, of this new informal learning environment is fragile, and it is good to remember this as a caution against overly enthusiastic approaches to new technologies in the peripheries of the world. From the perspective of local conditions of life, the emergence of this fragile and modest informal learning environment for literacy and communication skills is important, as it opens avenues of social development for individuals that could not be contemplated without it. In that sense, we see how stimulating and strengthening of such forms of informal learning can effectively contribute *something* to people living in conditions of marginalization and carrying with them histories of (formal) educational disenfranchisement. Informal learning, however minimal and constrained it may be, always results in new social and cultural resources and always carries a potential for empowerment and emancipation. Overly optimistic accounts of such potential, however, perpetually need to be checked against the actual structural constraints operating in specific environments. And pedagogies for informal language and literacy learning that do not take these actual contextual constraints serious will quickly turn out to be irrelevant.

Notes

(1) Research for this chapter was done with the support of SANPAD, whose commitment to this project is hereby gratefully acknowledged. We are also grateful to Christopher Stroud, Anna Deumert, Charlyn Dyers and the members of the Cape Town SANPAD team and the Tilburg TRAPS group for their continuous input and feedback. An earlier version of this chapter appeared as Fie Velghe, Deprivation, distance, and connectivity: The adaptation of mobile phone use to life in Wesbank, a post-Apartheid township in South Africa. *Discourser, Context and Media* 1: 203–216 (2012).

(2) The Reconstruction and Development Programme, A Policy Framework. http://www.polity.org.za/polity/govdocs/rdp/rdp.html

(3) The term 'middle aged' in Wesbank is difficult to define or outline, as a lot of 40-year-old women have grandchildren already and are already retired owing to chronic unemployment. Most of the women questioned were between 24 and 60 years old, with an average age of 47.8.

(4) Wesbank High is the only secondary school in the area and was opened in 2003. The Hoofweg Primary School is one of the three primary schools in the area.

(5) The three main mobile phone carriers offer different amounts of free 'Please call me' messages a day. Vodacom offers 10 of them, MTN 2 and Cell C 5.

(6) Website of City of Cape Town, see http://www.capetown.gov.za/en/emergencyservices/Pages/Home.aspx.

(7) At the time of the fieldwork survey conducted by Hannelore Depypere and Fie Velghe in 2005 the Kuilsriver Police was still responsible for the area of Wesbank. Nowadays, the Mfuleni Police is responsible for the area.

References

Achmat, F. and Losch, A. (2002) Wesbank: Power is the name of the game ... Power is the name of the problem. In I. Davids (ed.) *Good Governance and Community Participation: Case Studies from the Western Cape*. Cape Town: Foundation for Contemporary Research.

Aker, C.J., Ksoll, C. and Lybbert, T.J. (2010) ABC, 123: The impact of a mobile phone literacy program on educational outcomes. *Centre for Global Development,* Working Paper 223. Available at http://www.cgdev.org/content/publications/detail/1424423 (accessed 5 October 2011).

Blommaert, J. (2003) Commentary: A sociolinguistics of globalization. *Journal of Sociolinguistics* 7/4, 607–623

Blommaert, J and Velghe, F. (2012) Learning a supervernacular: Textspeak in a South African township. *Tilburg Papers in Culture Studies, Paper 22.* http://www.tilburguniversity.edu/research/institutes-and-research-groups/babylon/tpcs/

Blommaert, J., Muyllaert, N., Huysmans, M. and Dyers, C. (2005) Peripheral normaitivity: Literacy and the production of locality in a South African townships school. *Linguistics and Education: An International Research Journal* 16 (4), 378–403.

Chigona, A. and Chigona, W. (2008) Mixt it up in the media: Media discourse analysis on a mobile instant messaging system. *The Southern African Journal of Information and Communication* 9, 42–57.

Chigona, W., Beukes, D., Vally, J. and Tanner, M. (2009a) Can mobile internet help alleviate social exclusion in developing countries? *The Electronic Journal on Information Systems in Developing Countries* 36 (7), 1–16.

Chigona, W., Chigona, A., Ngqokelela, B. and Mpogu, S. (2009b) MXIT: Uses, perceptions and self-justifications. *Journal of Information, Information Technology, and Organizations* 36 (4), 1–16.

Davidson, C. and Goldberg, D.T. (2010) *The Future of Thinking: Learning Institutions in a Digital Age.* Cambridge MA: MIT Press.

Depypere, H. and Velghe, F. (2006) Passed and past in the present: Persistence of history in Wesbank, a post-apartheid township in South Africa. Ghent: UGent. Unpublished master's thesis.

de Souza e Silva, A., Sutko, D.M., Salis, F.A. and de Souza e Silva, C. (2011) Mobile phone appropriation in the *favelas* of Rio de Janeiro, Brazil. *New Media & Society* 13 (3), 411–426.

Donner, J. (2005) The social and economic implications of mobile telephony in Rwanda: an ownership/access typology. In P. Glotz, S. Bertschi and C. Locke (eds) *Thumb Culture: The Meaning of Mobile Phones for Society* (pp. 37–52). Bielefeld: Transcript Verlag.

Donner, J. (2007) The rules of beeping: Exchanging messages via the intentional 'missed calls' on mobile phones. *Journal of Computer-Mediated Communication* 13 (1), 1–22.

Donner, J. (2008) Research approaches to mobile phone use in the developing world: A review of the literature. *The Information Society* 24 (3), 140–159.

Donner, J., Gitau, S. and Marsden, G. (2011) Exploring mobile-only internet use: Results of a training study in urban South Africa *International Journal of Communication* 5, 574–597.

Ekine, S. (ed.) (2010) *SMS Uprising. Mobile Activism in Africa.* Cape Town, Dakar, Nairobi and Oxford: Pambazuka Press.

Esselaar, S. and Stork, C. (2005) Mobile cellular telephone: Fixed-line substitution in sub-Saharan Africa. *South African Journal of Information and Communication* 6, 64–73.

Hodge, J. (2005) Tariff structures and access substitution of mobile cellular for fixed line in South Africa. *Telecommunications Policy* 29 (7), 493–505.

Hymes, D. (1966) Two types of linguistic relativity (with examples from Amerindian ethnography). In W. Bright (ed.) *Sociolinguistics* (pp. 114–167). The Hague: Mouton.

International Telecommunication Union (2010a) *The World in 2010: ICT Facts and Figures*. Available at http://www.itu.int/ITU-D/ict/material/FactsFigures2010.pdf (accessed 23 September 2011).

International Telecommunication Union (2010b) *Mobile Cellular Subscriptions 00-10-1*. Available at http://www.itu.int/ict/statistics (accessed 23 September 2011).

Katz, J.E. and Aakhus, M. (2002) *Perpetual Contact: Mobile Communication, Private Talk, Public Performance*. Cambridge: Cambridge University Press.

Kress, G. (2003) *Literacy in the New media Age*. London: Routledge.

Lankshear, C. and Knobel, M. (2011) *New Literacies* (3rd edn). Maidenhead: Open University Press.

Miller, D. (2007) Mobiles and impoverished households in Jamaica. *ID21 Insights* 69, 1–6. Available at http://www.dfid.gov.uk/r4d/PDF/Articles/insights69.pdf (last visit: 26 September 2011).

Minges, M. (1999) Mobile cellular communications in the southern African region. *Telecommunications Policy* 23 (7/8), 585–593.

Newton, C. (2008) *Social Housing, Urban Policy and Social Capital: Spatial Interrelations in a Third World Context (Cape Town)*. Leuven: KUL.

Nina, D. and Lomofsky, D. (2001) *A Sustainable Development Strategy for Wesbank in the Oostenberg Municipality. City of Cape Town*. Project Hope, unpublished final report.

Nkwi, W.G. (2009) From the elitist to the commonality of voice communication: the history of the telephone in Buea, Cameroon. In M. De Bruijn, F. Nyamnjoh and I. Brinkman (eds) *Mobile Phones, the New Talking Drums of Africa* (pp. 50–68). The Netherlands: Langaa, Cameroon and African Studies Centre.

Rampton, B. (2006) *Language in Late Modernity: Interaction in an Urban School*. Cambridge: Cambridge University Press.

Reuben, A. (2007) Mobile phones and economic development: Evidence from the fishing industry in India. *Information Technologies and International Development* 4 (1), 5–17.

Samuel, J., Shah, N. and Hadingham, W. (2005) Mobile communications in South Africa, Tanzania, and Egypt: Results from community and business surveys. In *Africa, The Impact of Mobile Phones. Moving the Debate forward: the Vodacom Policy Paper Series #3*. Available at http://www.gsmworld.com/documents/GPP_SIM_paper_3.pdf (accessed 3 October 2011).

Sey, A. (2007) What have mobile phones wrought? Innovative calling practices to manage cost. Paper presented at 57th Annual Conference of the International Communication Association, May 24–28, San Francisco.

Sey, A. (2011) 'We use it different, different': Making sense of trends in mobile phone use in Ghana. *New Media and Society* 13 (3), 375–390.

Slater, D. and Kwami, J. (2005) *Embeddedness and Escape: Internet and Mobile use as Poverty Reduction Strategies in Ghana*. ISRG Working Papers: Information Society Research Group, Adelaide, Australia.

Ureta, S. (2008) Mobilising poverty? Mobile phone use and everyday spatial mobility among low-income families in Santiago, Chile. *The Information Society* 24, 83–92.

Velghe, F. (2011) Lessons in textspeak from Sexy Chick: Supervernacular literacy in South African instant and text messaging. *Tilburg Papers in Culture Studies, Paper 1*. http://www.tilburguniversity.edu/research/institutes-and-research-groups/babylon/tpcs/

Zainudeen, A., Samarajiva, R. and Abeysuriya, A. (2006) *Telecom Use on a Shoestring: Strategic Use of Telecom Services by the Financially Constrained in South Asia*. WDR Dialogue Theme 3rd Cycle Discussion Paper, WDR0604, Version 2.0. Available at http://ssrn.com/abstract=1554747 (accessed 3 October 2011).

Author Index

Subject Index